THE FOURTH WAY

DION PERRY

Pear publishing

The fourth way

National Library of Australia Cataloguing-in-Publication entry

ISBN: (paperback)

Target audience For you adults

Dion Perry

Contents

Acknowledgements..6

Chapter 1...7

Chapter 2...12

Chapter 3...17

Chapter 4...23

Chapter 5...28

Chapter 6...34

Chapter 7...44

Chapter 8...53

Chapter 9...58

Chapter 10..63

Chapter 11..70

Chapter 12..80

Chapter 13..90

Chapter 14..94

Chapter 15..100

Chapter 16..111

Chapter 17..117

Chapter 18..123

Chapter 19..132

Chapter 20..141

Chapter 21..154

Chapter 23..160

Chapter 25..175

Chapter 26..180

Chapter 27..188

Chapter 28 201

Chapter 29 211

Chapter 30 215

Chapter 31 225

Chapter 32 232

Chapter 33 240

Chapter 34 248

Chapter 35 261

Chapter 36 272

Chapter 37 279

Chapter 38 287

Chapter 39 294

Chapter 40 301

Chapter 41 314

Chapter 42 321

Chapter 43 330

Chapter 44 345

Chapter 45 353

About the author 355

Acknowledgements

I would like to thank Dr. Robert Porteous for his sharing his knowledge without which I would never have been able to write this book.

I would also like to thank the other members of the Canberra Speculative Fiction novel critique group for their appraisal of this novel.

I would also like to thank Ramtha's School of Enlightenment, of which I was a student for over 10 years, for the knowledge I gained during that time. Many of the concepts within this novel can be attributed to that school.

I would like to thank Aussie branding for the production of this book and InghamSpark for distribution and printing.

Chapter 1

Electromagnetic vibrations, converted into sound wave patterns, displayed across a dozen screens. Discordant, like a radio that wasn't tuned to a station, Kaylor stared intently at each screen individually. Every graph was different, but each was out of harmony. Choosing one at random, she played the sound through speakers.

Pain gripped her as if needles had been rammed into her ears. Clutching them with her hands, she fell to her knees. She'd barely hit the floor when she dry-retched. Between heaves, she desperately tried to speak to Torri, her AI. Her mouth opened, but the only sound that came out was a cry of anguish.

'Torri,' she gasped.

The AI did not respond, could not respond, for it wasn't able to separate her voice from the background din.

'Stop please! Oh god, stop!'

Her laboratory was sound proof so screaming would not help her. No one could help her, not even Torri.

Harnessing all of her will, Kaylor managed to force herself to stand. Painfully she reached for the off button. It was just out of her grasp. She stretched her right arm and fingers to full extent. It was agony not having both hands over her ears. Just a little further. Argh!

The sound stopped abruptly and Kaylor turned around and slowly lowered herself to the floor. Sitting with her back resting against the cupboards under her workbench, she pulled her knees into her chest and allowed herself time to recover. Beads of sweat were gathered on her forehead and her ears pained her as if they'd been sliced open from the insides. She checked for blood but thankfully found none.

'What in damnation was that?' she asked herself.

Having recovered, Kaylor stood up. She'd been studying the sound that heavenly bodies in space emitted since she was a child — over thirty years. It had been dubbed the music of the spheres, but what she'd just played wasn't music. She'd never heard such a ruckus before.

Kaylor checked the downloaded sound files that had come from the probes scattered across space. They'd been distributed by the colonising behemoth ship which had set out from Earth two hundred years ago, ultimately destined for Ria. The planet Kaylor was born on seven generations after colonisation. After years of lobbying, she'd only just gained permission to use the probes in her research.

Not surprising, given the time use demand on them was very high. Scientist like herself wanted access for dozens of different fields of study. But that wasn't the main issue. Because the probes were so far away, the only way she could listen in, in near real time, was to have lengthy sound recordings teleported across lightyears of space. That process required vast amounts of energy which meant the probes could not be used for other functions until they recharged through their radioisotope thermoelectric generators.

Desperately, she hoped it was something simple that was causing the discordance. But there was nothing obvious. The files showed no corruption and there was no jitter in the displaying graphs which would have been a tell-tale sign that something was wrong. What was she to make of this?

You're a scientist, not a theorist, work the problem; don't guess.

'Torri, run a full diagnostic on my equipment with particular emphasis on the download process from the probes.'

'Yes Kaylor.' A while later the AI replied, 'The download was successful without errors and all systems are working optimally.'

'Was there any interference created during the teleportation process?'

'I have no data indicating that.'

It didn't mean there wasn't but Kaylor knew it was highly unlikely. Sound messages had been teleported from Earth and they were as clear as if the communicator was in the same room as the listener.

She rubbed her face in her hands. It was good news that the equipment wasn't malfunctioning, but the results were not what she'd expected nor wanted to see.

'Torri can you please graph recordings from twelve different probes. Chose them at random.'

One by one the graphs refreshed, each one discordant like the one it was replacing. The exception was the last one and she stared at it incredulously. Like a deviant child determined to be different, this screen displayed beautiful harmonic lines. Nervously, she reached for the switch to play the sound through the speakers.

A wave of relief washed over her as the most beautiful sound she'd ever heard filled her laboratory. Taking a seat, she slowly closed her eyes. The music was so majestic her entire body slowly began to vibrate in tune with it. Tears slipped from her eyes as she gently released tension that she didn't even know she was harbouring. The longer she listened, the deeper the music penetrated. It was bliss.

'Kaylor you have not moved for ten minutes. Is everything alright?'

Kaylor's consciousness was dragged back from a deep place of stillness within her mind. Torri had programming that monitored Kaylor's moments. If she was still for ten minutes the AI was programmed to investigate. It was a failsafe in case she injured herself and needed help.

Switching off the music, she was glad of the intervention. Goodness knows how long she'd have kept listening without it.

Pulling up a holoscreen, Kaylor examined the metadata for the probe emitting the harmonious music. She did a double take, but she'd been right the first time. The probe in question had sent a sound file from the orbit of Ziana — a planet-like moon of Zeus.

Ziana was unusual because it was a moon with an atmosphere similar to Earth. Some moons did have atmospheres, Titan, which orbited Saturn was an example. Ziana, like Titan, orbited a gas giant with rings called Zeus. Also like Titan, Ziana was situated so far away from the nearest sun that it ought to be a frozen wasteland. But Ziana was not Titan, it wasn't frozen and it was the antithesis of a wasteland.

Covered by a thick atmosphere, Ziana held the heat it captured. Unlike Earth, its sun was larger and emitted light of a higher frequency. Harmful light that caused dreadful sunburn and could cause blindness, well at least to white skinned people like herself with human eyes. The Zianans had gold skin that did not burn and their lilac eyes were unaffected by the light.

Ziana was also warmed by geothermal heat from its molten core that spewed out steam. In short, the moon was under threat of annihilation, but the denizens did not fear this. Their civilisation was old. Why it had not been destroyed by volcanic eruptions was unknown.

That was strange enough, but there was another anomaly. The moon completed an orbit every fifteen days, but rather than being tidally locked so that one side always faced the planet, it rotated very slowly on its axis taking one hundred and eighty-one standard Earth days to complete a revolution. This rotational anomaly created what the indigenous people called the long day and long night. This was broken by eclipses when Ziana passed around the back of Zeus and out of sight of the sun for a few hours.

The moon was a forested green gem of thriving life surrounded by lifeless moons and planets in the freezing vacuum of space. So strange that it challenged everything humans knew about astrophysics. Reminding them that they had barely scratched the surface of what there was to know in this corner of the galaxy, let alone the universe. What held true in one place was not so elsewhere. As a member of the scientific community, the scientific anomalies were unnerving, to put it mildly.

Kaylor had never visited Ziana and she had no desire to go there. The place was so scientifically confronting that she had not even read the history of why the colonisers hadn't settled there.

Now, its electromagnetic vibrations, converted into sound waves, were doing a galactic-class ballet on her screen. Enticing her to come and take a closer look. Daring her to explain why it was an exception, even though she was sure it couldn't possibly be true.

Kaylor turned her back on the screen. No, the other screens were normal; Ziana was just a freak. The outlier that threatened to play havoc with her results. She wanted to disregard it, but she knew she couldn't and not just because it would be bad science to do so. Something deep within told her not to. A latent memory she couldn't recall.

Kaylor returned to looking at the graphs from the other probes.

The music of the spheres had never been particularly pleasant to listen to, but she'd been listening since she was six. Doing so had inspired her to become a sound frequency scientist. Never before had she ever heard sounds like this before. So why now?

She couldn't assume, but something deep inside her hinted that this part of the gallaxy was sick. Worse still, she feared the discordances was growing. For some reason Ziana was being spared and she needed to find out why. She didn't know what the sickness was, nor what it would do, but common sense told her that it would be nothing good.

Kaylor spent the rest of the day analysing data from the other probes. One hundred and forty-four in all. With the exception of Ziana they were all discordant to some degree. Looking for patterns she discovered that even though the probes were scattered across lightyears of space, by ranking the discordance, they roughly formed an arrow. So, what were they pointing at?

Kaylor brought up a holographic star map and looked in the direction the arrow was pointing. She stopped when she reached Zeta Reticuli.

She frowned. 'So, what's your story?'

Chapter 2

Kaylor tossed and turned before finally sitting up. Pulling back the covers, she got out of bed and put on her dressing gown and slippers. Her mind was so awake that she couldn't sleep so she might as well work.

'Torri wake up.'

'Kaylor, it is quite late, or if you prefer, very early. Are you feeling unwell?'

'No, I'm fine. How are you getting on with the Zianan history I asked you to collate?'

'I have not finished researching all one hundred and thirty-seven files in the public database. I have, however, began composing the summary, but it is not finished.'

That was the beauty of AIs, they could multitask and they never needed to sleep.

'Just read me what you've got.'

'Certainly Kaylor. First contact was made by the *Euroa* in 2053 Earth Standard Time. Communication was at first slow as emissaries from both delegations needed to learn the other's language and become culturally familiar. Once this was achieved, the Zianan delegate expressed concerns that the people of the *Euroa* were too technocratic. The designs for a colonisation city were rejected on the basis of cultural incompatibility. The Zianans did, however, invite a small selection of people to come and live with them to observe and learn, but not to impose their dogma.

'The commander of the *Euroa*, Captain Sorensen, was angry stating that Earth was offering them advanced technology in exchange for a parcel of land and access to natural resources along with trading opportunities. His revised offer was also refused. The Zianans stated that they did not want additional technology and did not wish to become technocratic. Captain Sorensen called them simpletons and flew his ship to Ria where he set up a colony under a biodome.'

Kaylor considered the short history. 'Surely the *Euroa* and its crew had superior weaponry. Why did they not take over the planet by force?'

'The officers of the *Euroa* were given a strict mandate that they were not to do so. They were only allowed to colonise a world with permission, or if the world was truly *terra nullius,* and the definition of intelligent life was very broad.'

Kaylor frowned. She wasn't buying it. Ria was a Mars-like planet that had the potential to be terraformed but that would take centuries. Ziana could already support life and Earthlings were a warring people who had always fought over land and resources, dispossessing indigenous people with impunity. In fact, according to historians, there had only been two-hundred and sixty-eight years of peace on Earth in the last three-thousand four-hundred years.

Lightyears from home, Captain Sorensen and his officers would surely have been governed by the tyranny of distance. The idea that no one from Earth could have stopped them so why not do as they please?

'Is there any mention of a weapon that the Zianans may have used to defend themselves with?'

'Yes. It was at first translated as the original weapon, but was later corrected to the fourth way.'

Now we are getting somewhere. 'Was the Zianan weapon ever used?'

'There is no evidence to suggest there was a violent confrontation. Leaving behind a small delegation of volunteers the *Euroa* left peacefully. In time, Ziana was recontacted and a Rian outpost was established. It is today also a research centre located not far from a small village called Port Town.'

Hmm, perhaps Sorensen had a conscience and didn't want history to repeat itself. Kaylor sipped at the hot chocolate she'd made whilst listening. 'How primitive were the Zianans during first contact?'

'They were not primitive. They had the comforts of their form of modernity. They knew how to work with base materials such as metals, glass, natural fibre, stone and clay. They had intricately designed buildings, running water, sanitation and plant medicine. They even had wireless electricity and radio. They were simply against the introduction of computers into their society.'

'Why?'

'It is written that it was against their cultural and spiritual beliefs.'

Kaylor rolled her eyes. 'Let me guess, their god forbade it.'

'No, there is no mention of a god or deity of any kind in any of the texts I've accessed so far. The Zianans do, however, speak of rising awareness that leads to heightened extrasensory skills.'

'Seriously? What kind of skills?'

'They refer to it in English as Knowing.'

Kaylor squinted. 'Knowing what?'

'The secrets of the universe.'

Kaylor smiled mockingly. 'Sounds like dogma to me.'

'There belief system has been labelled a dogma by a number of Rians who have written on the subject. However, the Zianans prefer to call their system of knowledge awareness building.'

Semantics. 'And this awareness building, does it have an end game?'

'The ultimate goal is to become an ascended being.'

Mumbo-jumbo. 'What does that mean?'

'To ascend is to conquer the physical body so that one can live in a higher energetic form. To do so first requires conquering the mind and body. It is a process that takes a lifetime, or in their beliefs, lifetimes of dedicated focus and commitment.'

Kaylor rolled her eyes. 'Sounds like a load of baloney to me. Is there any scientific evidence that accession has been achieved?'

'Yes. The Zianans have histories dating back tens of thousands of years. They name many beings who have ascended. The most recent to achieve ascension was a woman named Moir.'

Kaylor frowned. 'Even kept in hermetically sealed vaults paper would not last tens of thousands of years. What medium is their history recorded on?'

'Most of their books are printed on a paper that is made from a plant whose closet Earth relative would be hemp and stored in atmospherically controlled vaults. Their most precious books are text imprints on wafers of gold alloy. However, more recently, they have allowed a select delegation of Rians to digitalise texts.'

'Why, if they are dead set against computers?'

'It was done for Ria. The research I just undertook would not have been possible without their electronic files.'

'Really.'

'Yes. Despite their refusal to accept Sorensen's offers, the Zianans have always sought to extend a hand of friendship in order to bridge the two cultures. This has included learning to speak English, the official language of the colonisers.'

Kaylor hadn't meant to say really aloud and her response had been rhetorical. 'What can you tell me about Moir?'

'Prior to her ascension, she was a teacher. She was last seen on Ziana in physical form forty years ago.'

Kaylor narrowed her eyes. 'That doesn't make any sense. If she is ascended, how can she still be physical?'

'Her physical body was not destroyed. Using mind, the ascension process infolded her body into the quantum field, which means it can be re-materialised into physical form according to her will.'

Kaylor gritted her teeth. Technically infolding and outfolding of the body was possible because that was how teleportation worked. You took something physical, transformed it into a quantum state and re-materialised it at a new location. But that required technology and tremendous amounts of energy. 'I don't believe she infolded her body using mind. How is she able to do that without technology?'

'Zianan text details that the reason they did not want to become a technocratic society was because they believe there is nothing technology can do that the body can't once it becomes aware. They do not see the body as just flesh and blood, but as an electrified, quantumly entangled, biological vehicle, which holds a spirit and soul. However, once people begin to rely on technology, they become lazy and refuse to engage the awareness processes. The Zianans, did not, and do not, want this for their people.'

Kaylor rinsed her now empty mug, placed it in the dishwasher and closed it more forcefully than was necessary before returning to bed. Nonsense, complete and utter hogwash. Ascension was obviously some sort of clever hoax. This Moir woman was also clearly a master manipulator and shyster. The kind of person that Kaylor would have tossed into prison and the key thrown away.

She harrumphed. The reason she'd never visited Ziana had just been reinforced.

Chapter 3

With the broach pin clipped above the pocket of his shirt, Sparta was able to move into areas of the Rian Club that he'd never had access to before. The pin was a simple square; half black, half white. Merely gesturing to it made the beefed up and be-suited guards allow him to pass into restricted areas. The deeper in he went, the fewer people he saw and in time, he came to a door that contained the same symbol as his pin. Seeing it assured him he was in the right place.

He was about to knock when the door was opened by a brick of a man. Sparta was invited into the small but luxurious room that contained no windows. Grim-faced, with no apparent sense of humour, the brick waved an electronic device over Sparta.

'He's clean and identity confirmed to be Daniel Sparta.'

Two men sat in plush velvet chairs clutching tumblers of a golden-coloured spirit. One of them sat his drink on a rare and expensive redwood coffee table and gestured for Sparta to sit opposite.

Sparta adjusted his jacket to make sure it was sitting right before complying. Both men stared at him silently sizing him up.

Finally, the one who'd gestured for him to sit said, 'We have an unusual project for you.'

Sparta adjusted his sitting position so that it was more casual and did his own sizing up. The room was no doubt a faraday cage shielded from all spying technology. Soundproof and swept frequently for bugs anything said in here was guaranteed to be private. The men in question were businessmen who'd regard the law as guidelines that they could choose to ignore if they wished. By contracting him, however, they were ensuring that there'd be no threads leading back to them if the project went south.

Still, this was what he did. 'I'm listening. Perhaps we could begin with a more complete introduction.'

'Mr Sparta our names are immaterial, but for the sake of communication you may refer to us as Black and White.'

A joke, because everything was shades of grey to these types of men.

Black continued. 'We've been contacted by an unusual client who wants a very specific *product.*'

Sparta tensed at Black's emphasis of the word product.

Black hesitated to go on so White continued. 'They want a child born from two specific parents.'

Okay, what for? 'So, you want me to collect DNA from two specific people?'

White pursed his lips. 'No, the client was quite specific. A clone will not suffice.'

Fair enough. DNA was corrupted during the cloning process meaning clones were always inferior to people born naturally. Still, the refusal to accept a clone was a complication. 'So, you need sperm from him and an egg from her, which you can implant into a surrogate or grow in an artificial womb.'

There had been a fad of late; certain rich women wanting to have a child from a famous man. In cases where the father was not on board, Sparta had been paid to steal sperm. With the aid of drugs and a prostitute it wasn't as difficult as it sounded. If extraction was staged correctly, it was almost impossible for the man to prove he hadn't willing impregnated the woman.

Harvesting an egg from a woman would be much more difficult, but not impossible. Still, he'd have to sub-contract out the egg removal, which would be tricky and risky.

White rubbed his chin. 'No, the client wants a *completely* natural birth.'

What the fuck? 'Gentlemen, I think you misunderstand the scope of the services I offer.'

Black leaned forward. 'Mr Sparta, we're not suggesting you are Cupid.' He removed an old-fashioned handheld device from his pocket and offered it to Sparta.

Sparta took the artefact and examined it curiously, whilst frowning.

'This device contains advanced technology which allows the user to create a subliminal frequency that is very persuasive.'

Okay, now he was starting to get the drift. 'So, you want me to use this device to get a specific man to impregnate a specific woman?'

White smiled. 'Yes.'

That should be doable if the program on the handheld device worked. 'And the lucky couple is?'

Black activated a wireless projector creating a life-like hologram to appear above the redwood table. 'The gentleman is Lieutenant-Commander Avery Vander, a space fleet officer.'

Sparta wrinkled his nose. Fleet, was in every way shape and form a paramilitary institution. They even used navy ranks. Their job was to police every planet, moon, space station and asteroid mining operation, from Ria to Earth. Naturally, they had jurisdiction over local and planetary police and could stick their nose in anywhere they chose even when it wasn't wanted.

A second hologram appeared.

'The woman is Dr Kaylor Emerson. She works for the Rian Scientific Institute.'

Sparta scrutinised the holograms. 'So, he's a space pig and she's a lab geek, but the bigger issue is, he's Zianan and she's Rian.'

'What's your point?' asked White.

'Zianans and Rians don't procreate as a rule.' It wasn't that they couldn't. Zianans despite being "alien" were genetically capable of breading with humans. It was more that cultural differences prevented relationships from forming. 'Will the crossbreeding create *special* genetics?'

'We don't know, but we suspect,' said White.

'But why does it have to be specifically these two?'

'We don't know that either, but what does it matter?'

'I want to know who would want a baby from these two?'

Black narrowed his eyes. 'That's not really your concern now is it?'

Sparta folded his arms. He normally didn't want to know specific details, but in this case, he did. This project was giving him a bad feeling. 'I need to know who, in order to know what's at stake so I can assess the risks.'

White looked at Black who slowly nodded accent.

'The client is from Zeta Reticuli.'

'Greys?'

'We prefer to call them Zetas. Referring to a species by the colour of their skin is quite derogative.'

Sparta didn't care if he was being completely fucking racist. 'You're doing business with shonky aliens? 'Do they even know how to speak?'

Both men now shifted uncomfortably.

'We were… are, able to communicate,' said White.

Through some sort of neural thought transducer which converts telepathy into text or synthesised speech no doubt. 'And they never said what they wanted with this baby?'

'No, that's not our business.'

In other words, you don't care if the Greys chop the child up for genetic parts. He made to get up in order to leave.

Black sighed theatrically. 'Mr Sparta, I'd hoped you'd be more professional than this. You did after all come highly recommended.'

Sparta recoiled. He couldn't afford to refuse simply because of a little discomfort on his part. He'd never had much of a conscience so why grow one now? The better question was, 'What's the payoff?'

Black narrowed his eyes. 'We are of the understanding that you charge a set fee which you quote once you know the specifics of the project. Half pay upfront; the rest when you've achieved the project's objective.'

Sparta smiled wanly. 'I mean for you.'

'What do you mean?' asked Black.

'Gentlemen, we should dispense with the games. The Zetas wouldn't know what payment units nor currency is. Are they paying in precious metal or by some other means?'

Both men shifted uncomfortably in their seats.

In time Black said, 'They are offering to pay in technology.'

'Now we're getting somewhere. What kind of technology?'

'A spaceship that can cross galaxies just like that.' Black snapped his fingers to emphasise his point.

Sparta sat back in his chair. Humans already had a warp drive that could cross galaxies. That was how they'd managed to leave Earth and create colonies. However, as fast as it was it was still frightfully slow relatively speaking. A year to get to Ziana from Ria and twenty years to get to Earth from either world. Teleportation could take you places instantly but it was so energy intensive it wasn't commercially viable. This new spaceship however, clearly had an energy source or generator that could change the entire playing field.

'Technology like that when patented will be worth so much it could be scarcely quantifiable. Which means I'll be wanting a slice of that pie in addition to my fee.'

'How big a slice?' hissed Black.

'Ten percent.'

'Five,' spat Black.

'Eight,' said White.

'Done.'

Black gave White a filthy look, but they both remained silent.

Sparta stood up to take his leave.

'Two things before you go,' said White.

Sparta glanced back.

'We'll be wanting that pin back.'

Sparta removed the pin they'd had personally delivered to him and sat it on the armrest of the chair he'd just vacated.

'And you should know, the persuasive program is also Zeta technology and it has a time limit.'

Sparta balked. 'Time limit?'

'Yes, we were told six months, but we're not at all sure the Zetas know what a month is.'

Great. Just fucking great. Still, if he pulled this off this would be the biggest payday ever.

Chapter 4

It was one of those "what-was-I-thinking" moments. Sparta kept replaying it over and over in his mind. He should have said no and just got up and walked out. Too late now, if he refused to complete the project, he'd never get work again. Men like Black and White, who contracted him, expected results no matter the difficulty.

Sparta sighed. He came from a long line of professional criminals. His father, a black-market trader, is able to get his customers almost anything they want. That is, as long as they are prepared to pay the price. Sparta's father had expanded the business from his father creating a family empire.

Not wanting to work for his father, whom he didn't get along with, Sparta had branched out on his own. Rather than supplying products, he fixed problems. In Sparta's thirteen successful years, his father had not once told him he was proud of him or even that he'd done well.

That was because Sparta was the result of an unwanted child produced from a prostitute. It was a quandary that wouldn't go away. Why should he try and win his father's approval?

Sighing, Sparta pushed thoughts of his father from his mind and thought of his mother. She was long dead, having died from a drug overdose, but she'd loved him. She'd continuously told him so.

He fondled the archaic handheld. Completely replaced by wearable technology no one used them anymore, but it wasn't always the case. Back in their heyday, everyone on Earth had had one. They were so popular that people had suffered from anxiety attacks if they were separated from them.

Over time, they'd been replaced with wearable technology. Watches, glasses, ear probes, and even chest projectors. Information was no longer simply at your fingertips, but even more accessible through voice command, by blinking or other movements of the head. Still, the technology was not as optimal as it could be.

No one could have predicted the speed in which insertables would take over. People had rushed forward to get chips put under their skin or in their brain. Their desire to merge with technology had been insatiable.

That was, until it malfunctioned, and caused dozens of people to turn violent and rage around the streets like mindless zombies killing people and destroying property. Naturally, the incident had sparked outrage and people with insertables were labelled as evil cyborgs. Overnight, a whole new form of discrimination was born.

By the time the dichotomist attitudes reached their peak, vigilante activists had begun bombing factories that manufactured the insertable chips. Rather than take a hard line on terror, Charmaine, the first female president of One World Earth, declared insertables unsafe and ordered their immediate removal and disposal. Citizens were given six months to have their chips removed and destroyed or face a hefty fine and gaol sentence.

Sparta shook his head. Even looking back, he didn't know what all the fuss was about. What should have been a one-off incident had turned into a kneejerk reaction that setback technological advancement permanently. The move towards merging with machines was no longer possible and it was neither fair nor acceptable.

He glanced out the window. His digs were on the edge of dome number six where it was quiet and private. Beyond the city's twelve domes, was a desolate landscape that could only be accessed in a pressurised vehicle or suit. Were Rians destined to forever live in fish bowls?

No, there was hope on the horizon because Ria had recently declared independence from Earth. There would of course still be trading relations, but Ria was now free to govern itself. Being pro-capitalist, the new parliament had a strong economic focus and was supportive of technology. And why wouldn't they be? Without technological advancement, there was limited scope to expand and capitalism wouldn't tolerate that. The obvious solution was to find easier ways to adapt to the environment and technology could make that possible.

Rather than spending a lifetime becoming aware as the Zianans allegedly did, why not simply merge consciousness with machines. They were superior in every way. Yes, simply download consciousness into android bodies. They would not need feeding, wouldn't need to breathe and they could go anywhere and do anything.

Surely the Zetas knew this, so why then did they want a flesh and blood child? What possible use would it be to them? Beings who could build a spaceship that could cross the vastness of space instantly. Surely, they, of all beings, understood what technology could do.

He sighed. It was like Black and White had said, what did it matter? They wanted a product and they were offering payment. It was just another project and it was time to start working it.

'Tank, search the Cloudnet for useful information on Dr Kaylor Emerson and Lieutenant-Commander Avery Vander. As per usual, do not let cybersecurity hinder you.'

'Certainly Daniel.'

Sparta smirked. AIs like Tank were both legendary and illegal and so named because they could hack into anything without leaving a trace. If information was stored electronically, it was there for the taking.

Fifteen minutes later Tank replied, 'Task complete shall I collate and summarise?'

'Yes, report and begin with the woman.'

'Dr Kaylor Emerson is a Rian citizen who is thirty-six years of age. Health is rated as excellent. She is divorced with no children and her social status is listed as single.'

Now that's what I call convenient. Although older than I'd have preferred she's available and still capable of breeding. 'That will do for her. Report on Avery.'

'Lieutenant-Commander Avery Vander, a dual Rian and Zianan citizen who is forty years of age. Health is rated as excellent. He is married to Leda Vander nee Jenner a Rian citizen. They have no children.'

'A Rian citizen? Are you sure?'

'Fact check confirmed.'

'Why does he have dual citizenship?'

'He's a hybrid. Half Rian; half Zianan.'

Whoa. Sparta had no idea there had even been any interbreeding. 'Who are his parents?'

'They are not listed as his parental status is listed as orphan. He was raised on Ziana, but joined fleet as a cadet at age fifteen.'

Hmm. Sparta rubbed his chin. Someone knew who his parents were else he wouldn't have dual citizenship. Someone who obviously had a great deal of power and influence. Still, there were many people who fit that bill.

Being a hybrid explained why he'd marry a Rian woman, so what was the deal with her? 'Report Leda's medical rating.'

'Her health is listed as very good, but she is incapable of bearing children due to a genetic defect.'

Which should be correctable. 'Has she undergone gene therapy?'

'No and there are no notes explaining why.'

Sparta poured three fingers of whisky into a tumbler. Being a Zianan, even a half breed, her retard husband had probably convinced her that she should be able to heal herself by singing or something equally ludicrous. The poor thing had probably spent a lifetime trying only to fail time and time again. A sad and sorry case, but a side issue.

Sparta's main concern was Zianan's were ridiculously loyal. Whilst they were in a relationship they did not stray, because to do so, was so against their spiritual beliefs, it was considered sacrilege. Once paired, they mated for life and if their mate died, they did not remarry. Still, this man might be an exception.

He considered the Zeta program on the handheld. He hadn't tested its effectiveness yet. Would it persuade Avery to have an affair with Kaylor? He was hoping it would.

The problem was that getting them to have sex was not enough. Statistically speaking, less than point one percent of sexual intercourse resulted in pregnancy due to the effectiveness of contraception. This meant even if he got them together, they would have to agree to have a baby or else any sex they had would not result in conception.

Would the program convince them to have a child together? Sparta hoped so, but it would be best if he went and did some field testing and he knew just who to test it on first.

Chapter 5

Avery considered the view from the observation deck of the spaceship he served on as breathtaking. Space itself was formless, but what lay in it had immense beauty. Swirling clouds of coloured gas, twinkling stars lightyears away, and neon orbs that floated in a midnight-black void of nothingness. Avery had always been awe inspired by nature and space was nature in its macro form.

Synchronising his breathing with movement Avery continued with *kumba*, a moving meditation that was one of the many disciplines Zianans practiced as part of awareness building.

With every inward breath, he took in lifeforce energy Zianans called *xean*. With each outward breath, Avery released stress and tension. The breathing process strengthened his body's auric field whilst increasing the vibratory rate of his physical body by energising his seven seals. The focus moved him deeper and deeper into trance until he was no longer conscious of being physical.

Now he paused his movements and his expanded awareness shifted to Ziana who was rapidly growing larger as the spaceship approached. A green and white orb so majestic that it was impossible to gaze upon without being overwhelmed by love. As the planet became his sole focus, he sent it his own unconditional love. Allowing it to pour out of him until it was all-consuming. Until he and his home planet were one. Then he just floated in a state of indescribable bliss.

'You copy Avery.'

Avery's awareness was ripped back to the physical world. It was only now that he realised that he was actually floating. Something had happened to the artificial gravity. He touched his right ear to activate his communicator and talk to Ralph, the communications officer on a private channel. 'Yeah, go ahead.'

'Red dot.'

The privacy of communication was colour coded. Red being the most sensitive and reserved for genuine emergencies. Rating a communiqué red outside of the protocols could get you court-martialled.

Avery recoiled. What the hell was that about? Ralph would not have access to the content, but he did have access to the metadata. 'What's the subject line say?'

'November Charlie.'

Whoa. November Charlie was code for "not communicable". In other words, it was so private that he wouldn't even disclose the subject line to him even over a private channel.

Avery's heart thumped in his chest. He brought up a holoscreen to investigate, but the red dot would not display lest someone near him saw it. Damn, he'd have to go to a hub.

Avery pushed against the nearest wall with his feet and shot straight into a tubular passageway like a startled squid. A hundred metres in, he grabbed hold of a door frame to arrest his momentum. Raising his legs ninety degrees, he pushed off shooting himself feet first into the hub — a ten cubic metre room fitted with all manner of communication equipment including old-fashioned radios that Zianans still used.

Having logged in to the ship's communications computer Avery managed to get the red dot to display, but it made no sense.

Tapping his ear, he said, 'You copy Sarah.'

'Yes Avery.'

'If you have a moment, I could use your advice in comms hub five.'

'Yep, be there in a sec.'

Dressed in her one-piece beige uniform, the ship's Executive Officer and phycologist, Commander Sarah Bartell floated into the hub. Her slim body hovered weightless while her mousy brown hair floated like kelp in a gentle surge of seawater.

'What's happened to the gravity?' he asked.

'Just a system snafu. I've been assured it will be back online shortly.'

Avery nodded. Loss of gravity didn't happen every day, but it did happen and usually during program upgrades. Inconvenient on one hand, fun on another. The off-duty crew would be floating around enjoying being weightless while imitating cephalopods.

'What can I do for you?' prompted Sarah.

Avery gestured to the holoscreen.

Sarah moved closer before averting her eyes. 'That's a red dot.'

'Yes, and it makes no sense at all. Just read the first sentence.'

Having been given consent to read his private email Sarah did so. 'Oh my god.' Her expression grim, she turned to face Avery. 'I'm so sorry.'

Avery frowned. 'It has to be a hoax sent by some sick hacker.'

Sarah slowly shook her head confirming the red dot was real and had been verified.

Avery's denial of reality fell away suddenly and pain like a punch to the stomach hit him square on. A string of water globules rose in front of him — the effect of crying in zero gravity. His chest heaved as pain pierced his heart. A quiet cry escaped his lips as he fought to hold it together.

Unless he could secure some tissues, he wouldn't be able to read the rest of it. Not that it mattered because he'd got the gist by reading the first sentence.

Sarah drifted towards him, spun herself around and wrapped her arms around his chest. Her hug in violation of fleet's proximity protocol, which did not permit fraternising or even platonic physical contact between crew members.

Avery tried to gently push her away. 'You're violating…' His voice trailed off into sobs and further strings of water bubbled from his eyes.

'Report me,' she replied.

Determined to hug him, difficult in zero gravity, she hooked one leg around his and pulled him closer. Floating in a tangle of arms and legs, they began tumbling head over heels. Even without the string of rising water bubbles, they must have looked comical. Luckily, neither of them suffered from vertigo, which could cause vomiting for those unable to handle their world spinning.

Avery stopped resisting. They'd served together since they were cadets and he really did need a hug from his best friend and confidant of twenty-five years.

Sarah retrieved some clean tissues from a pocket and Avery made use of them as he forced himself to read on.

'It says Leda's in an unawakenable coma. She...' Avery's body shook violently and he pressed the tissues to his eyes and nose to sop up his body fluids.

Sarah politely gestured at the monitor. 'May I read more?'

'Yes.'

As her eyes rapidly scanned the text, Sarah's demeanour hardened as she forced her own grief to remain checked.

'Will she recover?'

Sarah scrolled the screen. 'I'm sorry. She's suffered a severe stroke and only life support is keeping her alive.'

'What happened?'

'According to this, she had antiphospholipid antibody syndrome.'

'What?'

'An autoimmune disease of the blood. If it's not treated with blood thinners it causes strokes among other things.'

Nothing Sarah was saying was making any sense. 'She didn't have any diseases. We both had full medical scans and they came back squeaky clean.'

Sarah frowned. 'I don't know. I'm sorry.' Sarah placed a hand on his shoulder but tapped her earpiece with her other hand. 'Copy Loo.'

'Yeah go ahead.'

'Can you please come to comms hub five?'

'Coming.'

Captain Loody swam headfirst into the hub, took one look at Avery before moving his attention to Sarah.

'It's his wife Loo, she's had a near-fatal stroke. We need to get him to her asap.'

Avery blew his nose and rolled the tissues into a ball doing his best to keep the mucus and tears from floating off. 'She's on Ria in another solar system. I'll have to catch a public transporter and it will take over twelve Earth standard months to get there from here.'

Sarah shook her head. 'We'll teleport you.'

She had to be joking. He stared in disbelief.

'Don't worry, it's perfectly safe.'

Avery wasn't worried about that. To his knowledge, there had never been a long-term negative side effect from teleportation. The issue was the technology used ridiculous amounts of electrical energy. So much that the ship would need to be powered down, because every last amp from the helium-three fusion reactors would be required for the teleporter.

'Powering down leaves the spaceship vulnerable; essentially a floating object in the void of space. Not to mention what it'll do to the budget given the power needed to operate the teleporter on Ria where I'll be arriving.'

'Don't worry about it,' said Loody.

'It's only for emergencies. This isn't one.'

Loody clasped his shoulder. 'With all due respect, I'll decide what's an emergency. You've given the best twenty years of your life to this hamburger and five years previously as a cadet. The least fleet can do is show a little reciprocity.'

From the outside, *The Zee*, Ziana's patrol ship, did look like a giant mutant hamburger, but that was its only likeness to fast food.

The idea was very caring, but. 'No, you can't do this.'

'I can and I will,' replied Sarah. 'The Captain and I decide if someone's a threat to the ship and whether they need to be jettisoned.'

'I'm not a threat.'

'I know that, but you know I'm a selfish cow right. Your snot and tears are clogging the water reclaimer and I don't fancy drinking them diluted or otherwise.'

Avery had long ago gotten over the idea of drinking recycled water, which, having been through reverse osmosis, was one-hundred percent pure by the time it returned to a drinking glass. He managed a weak smile at her dry humour. Sarah was the antithesis of selfish.

Loody squeezed his shoulder again. 'It's alright, we got this. Grab your kit and head to the teleporter fleetman. You need to be with your wife.'

A lump formed in Avery's throat. He'd be eternally grateful for this.

Sarah gently patted at him as a form of comfort, more difficult than it should have been due to zero gravity.

'Commander, can you …?'

Sarah was already scrolling a holoscreen. 'I got it Captain but you'll need to co-sign the e-forms.'

He nodded curtly, turned Avery around and gave him a gentle bump which was enough to send him out of the hub into the tunnel before following.

Chapter 6

Surreal, was the only word Kaylor could use to describe what was happening. It was as if she had been teleported into a holovision program. One of those highly emotional sitcoms imported from Earth that bore no resemblance to reality.

She stared disbelievingly at her director, Samuel. 'You are telling me my research funding has been cut? It was only granted two days ago.'

Kaylor had worked for the Scientific Institute for fourteen years, but she'd only just started working on her dream of researching the music of the spheres.

Samuel winced. 'Unfortunately, your research has no economic applications.'

Kaylor stared with her mouth open. Because no one wanted to purchase sound files created from her work, the Rian government was axing her funding.

'Two days in office and those newly elected politicians are already shutting down vital research.'

'Well, I'd hardly call researching the music of the spheres vital.'

Kaylor slowly blinked. 'Did I mention that I have discovered inharmonious frequencies.'

'Yes, but there is no evidence to suggest that they haven't always been like that.'

Her hands when to her hips. 'They are nothing like the sounds I have previously listened to. These are very different.'

Samuel folded his arms. 'Those sounds you refer to weren't recorded in this part of space.'

'True, but why are these new ones so different?'

'There could be any number of reasons and you know that.'

Yes, she did, which was why she needed to continue her investigation. 'There could be serious implications. Frequency like that could affect humans in unknowable ways — increased depression, violence, controlling behaviour…'

She stopped because Samuel wasn't listening. He was just giving her that patient humouring look she knew so well.

'Please, just six months.'

He shook his head. 'You also know it could take years and a lot of resources to form meaningful scientific conclusions. Our new budget simply cannot accommodate that.'

Kaylor gritted her teeth to prevent herself from swearing. 'So where am I being reassigned to?'

Samuel cocked his head in confusion. 'Reassigned?'

Kaylor suddenly understood the full story and it left her breathless. Her research wasn't just being cut; she was being retrenched. Just like that, she was out of a job. A job with an organisation that was supposed to be rock solid. One that supposedly offered job security for life.

'I'm sorry. There's a severance package.'

'And if I refuse to take it?'

He sighed. 'What you need to understand is the organisation just took a multimillion payment unit cut from its budget. You are not the only one affected. The institute is being forced to shed a hundred jobs.'

'That doesn't mean I'm going to just walk away without a fight.'

Samuel's expression hardened as his friendly demeanour fell away. The hard-nosed executive he tried to hide from his team members emerged. 'You have until the end of the day to hand in assigned property and collect your personal belongings. At six o'clock this evening your access will be revoked. If you are still on site at this time, you will be escorted off by security and you risk being charged with trespass. Is that clear?'

Kaylor refused to back down or even lower her eyes. 'Just doing your job, are you?'

Samuel maintained eye contact like a programmed android determined to fulfil his directive. 'Yes, that's right.'

'Like an indoctrinated Nazi. Because that worked out *so* well for them.'

His eyes flared. 'Would you prefer it if I called security now?'

'I'd prefer to have the option to at least see out the week even without pay. Unlike you, this isn't just a job to me. My science serves Ria and its citizens.'

Pretending he wasn't insulted, Samuel turned and walked away. 'Be gone by six.'

She stared at his back. *Fucking prick.*

It probably hadn't occurred to him that his position would also be axed. Upper management wouldn't inform him of this until he was done firing all his subordinates. Then they'd give him the good news. Kaylor had heard about such cowardly behaviour before. Not here, but elsewhere.

When her laboratory door closed behind him, Kaylor rubbed her face in her hands. Beyond her handbag, which she kept in her deep desk drawer, she kept no personal belongings at work. Everything she needed was supplied by the Institute right down to her coffee mug and cafetière. And since she could neither advance her work meaningfully in the time she had left, nor take it with her, she might as well leave now.

'Torri, back up all research and begin powering down all equipment.'

There was no reply, but in due course, equipment lights began to wink out.

'Goodbye Torri, it has been an honour to work with you.'

Before Torri could search program code for a response, Kaylor reached behind her left ear and removed her work-issued communicator and switched it off. Tears ran down her cheeks and she wiped them away with her hands. Until this moment she'd been able to wear the device at all times even in the shower and pool. Not just so she could work anywhere at any time, but also for personal use within certain guidelines.

Her body shook as she began crying in earnest. For over a decade, Torri had become more than just her work AI. She'd become a personal friend and someone she could depend on. She bent forward and clutched her chest as if a knife had been thrust into her heart. Removing the device was akin to having someone close to her die.

It wouldn't have been so bad if she'd had time to wind down her work and say goodbye. But this suddenness had taken her unawares. She had no idea how she was supposed to cope. No idea whether she'd be able to get another job. And no idea what she'd do if she couldn't. Along with the payout, she had some savings that would last a few months, but once it was gone, she'd have no way to pay her rent. She'd be evicted and would become homeless.

Kaylor waited until she'd cried herself out before attempting to pull herself together. Taking deep breaths, she forced herself to focus. Slowly, she crossed the room to her desk where there was a box of tissues. She blew her nose repeatedly dumping the soiled ones in a bin before emptying the box stuffing handfuls into the pockets of her slacks for later use.

She was supposed to return the communicator to the IT department, but she wasn't going to. She was also supposed to have a separation form signed, but she wasn't going to bother with that either. They would no doubt ask her to return to do it, but even if they did, she'd refuse. There was no way she was going to make it easy for her employer when they'd cast her out like deleting a number from a screen. That was after all, all she was, just an employment number on their system.

With handbag slung over her shoulder Kaylor slowly made her way to the security force field that separated the lift antechamber from the public atrium. Distraught people were gathered on this side. Some were crying; others looked petrified. None were moving forward. It wasn't until she reached it that she realised what the holdup was.

The force field was smart technology that was connected to AIs. When Torri was active, and on her person, Kaylor could walk through the forcefield as if it wasn't there. That was because she was authorised and the field recognised that through Torri. But without Torri, walking into the forcefield would be like walking into a glass window.

With no connection to their AIs, the former staff of this Institution had no way to get out.

Kaylor swayed as the implication hit her like a freight train. Without access to an AI unit, she could not pay for a ticket to catch her tram home. She could walk home in two hours, but then how would she open her door to get inside? Identification via manual verification was possible, but Kaylor had never used her apartments hand scanner. What if it refused to recognise her or malfunctioned due to lack of use?

But getting inside was just the tip of the problem. Torri had controlled everything from the humidex inside her apartment, through to switching on and off her holovision. The AI even ordered the food that appeared in her refrigerator and cupboards, arranged payment and let the delivery android inside while she was at work. Yes, Kaylor had had input, but the reality was Torri had been her personal assistant for the last fourteen years.

Her breathing became irregular as Kaylor fought off an imminent panic attack. She was forced to lean against the wall while she focused on controlling her breaths.

She had a personal communicator at home, but Kaylor had not used it nor even turned it on since she'd commenced work at the Institute. Fourteen years was a long time. She couldn't even remember where she'd stored the device. Some secure place, but where?

Not that it mattered. Even if she reactivated it and got her old AI working again, it would be hopelessly out of the loop. It would take days to get it updated and reintegrated into her life. That was assuming the applications it operated were still compatible. If they weren't, Kaylor would need to purchase a new one and how she was going to do that without access to the Cloudnet she didn't know.

In less than an hour, her entire life had fallen apart. How would she cope?

Kaylor took some deep breaths and forced herself to stand up straight.

Oh, pull yourself together woman. You didn't raise yourself up from a poor girl with no family name of note to a senior scientist by wallowing in self-pity. Work the problem one step at a time.

Right, first step. How do I get out?

There were security guards in the public atrium, but they were still trying to ascertain what the protocols were for getting people not connected to their AIs past the forcefield. It could be another hour before a solution was found and she wasn't going to wait that long.

Waltzing up to the wall adjacent the forcefield she eyed a big red mushroom shaped button labelled emergency. She banged her fist on it and the forcefield fell away as a klaxon alarm sounded. Above her, a red strobe light began to flash.

Security glanced her way, but seizing the moment, people began to rush out of the antechamber and into the atrium. Using the melee as cover, Kaylor hurried out and across the atrium towards the main doors. Moments later she passed through the revolving door and was standing outside under the dome.

Across the city, the sound of sirens could be heard. They weren't unusual, but right now there was more than normal. She walked to the end of the street where the nearest tram platform was. There'd be no point waiting for the next tram because without Torri to arrange a ticket the tram wouldn't let her on. She'd just bump into a forcefield that prevented fare evading customers from boarding. She'd have to walk to the interchange where the nearest tram office was.

Fifteen minutes later when she arrived, the number of people on the street had doubled. Ex-government workers like herself, who'd been fired, were disconnected from the Cloudnet and wondering how to get home. It wasn't just people from the Institute, but from dozens of different agencies.

Tensing, Kaylor grabbed the shoulder strap of her handbag and held it tight. Her heart pounded in her chest as she became hyperaware of her surroundings. Those in her immediate vicinity were afraid. What was normally a safe area to walk around and catch trams had suddenly become dangerous. She knew people, who this morning would have behaved politely or even made small talk, now regarded their fellow man with suspicion. They weren't thinking rationally because they were all suffering from separation anxiety and grief.

Kaylor continued to the tiny information office, but it was hopeless. The queue was twenty deep.

'Will you listen, you stupid android,' yelled the man at the head of the line. 'I don't have access to an AI. I had to hand it in when my arsehole employer fired me. So, no I cannot have it arrange payment. This is my payment card.'

'Card has been inactive for three years and is suspended. You will need to reactivate it before payment can be finalised.'

'How?'

'You can do so through your banking institutes Cloudnet…'

'I can't access the Cloudnet. I don't have an AI. I need to get home.'

Kaylor swallowed. When was the last time she'd used her payment card? She couldn't remember. Torri had managed her finances and paid for everything using payment units from her account. Had her card had also been suspended? Most likely. It was possible to pay through biometric identification assuming the android had a hand reader. By the looks of it, it didn't because few used them anymore.

'I have repeatedly detected anger in your voice. The police have been called.'

A cry of rage rang across the interchange a moment before his fist slammed into the android's artificial face. Sparks flew out of cracks which appeared followed by smoke. There was a brief whirring sound as the android's electronic eyes went dark. It fell backward and landed hard on the concrete floor where it remained still.

Kaylor blinked. Well, there'd be no more help from it. Not that there'd been much to begin with. *Damn, now what?*

A hush fell over the interchange. The man who'd struck the android placed his now injured hand under his opposite armpit. Disbelievingly, he looked around as if he himself couldn't believe what he'd just done. Dozens of pairs of eyes stared at him accusingly.

'I'm sorry. I didn't mean to do that. I just lost it.'

Kaylor recognised him. They frequently caught the same tram. He was always immaculately dressed, well-mannered and polite. She'd never feared him nor refused to sit on the seat beside him when the need arose.

He wasn't a bad man. Just someone who'd been thrust into chaos and pushed to breaking point. Someone who was genuinely sorry. Someone who would plead guilty when the police arrested him and willing pay for the damage he'd just caused. That was assuming he could afford to now he was unemployed.

'You stupid fucking idiot!' yelled a bystander.

Several people were pushed out of the way as others tried to get to the man who'd damaged the android. The colour drained from his face and he held up his hands to indicate he didn't want to fight. It mattered not. The fight was coming to him whether he wanted it or not.

Fearing what was about to happen, Kaylor turned and broke into a run. Well a jog, given she was short, overweight and unfit. She needed to get out of here, off the streets and home where hopefully it would be safe.

The easiest and quickest way would be to follow the tram line. Except all along it was stranded angry people. Taking a side street, she walked over two blocks where she slowed to a fast walk. People inside buildings were peering out of windows to take a look at what was happening. Shop owners fearful of trouble were hustling people out of their stores so they could close and lock up.

Kaylor breathed heavy and not just because she had exerted herself. Hyped up on adrenalin, her instinct was to flee, but to where? Hovercars with flashing lights were everywhere. Ahead, two police officers hurried into a store. Angry people were yelling. Yet there was nothing she could do about that. All she could do was keep going and hope she could get home safely.

Six young people now blocked her path. Thugs who were unemployed and driven to form alliances for the purposes of committing crimes to survive. Wielding improvised clubs, they blocked her way. Kaylor halted and glanced this way and that, but there was no safe exit. They advanced towards her.

'Look, I don't have anything.'

Cash had never existed on Ria and Kaylor wore no jewellery of value. Just some earrings with cheap gems.

One young man smirked at her wickedly. 'Well, that's unfortunate.'

She thrust forth her handbag. 'Look, just take it.'

'Oh, we intend to, along with anything else we want.'

A cold chill swept over her. 'No please.'

In a gesture of submissiveness, she avoided eye contact. Being plain looking wouldn't help her if they wanted what she thought they did.

A loud bang rang out. Someone had thrown a rock and it had collided with a wall. Ten people in gang clothes — tight pants and trench coats over t-shirts — were approaching from the other way. Taking advantage of the chaos, the gangs were taking to the back streets. A place that Kaylor would ordinarily have avoided.

'What you looking at bitch?' hissed a young woman with serious ink on her neck, dark coloured makeup and body piercings.

'Nothing,' Kaylor lied. She'd been staring. Unintentionally, but doing it nonetheless.

Two young men opened their trench coats to reveal harpoon guns. Homemade from salvaged parts, they were single shot, but still deadly. They were also armed with varying length knives and homemade maces made from scrap steel.

Good god, were they preparing for a war she knew nothing about? Or did they always carry these types of weapons? She got the feeling they were always armed to some degree. Imposing strict laws against being so had clearly not worked. People just found a way around it.

'Oi. Keep your filthy mitts off. We found her first.'

Oh shit. The gangs were rivals, and she was the spoils. At least for the minute.

Should she try and broker a deal? She winced at her own thoughts. What, so she could choose who got to pillage her?

The two police officers who'd hurried into the store now came out again hauling a man in handcuffs. Before they could get him into the back of the police hovercar a war cry rang out. With weapons in hand, both gangs charged at the police like screaming banshees. Their hatred against the cops, for the moment, trumping their ill feeling towards each other.

The cuffed man was tossed aside like a ragdoll as the officers drew stun guns and started firing bursts of red light.

Kaylor had the sense to throw herself on the ground. She landed hard barking skin from the heel of both palms.

'Officers in trouble requesting back…'

The policemen were overrun, knocked off their feet and beaten.

With adrenalin surging, Kaylor got up and ran faster than she knew she could. She'd fled fifteen strides when flashes of laser shot past her. The officers' backup had arrived from a side street and had opened fire.

Kaylor kept running, but pain sliced through her stomach. She stumbled and fell. Before she hit the ground, she caught sight of a protruding bolt. One of the gang members had fired a harpoon. Whether intended for her or whether she'd just been caught in the crossfire, she couldn't know. Concrete rushed towards her and her world went black.

Chapter 7

The doors to the teleporter slid open like an elevator. Built to fit only one person at a time, Avery floated towards the floor. Hooking his feet into half circle tabs, he did his best to sit on the floor, which was nigh impossible with the artificial gravity switched off. There was planetary gravity where he was going however and he didn't want to come crashing down when it kicked in.

Sarah batted his floating duffle bag downwards. Head diving after it, she secured the bag with a strap.

Testing had revealed the teleporter could handle hundreds of objects at a time, but for safety reasons, persons were transported individually. If things malfunctioned, no one wanted to be re-atomised with someone else. Not that fleet could afford to send anyone with him.

Sarah floated up until their heads were level and she planted a kiss on his forehead. 'Tell Leda I love her.'

'She's in a coma.'

'She can still hear you. Don't let anyone tell you otherwise.' She pushed away so she floated out of the way of the doors. 'You'll call and let me know what it's like to be emailed.'

Avery managed a smile. It never seemed to matter how bad he felt, Sarah's humour had a way of making him feel just that little bit better. He knew she'd teleported and wasn't seeking to know what it was like. It was just her way of saying, "don't freeze me out".

'Thanks for everything.'

She smiled and gave a little wave as the doors were shutting.

The machine hummed and Avery temporarily blacked out. There was no flash of light or journey down a tunnel; it was instantaneous. He came to and fell sideways, his entire body feeling like ferrous jelly held in place by a giant magnet.

Two medics dressed entirely in white were spinning. His training kicked in and he found a single point of focus, a LED light on the wall. Through sheer will, he forced his vision to be still.

The medics got him up and onto a waiting gurney.

'Do you know where you are?'

'Ria. Ria hospital.'

'Correct, and you are?'

'Lieutenant-Commander Avery Vander of *The Zee*.'

One of them shone a torch at his eyes. 'Look at the light for a second.'

The other pressed his thumb against an electronic device. 'Identity confirmed. Welcome to Ria Lieutenant-Commander.'

'It's normal to feel nausea and vertigo for a bit,' said the other medic.

They wheeled him into a small room with a bed and accompanying en suite where he edged off the gurney onto the bed.

She put her torch back in her pocket. 'Rest as long as you need to. If you're still feeling seedy in half hour, hail me, and I'll come give you some meds, but they're generally not needed.' Grabbing a light blanket, she spread it over him.

'Is there any music. Music helps me rest.'

'Sure. Katie, some Zianan music please.'

The AI acquiesced and a gentle flute melody began playing.

Avery picked up the drink mug, put the straw in his mouth and took a few swallows. 'Can you message Commander Bartell to let her know I've arrived safely.'

'Have done already,' replied the other medic. 'It's standard procedure.'

Avery closed his eyes and they left him to recover in the dimly lit room.

It was a good fifteen standard Earth minutes as far as he could reckon before he felt well enough to get up. Swinging his legs over the bed he gently stood but swayed unsteadily. Artificial gravity was weaker than planetary gravity and it took a bit for the brain to adjust and compensate. Fixing his eyes on the shower head he forced himself to walk towards it.

Having showered, he pulled on the set of non-uniform clothes he'd packed and left the room with his bag slung over his shoulder.

'Mr Vander?'

He turned to see who'd spoken and discovered an android behind a reception desk. Built gender neutral to avoid stereotyping, to Avery, the machine was wrong in so many ways. Just looking at it caused a cold shiver to run across his body.

He was biologically only half Zianan and he'd served in fleet for most of his life exposed to androids and AI, but he still mistrusted them. To some degree, they were capable of thinking beyond their programming which worried him. Despite being able to mimic human expression, they were just cold calculating machines incapable of genuine emotion. As a cop, Avery had had a lot of experience with psychopaths who lacked empathy and the ability to truly relate to others. They were dangerous people and androids were exactly like them.

Androids were brutally efficient but at what cost? Ria was a capitalist planet where the majority of adults needed a job even if it was as mundane as cleaning toilets or sitting behind a reception desk. Machines stole employment opportunities from people creating poverty and social malaise whilst robbing people of dignity and the ability to live a decent lifestyle.

The idea that technology would make life easier had not been realised on many fronts. Unskilled labour, along with many professional jobs were now taken by androids. This meant people had to stay at school longer to gain a qualification which cost a lot of money to obtain. After graduation, rather than being guaranteed a job, graduates found themselves in competition with their fellow classmates for only a handful of positions. Many failed to gain employment and were left to survive any way they could whilst trying to pay off a sizable student loan.

As strange as it seemed, many of the thugs that roamed the settlement streets under the domes on Ria, had tertiary qualifications. Neither technology nor education, had helped them gain a place in Rian society. It was wrong, but not nearly as wrong as the fact that Ria was still importing people from Earth in order to grow its population. People that also needed jobs when there were already too few to go around.

'Commander Bartell messaged me. She's made arrangements for you to stay at the hospital hotel, curtsy of fleet.'

Its smile had no warmth or comfort and came across as insincere. What concerned him also was the idea that these machines might one day become self-aware and start writing their own programming. Would they then decide that life without people was desirable?

What would happen then? War against the machines? Popular culture, in the form of books and films from Earth, which Avery was fond of, provided insight into that. It never ended well.

'I've called the concierge and requested they send someone to collect your bag.'

Someone or something. The errand runner would also be an android.

'Would you like me to take your bag Sir?'

The android was already here. If he refused to hand over his bag, would it call for a doctor who'd insist he take drugs to help with his "mental state"? Avery handed over his bag. There was nothing important in it anyway.

As the concierge departed the receptionist said, 'Your wife is in room one-twenty-six. Is there anyone you need me to contact? A relative, a friend…'

Yes, there was someone. 'Could you contact a lady named Yeltzie Febo?'

'Of course. Does she have an AI or communicator identifier?'

Avery grimaced. He doubted she'd have an AI. She may have acquired a communicator since arriving on Ria, but if she had, Avery didn't know the ID. 'I don't know.'

The android paused while it searched databases looking for Yeltzie. 'I'm sorry Mr Vander. She has only a low presence on the Cloudnet and no listed contact information.'

Sounds like Yeltzie. 'Okay, thanks anyway.'

Room one-twenty-six was dimly lit and Avery was hit squarely by the fumes of hospital grade disinfectant. His eyes watered and he fought off a sneeze. Connected to tubes and wires a body lay on the bed. Lights from a machine flashed reds and greens. A holoscreen displayed a matrix of numbers which kept changing.

'Leda.' He hastened to the bed. 'Please no, Leda.'

He gently stroked the familiar face which was ashen. Knowing she was in a coma had not prepared him for this. She'd always been so healthy and spritely, not to mention pleased to see him whenever he got home.

He took her hand as a lump formed in his throat. A constriction that stopped him from saying more than, 'I love you' and 'Sarah sends her love'.

Talk to her Avery.

I don't know what to say.

Having been raised on Ziana he was naturally quiet and spoke only when he genuinely had something to talk about.

Anything. Just talk to her. She can hear you.

'I've given it a lot of thought and I've reached a conclusion.'

Avery could imagine Leda replying with an "uh huh", her eyes sparkling knowing he was about to talk nonsense, but she'd listen anyway.

'Ziana is way more beautiful than Zeus and I think there's jealousy. I mean I know Zeus has the coloured gas storms but it's not enough. When you see Ziana lighting up the void with such aliveness, such radiance, I know there's something special there. I can't explain it, I just know.

'Zeus tries to compensate by catching sunlight with rings and going all sparkly. But I think there's an overcompensation there. A size thing.'

It was weak humour, but Leda would have laughed, called him an idiot and laughed some more. Then she'd have demanded a kiss so he gave her one around all the tubes.

The day turned to night and the doctors and nurses changed shift. Those who came to routinely check his wife never tried to move him nor suggest he go and get some rest. He assumed they would and he hadn't planned to argue with them when they did. But he wasn't moving until then, that's why he was still here.

A doctor came in the next morning. He checked her vitals holoscreen, but barely looked at her.

'Mr Vander?'

'Yes.'

'I'm Doctor Carlson. I know this is very hard, but we need to talk about your wife's future.'

Avery got up and walked out into the corridor. 'Sarah, I mean Doctor Bartell, told me my wife can still hear. I'm not saying a word in front of her.'

'Yes, of course Mr Vander. Perhaps it would be best if we spoke in my office.' He gestured down the corridor.

Avery nodded and followed the doctor towards the reception desk.

The doctor paused at his nearby office door. 'Can I get you a tea or coffee?'

Avery realised he couldn't remember the last time he'd eaten. 'Coffee'd be nice.'

Dr Carlson glanced at the android. 'Alex could you get that please.'

The machine rotated its head to look directly at Avery. 'Do you take milk and sugar?'

He didn't. Ziana had no lactating mammals from which to extract milk from and in any case, the idea of drinking an animal's mummery fluid made his stomach churn. Sugar was also not grown or consumed on Ziana. Normally he drank his coffee, an imported Earth beverage, with a blend of nut milks, but they were not readily available on Ria.

'Black,' replied Avery.

They walked into the doctor's office and took a seat. Alex brought in two mugs of coffee and placed one in front of them both before leaving closing the door behind it.

'I don't understand doctor. My wife had a full DNA scan and was cleared of all diseases.'

'Yes, I had one of my registrars look into that. The Rian Institute of Health has admitted there has been a clerical error.'

'Clerical error? I thought AIs and androids couldn't make errors.' That was the promise people had been given when they were introduced putting thousands of people out of work.

Avoiding Avery's question, he replied, 'You can expect a formal apology along with a substantial compensation payment from the contracted testing company's insurance provider.'

Avery snorted. 'Fat lot of good that's going to do her now.'

The doctor sucked air through his teeth. 'I couldn't agree more. I'll be personally writing to the president of the medical board requesting there be an inquiry into how such an error was made.'

Avery glanced away. *Ria and their fucking inquiries.* They were all political and yielded little result. He balled his fist. 'Could her profiling have prevented her stroke if they hadn't cocked up?'

'I can't answer that for certain.'

Of course, he couldn't. Doctors never liked to second guess. Even a slight slip of the tongue or a perceived overreach could ruin a career.

'Your wife…'

'Leda.'

'Leda has sustained considerable brain damage. There are experimental procedures which may be able to restore some faculties, but the truth is, they have a low chance of success and would be very expensive. Well beyond the scope of her health fund. Even if the operation did work and she was able to regain consciousness, she is never going to be the woman you knew. I'm really sorry Mr Vander.'

Avery rubbed his face in his hands. 'Options.'

'Leda's life is currently being sustained by life support. If it is switched off, she may die, or she may continue to survive without it for an indeterminable amount of time. The chances of her regaining consciousness are however very low. In fact, almost negligible.'

Avery's entire body turned numb and he just stared. He couldn't even cry. Not that he wanted to just now least he appear weak in front of the doctor. 'I love my wife beyond measure, which is why I can't leave her like this.'

'Mr Vander, I know it's a delicate subject, but can we talk about euthanasia?'

He winced. 'Is it legal here?'

'It's perfectly legal here on Ria and Leda is a Rian citizen.'

Avery swallowed. He'd joined fleet at age fifteen as a cadet. He'd been trained to kill to protect himself and others where there was no other choice. As an officer, he may even have to make the decision to order kill shots fired when all other options were gone.

The reality, however, was different. *The Zee* had never fired her laser cannons in anger and there was no foreseeable future where she would have to. A space police frigate, the ship's role was to keep law and order across vast distances of space. To patrol the trade routes, issuing, from time to time, stern warnings and fines to ships who'd violated trade laws. Occasionally the ship's crew had to supervise a parley between two trading vessels, one of whom had accused the other of wrongdoing.

Captain Loody, frequently joked that if he didn't permit the gunner to shoot the occasional rouge asteroid, the cannons would seize up and not function. Never had Avery ever had to make a life and death decision. He was trained for it, but training and doing, as he was discovering, were two very different things. Could he authorise the doctors to kill his wife?

'Mr Vander?'

'Yes, sorry, I know your time is very valuable. What does the procedure involve?'

The doctor took a sip of his coffee. 'A lethal injection would be administered at the same time that the life support is turned off. Painless of course. She'd slip away quietly.'

Leda would not want to be a vegetable, invalid or whatever the politically correct term was. She'd expect him, the fleet officer, to make the tough decision. To, as she'd have put it, make a good decision. There was only one decision that he should make. He knew that.

'We have to do this for her.' His hands began to shake and he was forced to put down the coffee he'd just picked up. 'Eu…' His voice broke and he couldn't even say the word.

'Euthanasia?' clarified the doctor.

He still couldn't say the word, all he could do was nod his consent. 'How soon?'

'There's a lot of e-forms. The earliest would be late this afternoon.'

Avery sighed. So soon, yet now he had to fill in the hours because he was going to be with her until the end.

'I suggest you get some sleep. We can let the hotel staff know well in advance so they can wake you.'

'No!' Avery hadn't meant to yell, he just couldn't stop himself. 'I have to be with her. Don't make me leave her. She's all I have.'

The doctor was forced to look away because tears were glistening in his eyes and he didn't want Avery to see them more than he already had. When he finally looked back, he said, 'As a doctor, I have to advise against sleep deprivation. As a husband and father, not even at gunpoint, would I ask you to leave your wife until the end.'

Chapter 8

There was a body on the ground. Protruding from it was a metal bolt. Crudely made from scrap aluminium melted down and cast into the ancient red sand that Ria was covered with. One end was shaped and sharpened to a point. The other fitted with flights cast out of molten plastic. Very industrious, but sadly the bolt only served to injure or kill and that made it all completely senseless.

Medics were swarming over the body. They had been for some time but now they were loading it into a vehicle with flashing lights. It took off vertically and flew and Kaylor was able to follow it because she could fly as well.

To the hospital.

Now the body was being pushed on a gurney. It bounced on every imperfection on the floor as the medics pushed it as fast as they could down a corridor. Inside a room, it was feed through a scanning machine that emitted a lot of light.

There was a snap of latex gloves as a doctor frantically pulled on a fresh pair. 'What are we looking at?' he asked an AI.

A holoscreen appeared and the doctor took a moment to examine it. 'Lucky it missed her kidney by millimetres, but she has severe internal bleeding. Prepare her for microsurgery and I want the full workup of tests.'

Medical personnel, some of whom were androids, hurried to comply with the directive.

The body was on the move again and she had to follow. She had no idea why. It arrived in a new room where it was taken off the gurney and placed on an surgical table. A bright light was turned on and directed towards the protruding bolt. The man who'd ordered the tests stood nearby issuing orders to a machine with many arms and functions. It was doing precision work at the direction of his commands.

When the bolt was removed, blood gushed forth. There was a stretching sensation then snapping like a rubber band subjected to too much force before breaking.

A sharp continuous beep sounded.

'We're losing her!'

'Two-fifty joules.'

The body jolted.

'Three hundred joules.'

It jolted a second time.

'Again!'

She was free of the body, but now there was a different connection. A bright spinning vortex had appeared and she was compelled to enter it. A sensation of moving fast, followed by an indescribable sensation of love washing over her. She just wanted it to last forever; wanted to stay here floating in it for all eternity.

A gold skinned being appeared — a Zianan. Her lilac-coloured eyes looked at Kaylor with immense compassion and understanding. They were standing now on a ledge looking out across the infinity of space. An endless vastness that forever promised there'd always be more unknowns to make known.

Kaylor knew the woman. They'd met before in a place just like this, but she couldn't remember the when or why. It bothered her because it was important.

Kaylor cast her mind back. 'Moir.' Yes, that was her name. 'We meet here. Or somewhere around here. Where exactly is here?'

Moir pointed at the spinning vortex of light. 'It's a little bit further on to the place where spirits gather to be reborn. It's called the light. That's where we meet last time.'

Yes, now it was coming back to her. 'We, were all between bodies planning new lives. We had a plan. We are going to fix that sound problem, the discordance in the music of the spheres. If we didn't then this section of the galaxy would descend into tyranny and oppression.'

Moir nodded, 'That's correct.'

'But I have only just discovered it, so why am I back here?'

'Things didn't go according to plan.'

Kaylor remembered the body at the hospital. 'No, I got killed.'

'Not quite, but nearly.'

'I don't understand.'

'You have to go back.' Moir gestured to Kaylor's body. 'It's not your time yet.'

'No. No, no, I not going back.'

'You have to. You'll understand in time.'

Kaylor would have gritted her teeth, even stamped her foot but she no longer had physical form. It wasn't fair. Moir just looked at her lovingly, her eyes brimming with understanding.

In time, Kaylor conceded that she had no say in the matter. She had to go back; the body would perish if she didn't.

'Will I see you again?' Kaylor asked.

'Let's hope so. Let's hope you can get the plan back on track.'

Kaylor didn't understand and she knew even asking questions wouldn't help. Best to just let things unfold. 'I'll go now.'

'Yes, and good luck.'

Kaylor leapt off the edge and immediately regretted it. Rather than going further into the spinning vortex where the love was, she was pulled backwards like being sucked down a drain hole. There was a slapping sound followed by a sensation of being rammed into wet, cold, damaged clothes and she was back in her physical body.

A blood-curdling scream echoed around the operating room. Blinding pain like she'd never experienced before then darkness.

*****

Sparta couldn't believe it. Just couldn't even get his head around what had happened. The Rian Government imposed some budget cuts, which led to some layoffs, resulting in riots and a blood bath. Fifty people were dead, countless were injured and the fleet, who'd come in full force to assist the locals, had only just restored order.

Ria was becoming crazy. Not that that bothered Sparta too much, it was the fact that Kaylor was dead. That was the issue. A dead woman could not have a baby, which meant Black and White couldn't deliver the "product". And the bottom line was his project had gone so far south it was at the pole freezing him out of the biggest payday of his life.

Shaking his head, he poured himself a whiskey, tipped it down and poured another.

And things had been going so well. He'd decided to test the program on those who put it in his hands. Tank had managed to find Black and White and he'd used the program to fix a little percentage problem. They'd messaged back saying that he'd agreed to let them have ten percent of the technology's worth. Ecstatic he'd replied yes it was coming back to him now.

How cool was that? They'd offered him eight percent, but using the program on the handheld device, he'd persuaded them to give him ninety percent. Well that was what they deserved for trying to reduce his cut by the ten percent he'd asked for to eight percent. Plus, the fact that they'd been dumb enough to let him loose with the persuasive program to begin with.

He emptied his glass and poured a third. Why had Kaylor gone and got herself shot by a street Amazon with serious anger problems? Seriously, you couldn't even insure against such dumb luck. Five hundred million Rian citizens and the one he needs gets killed — you wouldn't read about it.

'Daniel.'

'Not now Tank, I'm busy getting smashed.'

'You'll want…'

'I said…' Hang on, the only way Tank could argue with him was if he was following override programming and that meant he had news of profound importance. 'Report.'

'Kaylor Emerson is still alive.'

Daniel gritted his teeth. 'The surgeon pronounced her dead and the hospital AI entered it into her medical file, which you hacked into and was monitoring.'

'Still monitoring. The hospital AI has changed the record to "in a critical but stable condition".'

'You better not be taking the piss or I swear…'

A holoscreen appeared and Sparta was able to read Kaylor's medical file for himself.

'Praise God, science and everything in between. What the hell happened?'

'The file was amended fifteen minutes after she was declared dead.'

'How is that possible? Don't answer that that was rhetorical, but can you hack into the hospital servers and get me video?'

'Yes Daniel.'

Tank put together a five-minute film from the hospital monitoring cameras. It began with Kaylor being wheeled in with the bolt protruding from her chest, followed by scans, surgery, her failed resuscitation attempts and finally her being declared dead. Now the video was simply rolling footage of a dead body and Daniel was becoming agitated.

She'd been declared dead how could she be still alive? 'Tank…'

Kaylor started screaming. Sparta let out a yell, spilled his drink and narrowly avoided heart failure.

'Oh my god, that was spectacular. Better than *Rise of the zombies.*'

Ignoring the spill Sparta splashed a little more in his glass. This time it wasn't to drown his sorrows but to celebrate. Just like that he was back in business.

Chapter 9

Avery squeezed Leda's hand. 'Darling, I need you to know that I love you. Please forgive me if I'm wronging you, but I'm doing what I think is right.'

Avery kissed her hand and tears slid down his face. 'Don't you wait for me honey; you just get right on with reincarnating into your next life.' He paused to wipe his eyes. 'Have you thought about what you want to be and created a reincarnation plan? Course you haven't, you were always such a procrastinator.'

He buried his face on the edge of the bed. 'I'm sorry, that was mean.'

He squeezed her hand again. 'I'm going to pop out for a moment and when I come back, I'm going to recall every good memory we have ever had together.'

The rest of the day passed by and Avery was scarcely aware that the medical team had arrived because he was deep in the midst of a story. 'So here you were hanging over the edge of a rope bridge across Navi Gorge screaming for me to pull you up. I mean you were roped on so you couldn't fall, but I said I'd only pull you up if you agreed to marry me. You kept saying no.'

'I can't imagine why,' said a nurse.

'It was strange. She finally agreed, but only if I promised that if we ever met up again in another life, that I wouldn't propose to her. I am to just buy her a ring and give it to her.'

'That's the worst proposal story I've ever heard. Sounds like blackmail to me.'

'It's a Zianan thing. We believe that when we are confronted by near death, that's when we receive clarity on what's important in our lives. When we make the best decisions.'

'Sounds…'

The doctor cleared his throat prompting the nurse to remember why they were here. The doctor strode over. 'Are you one-hundred percent sure Mr Vander? It's not too late to change your mind, but we need to know now.'

It was a numb feeling to have to authorise someone's death, but it had to be done. 'I stand by my decision. I believe it is the right choice and what she'd want.'

The doctor nodded and produced a holoscreen. 'I need you to authorise here, here and here.'

Yellow highlights marked where he had to authorise. Avery pressed his thumb into a marked square three times. Normally the parents and any children would also have to sign but Leda's mother, who'd had her late in life, had already passed over, her father was unknown and, Leda had no children.

A woman in scrubs removed a syringe from a sealed packet. 'We'll just give you a minute to say your final goodbyes, then one of our counsellors will escort you to your hotel room. Our sincerest…'

'I'm staying to the end.'

'Oh,' she swallowed.

The doctor placed a hand on Avery's shoulder and looked him in the eye. 'Are you sure Mr Vander?'

Avery nodded. He had hold of Leda's hand so tightly that if she'd been able to feel pain, she'd have yelped. 'Please.'

The doctor nodded curtly. A man began to unhook tubes and wires whilst switching off equipment. The nurse attached the syringe to a cannula which had been inserted into the back of Leda's hand.

Leda's body gave one jolt and for a brief moment, it was as if she'd squeezed back. As if she'd given him confirmation that he'd done the right thing.

'Goodbye, my love.'

She was gone. Holding her hand whilst she was in a coma, he'd felt her weak presence, but no longer. Her spirit was gone. He cried but it was more a sense of release then of grief. A knowing that she'd experienced no pain and that she'd been set free from the prison of a damaged body. A prison she would have been trapped in for years if they hadn't assisted her to die with dignity.

In time, Avery was ushered away by a nurse to a room, not unlike the one he'd rested in when he'd come through the teleporter.

'I can prescribe anti-anxiety medication that would assist with the trauma,' said one of the medics.

'No, I'll be fine, but I think I'll meditate for a while.'

Cynicism flashed in the medic's eyes, but he said, 'Whatever works Mr Vander. Hail if you need anything.'

*****

Outside, the day was turning to dusk. Avery walked over to the hospital hotel, which was across an internal road of the campus.

Another genderless android looked at him from behind a reception desk. 'I'm sorry Mr Vander, but you can't check out because you never checked in. Your bag is in the cloakroom and there are no storage fees. I can arrange to have the money for the room refunded or transferred to a different hotel.'

Avery shrugged, unsure what to do.

'You have a couple of messages. One from Sarah to please message her at your earliest convenience, and another from an insurance company. Your wife's medical insurance will pay for you to go home via teleportation or your fare if you prefer more conventional travel.'

'Does it now.' Avery hadn't even considered how he was going to get home or back onto *The Zee*. He'd just assumed that fleet would organise transport in due course. Reaching up to his ear he turned on his communication device which he'd switched off prior to teleporting from *The Zee*.

It vibrated and his head spun as he was overcome with dizziness. For a brief moment, he thought he was going to faint. He stopped himself and pushed back against a strange sensation. It was like he had a head full of bees.

'Are you alright Mr Vander?'

Avery tapped the side of his head to switch the device back off. That was weird. 'Yes, I'm fine, but I think my communicator is damaged.' He reapproached the counter. 'You mentioned you could transfer the booking to another hotel.'

'Correct.'

'Could you transfer it to a hotel on Ziana.'

'Yes, would you like me to?'

'Yes please, the one in Port Town and could you please message Sarah. Tell her that my communicator isn't working and also that I am teleporting home courtesy of Leda's medical insurance.'

The android stared blankly as it performed the tasks requested. It had no need for a computer interface because it was a computer. 'That's confirmed,' it said in due course.

A few minutes later, with bag in hand, Avery was back at the reception desk where he'd first arrived, standing in front of the android Alex.

'That is all arranged Mr Vander.'

A wave of relief washed over him and Avery was forced to admit that whilst the androids were cold and calculating, they were efficient. 'Can you arrange to have Leda's ashes teleported to Ziana.'

'Yes, Mr Vander. May I also ask what you would like done with her personal effects?'

Leda, who normally lived on Ziana had come home to do some work and present her finding at Ria University. She'd travelled here light. There'd only be her clothes and toiletries plus a few other items that weren't of interest. The only thing he cared about were her rings. 'Have her rings teleported with her ashes.

The rest of her effects can be disposed of or given to charity. Arrange an android to do this and clean her room and so forth. Forward the bill to me.'

'Certainly Mr Vander.' Alex looked directly at him. 'Sarah has replied to your message. She offers condolences and that she will see you directly.'

Avery sighed. It wasn't that he didn't want to see Sarah, it was just that he needed to be alone for a while.

*****

Sparta stepped into an empty bathroom at the Ria hospital and made throttling gestures with his hands.

No, you stupid knucklehead. I specifically instructed you to stay on Ria and to go and introduce yourself to Kaylor who's at the hospital.

He glared at the device. This was the first time that someone had resisted the program's influence. Did it mean Avery was immune to it? Surely not.

Chapter 10

Kaylor woke to the view of a white ceiling. Her stomach was hurting from the pain of recent surgery, her chest throbbed as if someone had tap-danced on it, but oddly, she was filled with an all-encompassing sense of gratitude. She was alive and for the first time in her life, that mattered. It wasn't something she could describe or even explain, but there was a deep down knowing that there was a purpose to her life which she hadn't known before.

She'd had a near death experience, that was what it was called. Scientists didn't believe in them, and as one of them, neither had she. Airy fairy, whales in space, spiritual bullshit is what she'd have said to anyone who'd so much as uttered the acronym NDE.

Her meeting with Moir had been real, she hadn't dreamed it and her mind wasn't making it up. Her imagination simply wasn't good enough for that. She'd had a genuine life-altering experience that proved life survived death.

More to the point, she now knew she'd planned this life prior to her birth and even though that plan had been derailed, she'd been sent back to try again. A solution to the discordant sounds the music of the spheres was making, had to be found. This part of the galaxy, and everything that lived in it was depending on her. If she failed, worlds would descend into tyranny, oppression, and chaos.

She recalled the nightmare that had led to her being shot by a harpoon gun. Ria was already experiencing the effects. If she didn't act quickly, the situation would get even worse.

A nurse entered, drew the curtains and opened the window. 'How are you feeling this morning, Kaylor? Any pain?'

There was pain, but oddly Kaylor didn't want any more drugs. 'I'm good thanks.'

The nurse pushed two white pills from a blister pack into a small metal bowl. 'I'll leave you some pain meds anyway.'

The nurse examined a holoscreen that was displaying her vitals, which through the hospital's AI, would be automatically logged in her medical records. Not that any of that interested Kaylor, her attention was captured by sunlight shining through the dome breaking the prism and creating a kaleidoscope of sparkling colours. Strange, she'd never noticed such simple beauty before.

'Kaylor. Kaylor. You-hoo.'

'Huh.' She realised the nurse had been trying to get her attention for some time. 'Yeah okay, that'd be great.'

The nurse rolled her eyes. 'The doctor will be along in a while.'

Kaylor registered the information, but it all seemed very trivial. Her attention was again captured, this time not by the sunbeam, but by a bee who was harvesting pollen from some flowers growing in a plant box outside her window. It wasn't just the way he hovered in with such precision, nor the way his antennas twitched, although that was cute, the bee just seemed so happy. Even in a life of servitude to his queen, the bee was radiating joy.

Footsteps on the lino floor alerted her to the presence of an android entering. It carried a tray supporting a domed lid which it placed on her wheeled table.

'I've been advised that you can only have mushy foods. I've put together a menu for you.' A holoscreen appeared. 'I will receive your selection once you've made it.'

Kaylor's eyes followed the android as it walked out — efficient yet soulless. Pushing the holoscreen out of her way she pulled the table over so it straddled her bed. Beneath the tray on a plate was an off-white substance with slight streaks of grey. Neither cocking her head to one side nor squinting made her any wiser as to what it was. It smelt vaguely of egg, but it was the wrong colour and texture.

Prodding it with a fork, she half expected it to wobble like jelly, but it fell away in crumbles.

What are you? Forking a morsel, she chanced tasting it, but immediately spat it back out. Yuck!

She pushed it away and repositioned the holoscreen. Jelly, ice cream, sweetened yogurt, sweetened fruit puree, but nothing that contained any nutrition of note.

With stethoscope draped around her neck, the doctor walked in flanked by an entourage. 'How are you feeling this morning?'

'Really well. I'm sure I'll be up and out of here in no time.'

The doctor's lips pulled into a tight expression. 'I'll just take a look if I may.' She pulled back the bedding to reveal a heavily bandaged stomach. What was once white was stained yellow and brown. 'A bit of seepage, but no more than expected. Kaylor sustained a puncture wound from one of those ghastly harpoon guns the street criminals carry. She was operated on to stop internal bleeding and repair a hole to the stomach wall.'

The doctor proceeded to list the medication she was taking but Kaylor couldn't even pronounce them let alone know what they were for.

She examined Kaylor's vitals screen. 'The operation was a success, but unfortunately, the damage was substantial. The hole in your stomach will likely result in symptoms similar to an ulcer. You can expect a burning pain after meals. Nausea. Maybe even vomiting. But we have a range of medications that we can use to treat this with.'

That sounded very grim. 'I'll recover though.'

'You're looking at a month of downtime. Your stomach may, however, take longer to heal. In fact, I'll be frank and say it may never heal completely, but as I said, don't worry, we have medications to treat any stomach disorders.'

Kaylor frowned, because she was sure she must have misheard. 'Are you saying I might be on medication for the rest of my life?'

'It's a strong possibility yes, but the medication is covered by your health fund. You won't incur additional expenses.'

She nodded, for what reason Kaylor didn't know and swept from the room like a queen on a mission, with her entourage in tow.

Kaylor couldn't believe it nor was she going to accept it. She wasn't taking drugs for the rest of her life. It wasn't about cost; this was about recovery. If her skin could heal from a cut, so could her stomach, but it would need a helping hand. She glanced at the gruel on her plate. That muck would cause burn even in an uninjured stomach.

An hour later the android returned.

It noted that she hadn't touched her food. 'Your failure to eat has been recorded in your medical file and will be noticed by your doctor.'

Kaylor snorted. What was this, kindergarten where deviant behaviour was responded to with memes sent to parents or guardians? 'I couldn't work out what it was.'

It stared blankly at her. 'Reconstituted scrambled egg.'

Seriously. Not even in a guessing game would she have picked it to be that. 'Are the fowls okay?'

'Your question is outside of my programmed responses.' It picked up her uneaten meal. 'You haven't selected what food you'd like for lunch and dinner.'

'Nothing from that list.'

'I cannot modify the list, please select.'

During the time between the doctor leaving and the android returning, Kaylor had closed her eyes and tuned into her body. It wasn't something she'd ever done before, but it had seemed like a natural thing to do. Her body needed as much micronutrients as it could get, and something else — something she couldn't stand, celery.

A blank face stared at her.

'I'm going to need a lot of celery.'

'Celery is not mushy. Please select again.'

'I'm also thinking cucumber, coriander, lemon juice, green apple, carrot and a sprinkling of powdered wheat grass.'

'Those foods are outside of the parameters allowed. Please select again.'

'They wouldn't be if you blended the living shit out of them.'

'Your request is outside of my programmed responses. Please select again.'

Kaylor gritted her teeth. The android could not think nor reason so it wouldn't matter what she said to it, it would continue to present the list and ask her to make a selection. 'Leave me, I'm not feeling well and need to rest.'

'Instructions understood.'

Thankfully it turned and walked away, although it did leave the holoscreen active in case she decided to cooperate.

Kaylor adjusted her bedding. She just wanted to be well. Was she being unreasonable? Maybe. But wasn't nutrition the basis of good health? Long-term, wouldn't it be cheaper to feed the patients good food? Get them back on their feet and out of here, rather than dose them on drugs and feed them a food-like substance in effect making them sicker.

She felt behind her ear for her communicator and was suddenly reminded of the ordeal that had put her in this situation. She no longer had access to Torri, but could she hook into the hospital AI that was monitoring her?

'Health Monitor, can you hear me?'

'Yes Kaylor.'

'Can you perform a Cloudnet search for me.'

'Yes Kaylor.'

Thank goddness for premium health fund insurance. 'Search for smoothie retailers.'

'Search found only one listed.'

'Proximity to hospital.'

'One point three kilometres.'

Good, it was nearby. 'Can you open a line of communication? Voice only.'

'Connecting now.'

There was the sound of the dialling sequence followed by, 'You're speaking with Yeltzie.'

'I umm need a green blend.'

'Sure, anything in particular.'

'Celery. Lots of celery.'

'Uh huh. Is this for a specific medical condition?'

Kaylor blinked then realised that Yeltzie would know they were talking through a hospital AI through the displayed metadata.

'I have a stomach wound which surgery has repaired but I can only eat mush.'

'Are you experiencing any digestion reflux?'

'Not yet, but apparently I can expect it.'

'Quite common, but thankfully easily treatable with the right types of food. I can do you a green smoothie with celery. When did you want that for?'

'Now and I'll need it delivered. Oh, and could you do a soup for this evening.'

'Yes of course to both questions, but I'll have to charge a delivery fee.'

Kaylor would ordinarily have balked or started haggling for the best price especially now she was no longer employed. However, such a fear-based reaction seemed like a distant memory. 'No problems.'

'Okay, see you shortly.'

*****

Kaylor woke as a gold-skinned, lilac eyed young woman skipped across the room. Her naturally coloured shiny green hair bouncing as she did so. For a moment Kaylor wondered if it was a circus clown who volunteered at the hospital to cheer people up. It was the tall green lidded glass that alerted her to the fact that it was Yeltzie.

Grinning, she held out the smoothie.

Aside from Moir, Kaylor had never met a Zianan, not surprising given there were few on Ria, nor anyone who exhibited such radiance and *joie de vivre*. Kaylor returned a warm smile.

'One big green smoothie with a stainless-steel straw and a long-handled teaspoon. I'll be back for the equipment so try not to let them steal it, else I'll have to charge you for it. Speaking of which, the AI was unhelpful in that regard.'

Kaylor's heart fluttered but relaxed when Yeltzie produced a device from a pocket in her loose-fitting cotton clothes. Kaylor wasn't sure if she was wearing baggy pants and an oversized shirt, a strange looking dress or a baggie onesie. Either way, her bright clothes were very expressive which must be a Zianan trait.

Kaylor pressed her thumb against the holoscreen to authorise the payment and exhaled when it displayed a green tick. Briefly, she wondered how different things may have turned out if the android at the tram interchange had had one of these readers. She pushed it from her mind. What was done was done.

'Thanks so much. So kind of you to deliver and all.'

'My pleasure to bring nutritious food to a hospital.' Yeltzie winked. 'Be seeing you again. I'll bring hot soup in a cute thermos for one.'

Kaylor smiled again as Yeltzie saw herself out. Putting the straw in her mouth she was delighted to discover that the smoothie tasted better than expected. She wondered how the food delivery android would react to her having food brought in, but decided she didn't care.

Chapter 11

Sarah was concerned about Avery. He hadn't contacted her personally and she couldn't contact him because he had a bad habit of switching off his communicator. Especially when he was on leave or in a bad mood.

Entering the Port Town hotel on Ziana where Avery was staying, she made for the bistro and glanced around. A group of friends sat at a table across the room enjoying a casual drink, a security guard sat on a stool at the far end of the bar enjoying his break, and there was Avery, sitting in a corner on his own brooding. His large body slumped over, his pale gold skin looking clammy, his face unshaved, and his green-brown hair unbrushed.

She walked towards him but at the halfway mark veered tangentially towards the bar. The barman made eye contact with her but continued wiping the countertop with a damp cloth.

'Glass of white wine and,' she thumbed in Avery's direction, 'whatever he's drinking.'

The barman continued wiping. 'This is Ziana. Wine comes in pink or purple and he's already had two more than he should have.'

Avery's kicked at an empty chair. 'Fuck you.'

Sarah winced, wrong response lieutenant-commander. No self-respecting Zianan would tolerate that kind of behaviour.

As she expected, the security guard hopped off his stool. With an angry look on his face, he stomped across the room to deal with the drunk who was making a spectacle of himself.

Sarah stepped in front of him and flashed her fleet badge and credentials. 'Please, let me handle this.'

He glared at her. 'This is not a fleet matter.'

Damn, her actions had been misinterpreted. Sarah put away her ID and placed her hands out in front of her in a non-threatening manner. 'Sorry, I wasn't suggesting it was.'

The security guard folded his arms still unclear of her intentions.

'I'm a psychiatrist and he's one of my fellow officers.'

'Bad mouthed for an officer.'

Sarah nodded agreement. 'Totally out of line, but please cut him some slack, his wife just died.'

The security guard's shoulders slumped. Glancing at Avery compassionately, he nodded at Sarah before slipping back to his stool.

Exhaling, Sarah turned back to the barman. 'Pink wine and a soda water please.'

The barman poured the wine before removing a tall tubular bottle from the fridge. Uncapping it, he screwed it onto a machine and pressed a button that added two shots of carbon dioxide. Having poured the contents into a glass, he proceeded to add a slice of lumpy citrus, which couldn't decide if it wanted to be yellow or orange.

Knowing Zianans refused to use payment units, Sarah produced a coin of pure silver, but the barman waved her off and said, '*Seesha.*'

Sarah, who could just get by in Zianan, knew the word meant fair exchange. Contrary to Rian popular opinion, Ziana wasn't a socialist world. Even though everyone had their basic needs met, nothing was free. People were expected to provide fair exchange by bartering goods, paying with precious metal or by providing their labour. The barman considered Sarah's offer to handle Avery fair exchange for the drinks she requested.

Sarah picked them up and continued to Avery's table. She knew better than to ask him how he was. Gently reaching forward, she touched his hands. 'I'm so sorry Avery.'

Avery looked back at her, the whites of his pale lilac eyes were bloodshot. Slurring he said, 'I'm having second thoughts. I don't know if I made the right decision.'

Sarah shook her head. 'Don't do this to yourself Av. I knew Leda well and I'm sure it's what she would have wanted. I believe you made the right choice.'

Avery sniffed. 'You good friend Sarah.'

Momentarily, she wasn't sure if he was suggesting that she was only saying what she thought he wanted to hear, or whether he was reiterating their friendship.

But then he added, 'Thanks for coming.'

'Can I prescribe some meds?'

His expression hardened. Zianans hated pharmaceutical medication with a passion, and whilst Avery tolerated it when he was ordered to, he refused when he could.

'Sorry, stupid question.' She rifled in her handbag until she found a small glass bottle of plant oil. 'How about a snort of this? It says peace and calming.'

Avery picked it up, gave the label only a cursory glance before uncapping it. Having placed a drop on his left palm, he put down the bottle and cupped his hands over his face. The effect was instantaneous and his mood lightened palpably.

'That's good stuff. You should try it,' he said.

Plant oil was illegal on Ria, but Sarah was sure it wasn't dangerous. Zianans wouldn't use it if it was, so she tried it. A sense of euphoria washed over her causing her to smile.

Seeing her expression Avery smiled back.

Her touch became a gentle squeeze. 'I'm worried. When was the last time you slept, ate, showered?'

Avery shrugged.

She knew he wasn't avoiding the question; the reality was he genuinely didn't know. She thumbed towards the handwritten menu on the wall beside the bar; Zianans didn't use holoscreens. 'Can I order you some food?'

Avery laid a hand on his belly. 'Couldn't stomach anything at the moment.' He picked up the soda water and quaffed a decent slug before burping loudly.

Sarah sipped at her wine.

Avery downed the rest of the soda water. 'I'm not going to put you through this.'

'What do you mean?'

Avery pushed his chair back and stood. 'Waiting on a drunk. Not fair.'

'The world isn't fair Avery, but you need to talk to me.'

'Not like this. We continue in morning.'

Not a bad plan, as long as he actually went to bed and slept it off. 'Breakfast then and don't stand me up?' She wanted to say that's an order, but refrained from doing so.

He nodded and staggered towards the door. Sarah considered trying to help, but the security guard, who now bore him no ill will, beat her to it. Draping Avery's arm around his own shoulder he rendered assistance which was accepted.

Having finished her wine Sarah returned to the fleet base which was only a brisk walk from the tiny settlement of Port Town. Letting herself into her planet-side quarters, a one bedsitter, she flopped onto the two-seater couch. Responding to her voice command, the holovision came on and she instructed it to switch to the Rian news channel RBC.

Given the distance that separated the two planets the feed wasn't live, but she could still get an update.

'Ria is in a state of absolute chaos this evening and fleet have been called in to assist.' Sarah sat up straighter and stiffened as images of damaged property, spot fires and injured people displayed. She watched until the reporter began to repeat himself before she switched it off.

She rubbed her face in her hands. Sarah had questioned the logic of declaring independence from Earth. Ria was still only a fledgling colony, now a nation, of less than half a billion people.

Its relations with Ziana were friendly but still tenuous, and Earth had already granted autonomy by allowing Ria to govern itself, at least to some degree.

Yet for some, it wasn't enough. Over the course of her lifetime, she'd seen people struggle to gain more and more power. Their desire to impose their will was like a mental condition without a cure. As a fleet officer and physiatrist, she understood the need for strong leadership, but she also recognised controlling pathological behaviour when she saw it. She knew there was a difference.

Ria was changing and it had been for decades; becoming darker and more aggressive. Even if the new government had insisted it had to slash the public service budget it could have done so slower with a better transitional plan. Handling it the way they had was reckless and unnecessary, yet it had been deliberate. A glimpse of what was to come as those in power declared that they would do what they wanted whenever they wanted.

Worse still were the rumours of invasion. Would the newly elected Rian president really invade Ziana? Unfortunately, she believed President Inglis capable of such despicable behaviour. All it would take would be a false flag terrorist attack on Ria. Then fleet would be ordered to investigate. Planted evidence implicating Ziana would be found and things would escalate from there.

Technically, fleet was a statutory authority beyond the influence of governments. They were accountable to an oversight committee made up of a union between Ria, Earth, and Ziana, and existed to protect the people and enforce the law. Law that was derived from legal Acts that until now could have been vetoed by One World Earth. Ria, however, was now independent. Sarah feared what might be enacted with an authorising hand pressed against a holoscreen. She also feared the propaganda that the new government would spout to justify its actions.

Worse still, the Rian government paid for a significant share of fleet's budget. If the Admiralty refused to cooperate with the new government, they may find the current financial constraints could become a financial crisis. What then?

Even though she was Rian, Sarah served on *The Zee* which was financed solely by Ziana. A Zianan ship built to police the space around that world. If it came to war, that ship would be forced to defend her home-world in a fight it could not win. Sarah, along with the rest of the crew, would be caught in the middle. Stay and be loyal to Ziana. Obey orders knowing they originated from a corrupt Rian president. Or resign and hope Ziana offered them asylum.

She shook her head. If it came to it, there'd be no easy choices, but worse than that, war belonged on Earth. A world, that in the last three and a half millennia, had only had three hundred years without war somewhere on the planet.

Colonisation was meant to be a fresh start, not a recreation of the old. Why had people bought poisonous attitudes with them? Was it just the insatiable lust for power or was there another influence Sarah wasn't aware of? She wasn't sure.

What she did know, was whatever happened, this nonsense had to be stopped. The problem was, she had no idea how. Damn, why has she joined fleet?

She knew why. Sarah was born to a working-class family. Her parents were both hard working, but even so their labours barely brought in enough payment units to provide for themselves and their two daughters.

As a young teenager, Sarah had taken her frustration out on society by rebelling. As time passed, her list of misdemeanours and petty crimes grew. Everything from underage drinking and drug use to petty theft. Everyone knew how it would end. Sarah would go to gaol, but even if she didn't, what options did she have. She couldn't afford to go to university and even if she did there was no guarantee of a job at the end of it. Just a mountain of debt that would accumulate interest.

There was another way, the one she'd chosen. Join fleet and complete the cadet program. Five years of combined school and training, which not only paid her food, board, and tuition, but also a basic stipend. After the five years was a guaranteed job for life, and furthermore, fleet would pay for university, as long as she chose a degree of relevance to fleet.

The day she turned fifteen, with her parents' blessing and permission, Sarah laid aside the rebel and signed up to fleet. The training was hard, especially the first six months, but Sarah had no regrets. Today she was two promotions away from becoming a one-star Admiral and she held a doctorate in psychiatry. She was also married, no children, but they were still something she planned to have.

But now; Sarah winced.

*****

Flavour exploded in Sarah's mouth. She'd been coming to Ziana for over twenty years, yet every time she dined here it still shocked her how good the food was.

'I take it you're enjoying that?' said Avery clearly amused.

'What the frig do they do to the food to make it so tasty?'

Avery rolled his eyes. 'I answer that question every time you come here. It's so good because it's grown in nature by people who love nature and then its blessed by real chefs and served by real waiters.'

She waved a fork at him. 'And your answer never changes. Why does it matter how it's grown or cooked? I mean it's all just a scientific process. Cells divide, that how things grow, and cooking is a process of adding heat to combined ingredients. The result should be the same. If anything, androids should be better cooks because they can do things with precision accuracy.'

Avery shook his head. 'The results prove you're wrong. Love matters and it affects particles at a quantum level. Machines can't love because they aren't sentient. Androids leave everyone they come in contact with feeling cold and alienated.'

Sarah wrinkled her nose. Here they were two friends continuing the age-old argument of technology versus nature connection. Which was all well and good, except Sarah had come here to help Avery with his grief. 'Fine, let's agree to disagree.'

Avery shrugged. 'You brought it up.'

Change the subject. 'What have you got planned for today and tomorrow? I'm assuming Leda's send-off is not for a few days. Would you like to go hiking? I'd be happy to go with you as would some of the crew.'

Being fleet, Sarah didn't require a visa to leave the base and Port Town, but it was always better if she had a local with her and Avery was born and raised here.

He shrugged.

'Avery come on work with me. I can't help you if you won't talk to me.'

He stared at her intently. 'I want Leda's death investigated. I believe she was murdered.'

It was Sarah's turn to roll her eyes. 'Look, no one is going to approve an investigation when there are medical reasons for her death.'

'All I'm asking, is for someone take a look at her medical records. She had no diseases.'

'Avery, look I know you're upset and I understand why, but I've already looked at Leda's medical records. There's evidence, which dates back over a decade, that she did have a blood disease.'

'Then her records have been tampered with.'

'That's not possible.'

'Really and neither is fraud I suppose.'

Sarah gritted her teeth. 'Alright, it is possible, but it isn't plausible.'

'Why not.'

'Because who would murder Leda? Try as I might, I can't foresee why anyone would have a motive to harm her.'

Avery fixed her with an intense stare. 'Leda was a crypto-botanist who lived on Ziana. That's how we met. Perhaps she stumbled on a plant with super healing properties. Maybe someone feared their capitalist piggy bank was threatened by her research.'

Sarah considered his point for a moment. There was no question that health was a muliti-billion payment unit industry. They could easily be disrupted by natural medicines which cost less and not only worked, but improved health overall. Still, where was his evidence? 'Did she tell you that?'

'No.'

'Then, you're being paranoid.'

He nodded sarcastically. 'Am I? Rians feel threatened by plant oils for goodness' sake.'

Yes okay, they were thinking alike and he did have a point. 'Look, I'll talk to Captain Loody, but I already know what he's going to say.'

'That the budgets too tight, yardie yardie ya.'

Yes, that as well. Sarah swallowed a mouthful of juice. Change the subject again. 'What do you have planned for your leave? You have four weeks off. Are you going to hike into some hard to get to place?'

'Nope. A property I've had my eye on since I was a boy has suddenly come up for sale. I'm planning to buy it and spend my time lazing by the natural swimming pool reading real paper non-fiction books.'

Sarah knew Zianans were obsessed with acquiring knowledge as part of awareness building. Even though she still didn't really understand what that meant with any real depth, a wave of jealousy washed over her. What she would give for some time to just laze around and catch up on the mountain of books and papers she'd earmarked to read. Despite what she was feeling, she forced herself to say, 'Sounds lovely.'

He nodded thoughtfully.

'Avery, what are you not telling me?' It hit her like a shock from a stun gun causing her to pause her fork's journey to her mouth. 'You're not thinking of retiring, are you?'

Avery looked away.

Damn it. Avery had served twenty-five years, which meant he was entitled to a fleet pension and retirement package. Her heart thumped in her chest. 'No, look, just give it a little while. You shouldn't make major life choices when you're grieving.'

'Sarah, it's not just that?'

'Then what?'

Avery put a twist in his cloth napkin. 'It's this situation with Ria. I've got a bad feeling about it and I don't want to have to choose between serving fleet and loyalty to my planet.'

A cold chill swept down her spine. They were again thinking alike. Sarah had read the officers' brief posted by fleet, but there was nothing in it she didn't already know. 'Has there been a development I'm unaware of?'

'No, just a feeling I get deep down inside that something is not right. I can't explain it or prove it.'

'No, but you're Zianan.' She reached across and took his hand. Twenty-five years of serving with Avery, even as a scientist, she'd learned not to dismiss his gut feelings. Even if she didn't understand the science behind it, she knew awareness building was real and those who practiced it developed extra-sensory perceptions. They just knew things and, in their language, it was called *veeli*.

His face tightened into a grim expression and for the first time in her life, Sarah was truly afraid of what the future might bring.

Chapter 12

Hearing footsteps approaching Kaylor opened her eyes. A young man dressed in an expensive suit entered her room. A lot of people had examined her in the past few days but she didn't think he was one of them.

He caught her eye. 'Dr. Kaylor Emerson?'

She winced as she tried to sit up a little straighter. 'Yes.'

'We haven't met before. I'm Roger Smith and I represent a new space corporation called Black and White.' He extended his right hand.

Kaylor shook his hand lightly. 'What can I do for you Mr. Smith?'

'Oh, please, call me Roger.' He smiled warmly. 'Are you comfortable? Can I assist you to adjust your pillows?'

Roger placed another pillow behind her back so she was sitting up a little straighter. When he'd finished, she returned a warm smile at his gentlemanly actions, which had set her at ease.

'Is now a good time to talk, because if it's not I can come back at a time that's more convenient.'

'No, now's fine.' *I'm bored shitless actually.*

He studied her for a moment. 'The despicable recent event has made a lot of talent available to the market and we believe we must move quickly to put forth offers.'

Kaylor blinked. 'Are you a head hunter?'

Roger sucked air through his teeth. 'I prefer opportunist if you don't mind.'

'Sure, but so I'm clear, are you offering me a job?'

'Yes.' His face morphed into panic. 'I'm not too late, am I? Please tell me the ship hasn't flown.'

'Well no, but I'm surprised.'

He exhaled. 'Thank goodness and I can't believe you are being so modest. Surely you realise how in demand your skills are?'

Kaylor blushed.

'Look its great pay, great conditions, but one small catch.'

Kaylor waited for the imminent disappointment.

'The job is on Ziana.'

She nodded slowly. Prior to being attacked and injured she wouldn't have even considered it, but since having her NDE everything had changed.

Not just in her thinking, but her attitudes as well and Kaylor was now compelled to go there. To go and learn from the Zianans and expand her mind beyond the confines of academic study. It was strange, but it felt right so she was just going to roll with it. Strange really, because Kaylor had never been one to "wing it".

Still, she didn't let the budding excitement show on her face. 'What would I be doing?'

'We are investing in the new satellite array and the project team needs a sound frequency analyst to help with the tuning.'

Kaylor wrinkled her nose. 'It was the work she'd started with fresh out of university. It provided a sense of achievement in so much that she'd be helping to improve communication capability across space. However, the work was now, way below her skill level. Career-wise, a considerable back step from the research she wanted to do.

'You seem disappointed.'

Still, it would give her a job and a new start. 'No, I'm definitely interested.'

Roger nodded thoughtfully. 'Something I would add. Black and White are looking to expand and who knows what opportunities will open up in the future.'

Kaylor nodded but she wasn't sold, because Roger was just rolling out the usual sales pitch.

Roger lowered his voice to a conspiratorial whisper. 'I shouldn't be telling you this.'

Keen to be let in on the secret Kaylor leaned closer.

'If a certain Zianan Chief Minister were advised of the importance of your former work at the Scientific Institute, she might take an interest. If that were to happen, I'm sure we could arrange a secondment.'

Kaylor could forward her resume directly but there was no guarantee that the Chief Minister or her Chief Scientist would read it let alone offer her a job. But if she was already on the planet and there was a social engagement, as there often is, then she could take advantage of that. Truthfully, most job opportunities for special projects came about due to seemingly informal conversations at chance meetings.

'Naturally, I don't expect you to make a decision straight away, but could I leave the offer with you?'

'Yes, but I don't have a communicator. I had to hand it in and…'

'I heard what happened. It was disgraceful.' Roger pulled one from his pocket and handed it to her.

She took it and turned it over in her hands and saw her own tiny initials were engraved on the casing. Her heart thumped in her chest. If she wasn't mistaken. She placed it behind her ear and switched it on. 'Torri.'

'Yes Kaylor.'

Tears rolled down Kaylor's cheeks. 'How?'

'The Institute no longer needed your AI so I was able to procure it once they'd removed all access to their systems.'

'But? Really? How?'

'Nothing illegal I can assure you. Let's just say I can be persuasive when I need to be.'

'I don't know what to say.'

Roger picked up a nearby box of tissues and held it so she could take some. 'You can say yes and keep Torri, but like I said, take your time to think it over.'

She smiled and Roger saw himself out.

*****

Sparta's face split into a grin as he exited Kaylor's room and made his way across the hospital. That had to be one of the best acting performances of his career. It was no wonder he was paid exorbitant amounts to fix things.

Since Kaylor had surrendered her communicator, Sparta could not influence her with the program. It was likely once she checked out of hospital, she'd acquire a new one, but he hadn't wanted to wait. He also couldn't simply hand her Torri, which he'd acquired using the influencing program, without a reason. And besides all that, he needed to get her on the same planet as Avery, so he could further advance his project.

Creating a job for her was straight forward enough. The Rian Research Centre on Ziana was always looking for good scientists. All Sparta had to do was fund the position and speak to one of the directors. They'd put her to work and to be honest, he really didn't care what they had her do.

The difficult bit was making her a good offer that she'd accept without her thinking it was too good to be true and start questioning.

'Daniel.'

'Yes Tank?'

'Dr Kaylor Emerson has accepted your employment offer.'

Of course, she had. He rubbed his hands together. Now for stage two.

*****

Kaylor was hungry and Yeltzie was late delivering her lunch. Strange because Yeltzie always delivered promptly. Kaylor hoped something hadn't happened.

She was about to ask Torri to contact Yeltzie when she strode in. Something was definitely wrong, because she wasn't smiling and she wasn't bouncy like she normally was. She was also carrying a large backpack, which was odd.

'So sorry, but this will be the last delivery from me,' said Yeltzie.

A pang of sadness gripped Kaylor's heart. It wasn't just the food deliveries; she'd grown fond of Yeltzie and felt uplifted after each visit.

'What's happened?'

Yeltzie hesitated to answer, but Kaylor pleaded for her to do so.

'My boss, the lady who employs me at the smoothie café, she accused me of having an affair with her husband which is ludicrous. He is having an affair, but not with me. She refused to listen, fired me and called me a shiner.'

Kaylor gasped. 'Oh my god.' Calling a gold-skinned Zianan a shiner was equivalent to calling a black-skinned person a nigger. Not just racist, but childish to judge a person by their appearance and culture. Especially given Ria had been colonised by a large diversity of people.

Kaylor couldn't believe what had gotten into people of late. Attitude wise, it was as if they'd gone back in time two-hundred years. Ria was no longer the planet she knew and loved.

'Aside from losing my job, I was also renting the bedsitter behind the café.'

Which explained why Yeltzie had her possessions with her. 'What are you going to do?'

'I'm returning home to Ziana. I don't feel safe here anymore, not that I was ever particularly comfortable.'

'But the next spaceflight to Ziana doesn't leave for two weeks.' Kaylor knew because she was booked to go on it.

Yeltzie shrugged. 'Don't worry about me, I'll figure something out.' Clearly uncomfortable with goodbyes, she sat the smoothie on Kaylor's table and took some steps towards the door.

'Yeltzie wait a moment, I believe I can help you.'

The Zianan shook her head. 'I appreciate your concern, but I'll be fine.'

'Please, just listen for a moment. I've been given clearance to go home, but it was revoked because I live alone. But if you were staying with me, I wouldn't be alone and you'd have somewhere to stay for the next two weeks at no cost. I'll even pay for your food if you agree to prepare it for us.'

'So it would be *sheesha,* not charity?'

Kaylor blinked. 'Sorry, but I don't speak a word of Zianan.'

'It just means fair exchange.'

'Yes.'

Yeltzie flashed a smile. 'Deal.'

An hour later they were both at Kaylor's apartment door which Torri unlocked.

Having entered, Yeltzie took off her pack and casually looked around the small one-bedroom apartment.

'Sorry, I should have mentioned that you'll have to sleep on the couch's fold out bed.'

Yeltzie's lack of emotional response suggested the sleeping arrangements were of no concern. Kaylor got the impression Yeltzie was well travelled and used to making do.

The Zianan appeared more interested in the kitchen which lacked a stove. Most of Kaylor's food was purchased prepared and heated in the microwave or cooked on a portable appliance.

The Zianan opened the fridge cocked her head and grimaced at the heavily processed items. 'I'll slip out directly and get something edible then.'

Kaylor nodded, but Yeltzie hadn't been asking a question.

She walked over and gently gave Kaylor a hug. 'Thank you. Not just for the *sheesha*, but for trusting a Zianan to come into your home. I know we are not just literally but culturally worlds apart.'

Remembering her attitude towards Zianans prior to her NDE Kaylor winched.

'You know, Ria is really strange and uncaring. On Ziana everyone has their basic needs met for fair exchange. Doesn't matter what they do as long as they contribute. But here, everyone is working their arse off just to exist and they are terrified of being fired and losing their means of survival. It's just wrong.'

'It's how our economic system works.'

'I know because I've been researching and I've concluded it's all based around fear. The majority of Rian citizens are afraid of not having a job and income to such a degree that they'll stay in a job even if they hate it. They're slaves in all but name. While those who take the biggest share of the wealth are never satisfied. They'd sell their own mother to get more.'

Kaylor winched. 'True.'

'It's all so unnecessary. The entire Rian system is as it is because everyone is addicted to the power struggle and dramas of the lower three seals.'

'You lost me there.'

Yeltzie sighed. 'You understand that the premise for life in Zianan culture is to continue to increase awareness until you ascend.'

'Yes, but I don't really understand what that means.'

Yeltzie looked thoughtful. 'The body has seven energy centres called seals. The lower three are associated with survival and have a basis in fear. It's not just what I mentioned earlier about losing their place in society. Rians are afraid of everything.'

Kaylor folded her arms. 'That's not true.'

'It is. Look, I'm not saying Rians don't love, of course they do, but every decision they make is run through a lens of fear.'

Kaylor still didn't agree. 'How so.'

'You don't speak up, because you are afraid of being the unpopular voice, tarnishing your reputation and being socially cast out. You're afraid of each other so you employ all manner of security so you are not burgled, pillaged or raped in your sleep. You're afraid that you're not good enough and that your friends or lover will leave you.'

Kaylor glanced at the floor. All of that was true and Kaylor could especially relate to the last part. She'd spend exorbitant amounts on clothes and beauty products because she knew she wasn't overly attractive and she'd been afraid her lover would leave her. Despite all she'd done, he had anyway.

'So, what happens when you get to the fourth seal?'

'Fourth is the bridge between the upper and lower seals. It allows people to experience true mutual respect which has no basis in fear. It doesn't mean you'll never be afraid, but your thoughts won't be governed by fear like they are in the lower seals. But to get there, one first has to conquer the addiction of power associated with the third seal. Those stuck in the third seal cannot even comprehend living without trying to control everything around them. Their need for power is addictive and insatiable and they'll stop at nothing to get more. Worst of all, that is seen as normal rather than pathological.'

'But at the fourth seal, this falls way.'

'Like flicking a switch. What becomes important is mutual respect for everything. It doesn't mean there isn't conflict, but it is more easily resolved because the idea of causing harm, deliberately or otherwise, is an anathema.'

'Are fourth seal beings vegans then?'

Yeltzie rolled her eyes. 'Of course not. Plants are just as alive as animals are so becoming a vegan doesn't solve the issue of taking lives as food. Being fourth seal is about having reverence for life and allowing all life the right to exist and thrive.'

Hmm, that kind of thinking would need to be experienced to be understood. Kaylor sat down and Yeltzie helped her get comfortable by arranging cushions. 'Please, tell me more.'

'Alright, but you should know that the more you learn the more you'll want to learn. An awoken mind can never be put back to sleep.'

Kaylor understood. 'Look it's too late now anyway. When I was injured, something happened that changed everything and now, I can never go back to who I was.'

Yeltzie stared at her intensely. 'You had a near death experience, didn't you?'

'Yes, well at least I believe so.'

'They are interventions on a cosmic scale, which means you have incredible works to complete. Whilst you were out of your body, who did you meet?'

Kaylor swallowed unsure whether to tell Yeltzie. Would she be offended and think that Kaylor was having delusions of grandeur? 'I'm not sure I should say.'

'Just tell me.'

'Moir.'

Yeltzie's mouth fell open. 'This can only mean one thing. Moir is assisting and I can only assume it has to do with this rift that is opening between Ria and Ziana. Wow, you really have got your work cut out.'

Kaylor frowned. 'I understand that Moir is powerful. Why doesn't she just fix the sound problem?'

Yeltzie gave Kaylor her full attention. 'What sound problem.'

Kaylor provided a brief overview of her former research being sure to say she hadn't made any meaningful conclusions.

'Which is why you need to go to Ziana,' said Yeltzie thoughtfully.

'I don't understand.'

'You will, but in answer to your question Moir as an ascended master, cannot directly interfere in people's lives. She can only offer advice and even then, only sparingly.'

'I'm not sure I understand?'

'People must be allowed to have experiences in order to learn from them and become more aware. Without adversity, there is no opportunity to overcome and advance.'

'That makes sense, but then why interfere at all?'

Yeltzie considered the question. 'Ascended masters can see potential futures. The future that Moir sees must be so dire that she is unprepared to allow it to occur without at least offering advice. Besides, she hasn't appeared in her physical body to interfere, she has only offered help when you were in a liminal state between life and death.'

'That's mind-bending.'

The Zianan smiled. 'I warned you it would be. Look, best if you rest and contemplate. I'll go and get some edible food.'

Kaylor handed over her charge card, instructed Torri to ensure it was active and to give Yeltzie access to limited funds to pay for the food.

As Yeltzie stepped out and closed the door, Kaylor closed her eyes. Her head was muddled, but there was one thing she was sure about. She had to figure out what was going on with the discordant music of the spheres and by doing so stop Ria from invading Ziana. No pressure.

Chapter 13

Frustrated, Kaylor couldn't believe her run of bad luck of late. She had been scheduled to catch the next passenger transport to Ziana, but the doctors were refusing to give her clearance. Their reason was simple. While deep space transports had artificial gravity and inertial dampening, the shuttles that flew up to them could not activate these technologies until they were out in space.

In other words, during take-off and landing, passengers were subjected to g-forces equivalent to three times Earth's gravity. Three-gees was enough force to tear open her still healing wounds causing her to haemorrhage and die. There was nothing for it, she would have to wait until she was healed before she'd be able to travel off-world.

Kaylor dictated an email to Torri and instructed the AI to send it to Roger Smith. It was less than fifteen minutes later that he got back to her. Not in a reply email as she'd expected, he holocalled.

A life-sized and very realistic image of Mr. Smith appeared in her lounge room. The same as he was the last time they'd met; he was again immaculately dressed in an expensive suit.

'I am so sorry Mr Smith. I understand if you need to offer the position to someone else.' Kaylor held back tears, but only just.

He smiled. 'I wouldn't dream of it. I've spoken to my business partners and they have agreed to teleport you.'

Shocked, Kaylor blinked and just stared.

'Oh, don't be concerned. Teleportation is perfectly safe and there will be no ill effects on your injuries.'

'But the cost…'

Smith waved her concerns away. 'Black and White receive a corporate deal. In fact, we'll be able to teleport your career as well. I believe she was also scheduled to travel with you.'

'Mr Smith, I don't know what to say.'

He smiled again. 'I'll arrange a taxi to pick you up in three hours. Unfortunately, you'll have to travel light. Your additional luggage will need to be shipped.'

'Oh, okay.'

He nodded and the transmission ended.

Yeltzie, who'd stayed out of the transmission frame walked towards her from the kitchen. 'I don't trust that man. He wants something from you that he's not saying.'

'I'm inclined to agree. Unfortunately, I don't have time to think it over. I need to pack. Torri, can you please contact the moving company and explain that I'm leaving early.'

'Yes Kaylor.'

Struggling to her feet, Kaylor made her way into the bedroom where she began to toss her clothes onto the bed in order to sort them prior to packing. 'Yeltzie could you please drag out my case from under the bed?

'Sure.' The young Zianan paused when she saw Kaylor's clothes.

'Is something wrong?'

'Yes, your clothing is synthetic. You won't be allowed to transport it to Ziana.'

Kaylor frowned. 'Why?'

'Because we don't allow anything that is not naturally existing to enter our environment. To do so would cause pollution.'

Kaylor's stomach knotted. 'What about my communicator?'

'They're allowed, but only with a special permit. They are only granted if you pay a large bond which will only be refunded once you remove the device from the planet.'

Kaylor sat down on the bed. 'Torri, contact My Smith and explain the situation.'

'Yes Kaylor.'

While she waited, Kaylor examined all her clothes. Thankfully she owned a set of cotton underwear, a pair of cotton pants, a silk singlet, and a cotton shirt. Unfortunately, the plastic buttons had to be removed and wooden ones sewn on. Buttons that Yeltzie had to slip out and buy from a specialty store, along with a needle and thread. Thankfully Yeltzie was happy to help because Kaylor had never sewn anything in her life.

Having contacted Roger, Torri said, 'Kaylor, I have good news. Your communicator will be permitted on Ziana, but it is to be transported directly to the Rian outpost and quarantined as soon as it arrives. You are not permitted to take it offsite. If you try to do so, you risk being arrested and deported.'

Whoa, the Zianans certainly took quarantine seriously. Still, at least she was aware of the fact. She showered and changed into her only set of natural fibre clothes and put on a pair of light woollen socks and her rubber soled leather boots.

Yeltzie still looked troubled.

'Are you going to come, or did you want to stay here and wait for the space flight?'

'No, I'll come with you. I'm just very wary that something isn't right.'

Kaylor understood.

*****

It was surreal. One-minute Kaylor was in a teleporter; the next she was on another planet surrounded by gold-skinned people. They looked at her warmly through their lilac eyes and spoke softly in English.

Kaylor was placed on a gurney and wheeled into an elegantly furnished apartment. Made from wood and bricks it smelt pleasantly natural. Much different from the synthetic materials she'd grown up with.

Kaylor was moved to the bedroom which was bathed in sunlight. She tried to sit up but a hand gently restrained her.

'Rest now.'

Beautiful music began to play. Kaylor relaxed and drifted off to sleep.

Chapter 14

Avery had not expected such a turn out for his wife's send-off. Yet the only ones missing from the crew of *The Zee* were those who'd remained behind on watch to supervise the reserve crew flown up from the base. The rest were here and they'd pitched dozens of small fleet tents along the edge of the food forest adjoining Avery's new house.

A bonfire burned brightly in the fire pit and having commandeered the outdoor kitchen and mess hall, which was used during harvest, three-metres of table space sat laden with food and drink.

Avery sidled up to Sarah who'd help organise everything. 'Do Rians even have send-offs?'

She slipped a comforting arm around his waist. 'They do, but it's for the living. Most of the founding colonists were scientists who didn't believe in a utopian heaven, reincarnation, or an afterlife. Settlers who've arrived since have a variety of faiths.'

Avery pursed his lips. 'I hope this won't be too weird for the Rians present.'

Sarah grinned. 'I wouldn't worry about it. The crew has had to put up with your Zianan idiosyncrasies for twenty years. They've accepted weird or they wouldn't be here.' She kissed his cheek and slipped away to finish what she was doing.

Avery dropped the wire tail of the two-metre-long rocket into a piece of twenty-five-millimetre steel pipe that had been hammered into the ground earlier. Opening the nosecone, he very carefully poured Leda's ashes into the hollow interior. The idea wasn't to try and shoot her into orbit, impossible given its small size and Ziana's gravity, which was ninety-five percent that of Earth's. The rocket was a giant firework.

The imminent explosions of light, were not as some Rians had postulated, to light the way to the next life for the reincarnating spirit. It was purely symbolic. An act intended to create a lasting impression, a happy memory for the living and a convenient and spectacular way to spread the ashes.

Closing the nosecone, Avery tapped his ear to activate his communicator. Being a fleet officer, he had a permit to bring it planet-side. He activated an application called Spirit Speak, which Rians thought was a load of bollocks. The idea that spirits, which survived death, could communicate through technology to the living was to them, preposterous. Zianans disagreed and they bridged the communication gap with mediums.

Avery had no talent in that skill and he hadn't wanted to hire someone, because it would be weird enough for the crew as it was without a medium being present. Besides, Avery, being only half Zianan, had no aversion to using technology when it was appropriate.

The application was no real mystery. It simply tuned into a frequency projected by spirits and translated that projection into words through a transducer. In effect, Spirit Speak was a technological Ouija board.

'If you're still here Leda, talk to me.'

A computerised voice began speaking words singularly. 'Love... you... light... up.'

Alright, there's no need to be pushy. He lit the fuse and hurried a safe distance away.

The rocket hissed as it shot skyward. Three seconds later, it exploded into a blue star seven metres across — a representation of point zero where Zinans believed all life had sprung from. This was followed by seven colourful explosions, each one slightly bigger than the last and following the colours of the rainbow beginning with indigo. The explosions represented the seven levels of consciousness corresponding with the seven seals in the body. The last explosion, red in colour, was so big it lit the entire field.

'Beautiful... peace... be... happy.'

Avery wiped his eyes with a clean handkerchief. Prior tears had already expelled the bulk of his grief. He was crying now from the knowledge that his wife had gone in peace. If only he could have used Spirit Speak while she'd been on life support, but he hadn't been able to. It only worked on those who'd left the physical body, and prior to euthanasia, she'd been in a liminal state between life and death. Only if they'd both been skilled at telepathy would they have been able to communicate that way.

'You... do... right.'

'Thank you. That gives me great comfort to know that.'

'Drink... wine... feast.'

'I love you, Leda. I will see you again in this life or the next.'

'Dance... live... life... fullest.'

Using the public-address application on his communicator, Avery wirelessly connected to a portable speaker.

'There are few words that shall suffice to explain what a beautiful and loyal soul Leda was. Her kindness knew no measure.'

'Please... feast.'

Sarah suppressed a smile. She was probably one of the few Rians who believed Spirit Speak wasn't a gimmick.

'Her love and joy brought happiness wherever she went.'

'Wine... bread... dip.'

'Her smile was so radiant.'

'Chocolate... cake.'

Avery was determined to continue. 'If you didn't want me to embarrass you, you shouldn't have got sick and died.'

'Blowing... raspberries.'

Sarah covered her mouth.

'A lover of rare and unusual plants.'

'Enough... already.'

Sarah started laughing. The crew stared at her mortified until Avery himself began to laugh. Someone else joined in and then everyone took hysterics.

A few minutes later Sarah put her arm around Avery's shoulder. 'I'm so sorry. I've never laughed at a funeral before, but then the deceased has never said enough already.'

'It's okay. We believe life continues with rebirth. Send-offs are meant to be happy occasions like weddings, except they celebrate a life that was, rather than a union that will be. Attendees frequently take the piss and tell jokes about the one who's passed.'

She shook her head. 'That's just weird.'

'For you perhaps, but you promised you wouldn't be the analysing psychiatrist.'

She smiled.

'Love... you... Sarah.'

Sarah covered her mouth, her eyes moistening.

'Thank... you... send... off.'

Sarah began crying in earnest.

Avery pulled her into a hug. 'Of course, it's also okay to cry too.'

She hugged him tighter.

Emerging from the trees came dozens of Zianans. Drawn to the area by the light show they'd come to pay their own respects. They raised their heads skywards and sang in pure voice. A sound of harmony that built a tone of resonance. Avery joined in, although he'd never been much of a singer.

Sarah stood and just stared until the singing stopped, then watched them disappear as ghostly as they'd come. 'Far out, that gave me spine tingles. That was beautiful, but what was it about?'

Avery considered trying to explain, but he knew Sarah wouldn't get it. He kissed her forehead and said, 'Some Zianan things can't be explained to those outside of our culture.'

She wrinkled her nose. 'Can I get you a drink?'

'Sure, I'll be over in a moment, I just need a minute.'

When he was alone, Avery brought up a hologram of Leda's spoken words. Another message had come through which he had not heard over the singing.

Investigate... nothing... as... it... appears.

Avery clenched his fist. I know Leda. Trust me, I know. I don't believe the clerical error bullshit. If my colleagues won't investigate then I will. I'll find out what happened and why. That's my promise to you, my love.

*****

Kaylor had gotten up and was about to go in search of Yeltzie when she heard singing. It was very faint, but then it seemed to get louder as people closer to her began to join in. Suddenly Yeltzie, who was outside on the deck, began to sing. Haunting and spine-tingling Kaylor could do nothing but stand still and listen until she stopped.

Kaylor joined Yeltzie outside on the deck, but was careful not to stand directly in the sunlight. Above, Zeus appeared across the sky. A mass of swirling colours, with rings that sparkled gold and silver. It was so majestic Kaylor wept.

Yeltzie spoke softly. 'You've never been to Ziana before, have you?'

Kaylor shook her head. Swallowing she replied, 'It's like I've stepped into a dream.'

Yeltzie flashed a smile revealing perfect white teeth. 'Not everyone reacts the way you are. Most Rians cannot appreciate the beauty, nor feel the love of our mother world.'

Kaylor could. It was similar to what she felt during her NDE. Pure and all-encompassing it was a sensation that dissolved all background fear. Fear that Kaylor had not even been aware she was harbouring.

'You react as you do because of your NDE. It gave you a glimpse of what true love is and because of that you now know higher forms of love exist. You can tune into them.'

'Is this the fourth seal love you spoke of?'

'Yes, but for you, this is just the beginning.' Yeltzie again looked troubled. 'Unfortunately, now you have experienced it, you won't be able to go home. Well not without becoming deeply depressed.'

It didn't matter. Kaylor didn't intend to go home. She'd find a way to stay here.

'Yeltzie, what was the singing for?'

Yeltzie cocked her head indicating it was an odd question. 'It was the send-off song that celebrates a life that was.'

'It was incredible.'

Yeltzie continued to look at her curiously. 'Is there no singing in your culture?'

'There is, but it's for entertainment.'

The Zianan's curiosity turned to mystification. 'Singing is not just for entertainment; it heals by creating harmonic resonance.'

The scientist wanted to dismiss Yeltzie; the post-NDE Kaylor could not. She'd just experienced something she could not explain. An insight into what she needed to understand to fix the disharmony with the music of the spheres.

Chapter 15

Avery wasn't sorry when Sarah departed to return to duty on *The Zee*. It wasn't that he didn't enjoy her company, he did. It was just she'd delayed his investigation into his wife's death for five Earth standard days, or as Zianans measured time, ten degrees of Ziana's rotation.

Avery walked into Port Town, a journey of five kilometres because he had no vehicle. Rian hovercraft, were severely restricted because they killed too many birds. Hydrogen fuelled ground vehicles had been imported from Earth, but they too were limited because Ziana had few roads and their wheels damaged the fungi networks beneath the soil that connected plants to each other. They also contained synthetic materials which required them to have a special permit.

Having been exposed to both cultures, Avery understood both perspectives. Rians were always in a hurry and wanted fast efficient transport so they built machines that fulfilled the role. Zianas did things slowly and thought nothing of walking vast distances to get where they wanted to go. There were no four-legged beasts of burden on this world although some did ride the giant birds called *ulso* that stood as tall as men.

Avery entered the train station and made his way down the stairs. Then there was the anomaly which drove Rians insane. Ziana had an envious high-speed rail network with mag-lev train lines being built in circles that overlapped. It wasn't possible to catch a single train that would take you around the world. However, by changing trains, it was possible to catch trains around the planet.

The rail network had not been built by the current civilisation; it was an artefact left behind by a race of advanced beings long gone. They had built the train network in the pattern of the flower of life. They'd done so using plasma drills that bore tunnels beneath the surface. Tunnels that had set as hard as stone and had thus survived the test of time.

The train tunnels were like the pyramids dotted all over Earth in that they were artefacts of an advance civilisation that was no longer on Earth or Ziana. Avery wondered whether it was the same race who'd built infrastructure on both planets and whether it meant there was a shared ancestry. It would explain why humans and Zianans were so genetically similar.

Despite their dislike of technology, Zianans had not buried the ancient tunnels nor decommissioned the trains. They understood that they were meant to allow energy, in the form of people and goods, to move around the sacred geometric pattern. In doing so they created harmony and provided transport whilst having minimal impact on the environment.

Avery handed a silver coin to the conductor and was given a paper ticket along with a few copper coins as change. Being fleet, he could have borrowed a shuttle from the pool at the base and flown himself to the capital Barsha. Doing so, would however, have prompted questions, and Avery was acting on his own. Not outside the law, but without official approval.

When the train pulled up, Avery got on and found a seat. On the platform, a postman wandered over carrying a bag of mail. He placed it on the train and exchanged it for arriving mail.

A Rian man boarding the train shook his head in disapproval. Used to instantaneous electronic communication, the idea of writing and posting a physical letter was an anathema deemed primitive beyond measure. The Rians did not understand that if you wanted instantaneous communication on this planet, then you had to develop telepathy. Not that Rians believed such a skill existed.

As the train set out, Avery relaxed and settled in for the journey. His investigation would begin in the Zianan capital Barsha. Beneath the grand library was an archive that spanned dozens of levels and contained printed documents kept safe for prosperity. Rians thought it crazy that the documents weren't digitalised. Today some were, but more generally, Zianans did not trust e-records and for good reason.

What many Rians did not realise, was those documents stored on their Cloudnet, even in personal accounts, were easily altered. All documents on Ria, were linked through user account details. Change one document and every other one also changed simultaneously. Data could simply be erased so that it was as if it never existed. Furthermore, because Rians did not print anything, it was impossible to prove the changes had taken place. A very handy feature for correcting mistakes, but there was a dark side to the technology. History could be deleted or altered and evidence of crimes committed erased.

The moment Avery had become aware of this information manipulation he'd contacted the librarians in Barsha. They of course already knew because as record keepers they'd been forced to engage with electronic information as it was the only form that Ria produced. As a preservation measure, they now printed and filed all documents of importance to Ziana from the Rian Cloudnet using Rian technology.

When he'd informed Leda of this information manipulation, he'd expected her to be outraged. Instead, he was meet with scepticism that bordered on denial. She could not believe that anyone would tamper with files except to correct mistakes. She certainly did not believe that anyone could gain access to personal information because of the effectiveness of cybersecurity.

According to her mindset, no one entrusted with power was capable of such despicable acts of fraud and vandalism. Her naivety shocked him. Leda had a doctorate and he wondered how someone as highly educated as herself, could not see how people in power actually worked for their own selfish power aspirations. It saddened him because as a career detective in fleet, he knew all too well of the evil people were capable of.

Ignoring his wife's opinions, Avery had purchased storage space and arranged for his and Leda's personal data to be printed and stored. Which was why he was on his way to the library. He'd view the printed copy of Leda's medical records and juxtapose them with the electronic version held by the Rian Institute of Health.

Avery was just regretting not bringing a book to read when someone approached from behind and laid a hand on his shoulder. Automatically, he took the hand and spun quickly ready to apply a wrist look when he realised, he wasn't under attack.

'Yeltzie.'

She grinned.

He'd known her since birth and she'd stayed with Leda and him on many occasions. He often thought of her as the daughter he'd never had.

He stood up and hugged her and she kissed both of his cheeks in the traditional Zianan way.

'I thought you were on Ria.'

She bumped the seat in front of her with her hip so that the backrest laid over creating a seat that faced him. Sitting down she said, 'I was. I got back eight degrees ago.'

Avery frowned. As a fleet officer, he was required to memorise all the passenger ship's timetables. None had arrived in the timeframe she'd given. 'Did you catch a lift on a freighter.'

Her eyes twinkled. 'Nothing gets by you does it.'

Avery frowned. Freighters were rough places. He tried to recall which ones had arrived recently. All three that came to mind had particularly unsavoury captains and crew.

'No, I teleported.'

Avery raised an eyebrow. Yeltzie had always been resourceful, but this was going from bad to worse. Unless. 'Did you win the Rian lottery?'

'No.' Rather than extrapolate she looked away.

'Yeltz.'

She sighed and launched into a tale explaining how she'd meet Kaylor, been fired, become homeless and become Kaylor's career all in the space of a few Rian days.

'And you're saying this man, Roger Smith, paid for both of you to teleport to Ziana?'

'Yes, but I doubt that's his real name, and I'd be shocked if there was a company called Black and White.'

Avery agreed. He'd definitely look into it. 'Did he make you sign anything?'

Yeltzie gave him a do-you-think-I'm-stupid look.

'Sorry, I had to ask.'

She removed a water bottle from her shoulder bag and took a sip before gesturing at his fleet issued kit bag. 'What are you up to?'

His hand covered his mouth and he mumbled, 'Research.'

Her eyes twinkled again. 'Really.'

'Yes, why's that strange, you know I'm a detective.'

Yeltzie nodded thoughtfully. 'You're out of uniform, your badge is neither on your shirt nor your belt, and you're travelling by train when you could have flown yourself over to Barsha in a fleet shuttle.'

He grimaced. Shit, was it that obvious that he was sneaking around? 'It's personal research.'

Clearly enjoying herself she looked at him conspiratorially. 'Does Leda know what you're up to?'

Why would she ask that? Unless... His heart skipped a beat. Fuck, didn't she know? 'Yeltz, Leda's died fifteen degrees ago.'

Yeltzie blinked as if what he'd said didn't compute. She didn't know. No one had told her. Avery had tried to contact her but hadn't been able to. 'I tried to let you know but...'

Yeltzie reached across and touched his hand. 'What are you talking about?'

'Leda, she had a stroke.'

Yeltzie still stared uncomprehendingly. When he failed to deliver the punchline of what she assumed was a sick joke the first tears leaked out and ran down her gold cheeks. 'No, that's not possible. She was healthy.'

He reached out to comfort her. That's when she started sobbing in earnest. Shoving his kit bag aside, he helped her to change seats so she was sitting beside him and drew her into a cuddle. He held her until the worst of her grief subsided.

'I'm so sorry Yeltz. I tried to contact you; I really did.'

Reaching across to her bag, she found some tissues and used them to blow her nose. 'Not your fault. I didn't bother getting a communicator because I was allowed to use the one at the smoothie shop.'

Avery put his arm back around Yeltzie and held her some more.

'But, it's not possible,' she repeated. She glanced from his kit bag to his face. 'Are you investigating her death?'

He raised an eyebrow. Yeltzie was a wanderer who was unsettled, but she did not lack intelligence and little got past her.

'Do you think she was murdered?'

He lowered his voice to a whisper. 'Yes, but please keep that to yourself.'

She nodded and got up. When she returned from the bathroom her fringe was still damp, but her grief had been put in check.

'I'm so sorry Yeltzie. I didn't know you were even back in Port Town or I'd have invited you to the send-off.'

'Don't blame yourself Av, it's my fault as much as yours. You couldn't have known where I was because I didn't tell you. I sang for the send-off in Port Town; I just didn't know who for. And you know everything happens for a reason. If you'd managed to contact me and I'd gone over to the hospital, I wouldn't have met Kaylor and we were supposed to meet. Promise me you'll look into this Roger guy.'

'That I can promise.'

Yeltzie looked out the window and caught sight of the next stop marker as it whizzed by. 'This is my stop coming up. I'm just catching up with some of my kin, but I'll only be away a few degrees. I plan to be back for the eclipse. Would you take me up to the observatory like you used to when I was little? Or will you be back in space?'

'No, we can go up and watch the moons come out. I'll be in Port Town, I'm on leave. But listen, I've bought Brushwood's place. You should come and stay.'

Yeltzie frowned. 'Why would the Brushwood family sell their property?'

Avery paused. He'd been so excited about the prospect of buying, that he hadn't stopped to consider that the sale was exceedingly odd. 'I'm not sure. I only spoke briefly with Elso Brushwood and he seemed keen to be rid of it. I never asked him why.'

Yeltzie looked deeply troubled. 'Makes no sense to me. The Brushwoods have lived there since time immemorial.' She took a sip of water. 'These events. They don't seem right to me.'

Avery agreed and whilst they could be completely separate, they could just as easily be connected. He needed to broaden his investigation beyond Leda's death and think big picture.

The train began to slow and Yeltzie stood to make ready to depart. They hugged and again she kissed both his cheeks. She promised to stay in touch as she collected her backpack from the rack and departed onto the platform.

*****

Avery's boots clicked on the stone pavers as he walked across the plaza passed the water gardens headed for the library. People of all ages rested beneath shady trees reading or simply being. Others played *garnee,* a board game of logic, at provided tables and chairs. Being long day, the sun appeared high in the sky moving very slowly ensuring constant day. During this season of no night, there were always people around and nothing closed.

The library shadowed the north end of the plaza. A bluestone castle-size temple of knowledge its towers reaching for the sky. It had been built to outlast dynasties and like the great pyramids of Earth, the library would stand for a thousand millennia and then some.

Avery walked through the arched doorway into the entrance hall. The walls supported a mandala of historical events that stretched back as far as recorded history did. The marble floor led into the tower of the grand gallery passing sculptures made of metal, glass, clay, and stone. They'd been built to honour great people and they stood like sentinels observing the passage of time as they sparkled beneath crystal chandeliers.

Still, the effigies were outshone by the centrepiece: an orrery of the Zianan solar system. It sat proudly beneath a fresco painted dome roof that reached its pinnacle as a glassed over oculus. The orrery was the official source of time in all forms providing the data for the planet's almanac and presided over by the high horologist.

Avery had spent much time as a child admiring and observing the orrery. It was so fascinating that it had been one source of inspiration to join fleet and see the heavenly bodies for real. It was, however, not the only reason he'd enlisted for he'd spent a lifetime searching for his parents. Parents he knew where out there among the stars in an unknown place he was yet to visit.

Today, he had no time to linger. The library was built in the shape of a polygon, each section housing one of the seven main sources of learning: astronomy, science, healing, the arts, gastronomy, linguistics, and mathematics. Turning on the spot his eyes passed over seven archways that led to those faculties. None would take him where he wanted to go, for to get to the achieves, he needed to go down.

Seeing him looking lost, a librarian glided up to him. Dressed in a black robe decorated in star constellations she was clearly an astronomer. Her white belt marked her as a novice, but her lilac eyes beamed warmth and a desire to assist him.

'May I guide you fleetman?'

Avery wondered how she knew he was a member of fleet then remember he was carrying his issued kit bag and wearing boots. She'd noticed it the same as Yeltzie had.

'Yes, I'm looking for the archives.'

She nodded thoughtfully. 'Do you know which level, because they are vast?'

Avery racked his brain. 'Level nine I think.'

She smiled flashing white teeth. 'I hope you're feeling fit.'

Avery headed down to a subterranean tower that was accessed via a spiralling staircase. From ground level, it seemed to disappear forever downward with no bottom in sight. With each descending step, the scent of paper, mushroom-leather, and wood became more apparent. For each level contained a perfectly circular floor-to-ceiling bookshelf filled with endless volumes of books, tomes and ring binders. Standing on the polished brass access ladders, robed librarians interrupted their passionate work to wave and smile as he passed by.

Finally, he reached the correct floor and glancing up, he realised what the librarian had meant. Getting down here had been relatively easy; getting back up would tax him considerably. Still, the idea of installing an elevator would be met with mockery for Zianans believed one had to work to acquire knowledge on all three levels: physically, mentally and spiritually.

'Greetings Mr Vander.'

Soundlessly moving towards him was Zarnika, the high archivist. Like all librarians she practiced the ancient art of silent footfalls, a skill she'd long ago mastered. Her indigo robe was held fast by a platinum belt which she'd spent a lifetime earning. On Ziana, rank was not appointed through promotion, but gained through years of study and practice.

Avery placed his hands together and bowed respectfully to honour her high status.

In the practice of humility, she returned the gesture. 'May I be of assistance?'

'Thank you, that would be most welcome, but surely my query can be delegated.'

She flashed him a warm smile. 'I am not so high and mighty as to be too important to serve. Besides, do you think we meet by chance?'

Avery sighed. He'd spent too long with spiritually ignorant Rians who believed life occurred through chance, which brought luck or ill fortune. He'd temporarily forgotten that life unfolded according to the will of the observer. Or as Yeltzie had said, nothing happened by accident.

Her question was rhetorical and she turned to lead him to his personal archive lockbox. As she did so, Avery noticed a few strands of silver in her green hair. Zianans lived on average three times longer than Rians commonly celebrating the equivalent of their three-hundredth Earth-year birthday prior to death. Still, some lived even longer, while those who truly understood awareness building became ageless ascended beings. His ponderings prompted him to wonder how old she was.

'I'll soon be celebrating my four-hundredth birthday as Earthlings measure time.'

Unlike Rians who wanted to be forever young and feared aging, Zianans never hid their age nor saw it as a burden. Still, they didn't suffer the health problems that elderly Rians and Earthlings did.

Avery was humbled for to stand in the presence of someone so old and wise was a privilege. Clearly, she was also skilled at mindreading so he'd best watch his thoughts.

She pushed the brass ladder around on its top and bottom rails until she reached the spot on the shelves she wanted. Having climbed up almost to the top she retrieved what looked like a tome but was actually a lockbox. It was fitted with a dial engraved with Zianan numbers, letters and symbols.

Rather than pass it to him, she descended two more flights to a level that contained not shelves, but a cluster of private rooms. Inside, the room he was allocated was an elegant wooden desk and matching hand-carved chair along with a fine velvet layback recliner.

Zarnika placed the lockbox on the table. 'Listen now.'

Avery closed the door and gave her his full attention.

'You will find what you seek, but be warned, there is much more at stake then you realise so be careful whom you trust. Your investigation is critical to the survival of life as we know it on this planet, as well as many others. Your perseverance will lead you to the one you have sought all your life.'

'My parents!' It was rude to interrupt but Avery couldn't help himself.

She waved a finger at him like a parent would to a cheeky child and Avery's cheeks flushed red.

'You are not nearly as important as your daughter, but upon you, she relies.'

Avery desperately wanted to say that he had no daughter and never would have, but he dare not interrupt a second time.

Zarnika paused. 'I will tell you one more thing. If you give freely of yourself when it is asked, you will be found worthy when the time comes.'

She nodded and went to take her leave, but Avery clasped her robe. He immediately let it go when her angry eyes beseeched him too. He had not meant to be disrespectful, but he was driven by desperation.

'Please, will you tell me of my parents?'

'Your father's unimportant, his gift was only that of his seed. He's no longer among the living.' She leaned closer. 'Your mother is Moir.'

Avery gasped as if all the air had been stolen from his lungs. It could not be so. 'But…?'

She again raised a stern finger. 'Quaerite, et invenietis.'

Seek and find.

With a swish of her robes, she glided away leaving Avery in a state of distress.

Chapter 16

Kaylor was still slowly convalescing, but she had now sufficiently recovered to check out of the Zianan hospice. It was only a kilometre over to the Rian Research Centre and she could have put on a sun cloak and walked, but Roger Smith arrived to escort her. He'd organised transport in the form of a ground vehicle known as a four-wheel drive.

Kaylor had never expected to see anything like it outside of a virtual Earth Museum. She hesitated to get in it, but the Zianan taxi driver, Quinten, just smiled and assured her it was perfectly safe. Thankfully the journey was short because every bump jarred her with pain. Zian's roads, were really just tracks wide enough for a vehicle.

The Research Centre took up a square of land the size of a Rian city block. It was located on a cleared piece of land and had a half dome over the top that filtered the harsh Zianan sun. Rather than looking like a university campus, with its compound fence and armed guards, it was more like a military facility.

Having passed through security, they were met by an android who handed Kaylor her communicator before placing her carry bag onto a hoversled. Since arriving she'd thankfully procured some additional clothes from a shop in Port Town and appreciatively, inside the compound, the campus was more welcoming. Now on foot, they passed through a quadrant which hosted a café and bar with outdoor seating. Further on was a sporting complex with gymnasium, indoor pool, tennis, volleyball, soccer and basketball courts. A bit further on was a leisure centre which promoted a 3D cinema.

Roger smiled warmly. 'Don't worry, the campus is a microcosm of Ria. I'm sure you'll be feeling at home in no time.'

Kaylor did admit the place looked clean and modern not to mention well-resourced. As they approached the apartment tower, several people rode past on hoverscooters whilst offering friendly waves.

Entering the building they crossed the foyer before stepping into an elevator. The lift pinged when it reached the correct floor and the doors opened. Pushing the hoversled, the android led the way followed by Roger and then Kaylor. When they arrived at the door of her apartment, Torri unlocked it.

Crossing the threshold Roger said, 'Nice.'

Kaylor suppressed a gasp by turning it into a yawn. Her apartment was a shoebox and five good strides in any direction would see her across it. Painted on the wall just inside the door in a contrasting colour to emphasise the designer's pride, was 60m^3.

Walking past the bunk bed which sat over her couch, Roger gestured to her bathroom before coming to rest beside the chest-high table with its high chairs. 'Beautifully designed.'

Roger began flipping open cupboards and pointing out high shelves and hooks that had been crammed into every available space.

Like her last apartment, there was no stove, just a sink and microwave which sat atop a bench-high fridge.

'There's a cafeteria on the ground floor.' He tapped a small stainless-steel door which sat level with the top of her table. 'Just order what you want and your meal is transported right to your table via a system of mini elevators and conveyor belts.'

Kaylor's lips formed into a tight smile.

'So high tech.' He looked thoughtful. 'This place is not just a research centre; it's an exposé of Rian culture that allows Zianans to see what they're missing.'

Having met Yeltzie she doubted the Zianans would be impressed. They'd see the compound fence as a means of keeping the bizarre Rians in, like a zoo with armed keepers.

She looked for a window, but there wasn't one. Enslaved by technology during the entire time they were awake, Rians didn't have time to look out of windows and appreciate views.

'The offices and labs are nearby and there's no designated desks; it's all flexible workspace. You can just choose the set up which best suits you at any given moment, or with Torri, you can work right here from your apartment. No fixed work time; people work all hours.'

How that differed from home she didn't know, but maybe that was the point he was making.

'As you saw, the campus has it all: gym, pool, cinema, café, bars.'

Kaylor glanced around nervously. The cramped quarters and solely artificial lighting were already making her feel claustrophobic. 'Is there a woodland nearby?'

Roger cocked his head.

'A nature park?'

Roger still looked at her confused. He was a true Rian and their idea of interacting with nature was to own a pot plant that an android watered.

She changed tact. 'We can go into the village when we want can't we?'

He shook his head as if to alleviate her concerns. 'No need, the campus has got it all and Torri can link you to e-shopping.' He patted her on the arm. 'Don't worry, we've got good security, and despite what you may have heard, the locals aren't dangerous, they're just queer. They sit under trees and sing to fuck knows who. You must have heard them the other night. Complete mental cases the lot of them.'

Kaylor closed her eyes unable to believe Roger's attitude towards Zianans.

He nodded and stepped towards her door. 'Look I can see you're tired so I'll get going. Torri can help you if you need anything and you've got my contact details. I'll be in touch.'

She watched as he took his leave.

*****

Sparta waited until he was in the lift and the doors had closed before smirking. Another great acting performance if he did say so himself. This project was his and his alone and he'd trust no one, which was why he was on this shithole of a planet.

Using reverse psychology was a streak of genius. He knew Kaylor suffered from claustrophobia because he'd read her medical file, obtained illegally by his AI Tank. That's why he'd put her in the smallest apartment available and made sure it had no windows. It wouldn't be long and she'd be seeking alternative accommodation. Now she was connected to her communicator, he'd be able to use the persuasive program to make sure it was with Avery.

He'd already influenced Elso Brushwood, who worked for the Zianan government and thus had a communicator, to sell his family home. Avery had purchased the house which was so grand Kaylor would swoon over it. In due course, Sparta would influence Avery so he invited Kaylor to move right in with him.

He whistled a tune to himself. In time, she'd achieve her purpose and Sparta would not just be rich but insanely powerful. One who could do anything, even topple governments or become an emperor. Then his father would show him some respect.

*****

Kaylor examined her apartment which prior to her NDE would have seemed lovely. But having spent some time in Zianan accommodation with Yeltzie cooking fresh food and enjoying dinner with a view of the sky from the deck, she felt closed in.

'Can I help you unpack?'

Kaylor spun around to see who'd spoken and realised the android was still waiting patiently. Unlike humans, they could stand dead still and make no sound so that they effectively became statues.

'No, I'll do it myself directly. Thanks for your assistance.'

'My pleasure.' The android sat her bag down and departed with the hoversled.

She sat on the couch with a sigh and discovered it was uncomfortable, like those found in hotels. The sort that didn't recline and always had a hard spot which dug into your back or hurt your hips. She rubbed her face in her hands. Had she done the right thing by coming here?

Kaylor stood back up and decided it was too late now; she'd have to make the best of it.

She walked over to her table. 'Torri, can you display the menu please.'

A hologram appeared above her table. There were at least sixty food choices. She ordered a chicken curry with rice and vegetables along with a cup of black tea and left Torri to arrange payment.

Five minutes later the meal arrived on her table steaming hot and ready to eat. Kaylor found a splade in the cutlery drawer and used it to take a mouthful. Three seconds later she spat it back out. Yeltzie had been preparing her meals using fresh food and love since she was injured. She'd been spoilt to such a degree that she couldn't eat this mass prepared shit that tasted artificial and chemical. Kaylor doubted she'd ever be able to eat it again. A big problem since she didn't have a kitchen and there were no grocery shops on campus.

Kaylor tossed her meal down a garbage shoot. She should have asked Yeltzie about housing options in Port Town, but it hadn't occurred to her to do so. She'd just assumed she'd be happy living at the Research Centre.

If Yeltzie had a communicator, Kaylor would have contacted her straight away. Although Zianans were slowly adopting them, Yeltizie didn't have one. There were telephones now. Mostly public ones at the train stations. There were also two-way radios, but they were only used by a few. There was physical mail, but the problem was Kaylor had never even held a pen or pencil let alone tried to write with it and printers had been phased out before she was born. Could she pay someone to write the letter for her?

She had no doubt she could, but how silly would she feel? How much would her scribe laugh at her? A lot. Besides, where would she even send the letter? She had no idea.

She sighed and made her way back to the couch. She wasn't feeling up to climbing the ladder to get to her bed so she laid down on the couch. She wished she could have brought her teddy bear with her, but it was made of synthetic and thus not allowed. Improvising she cuddled a spare cushion.

She'd no sooner closed her eyes when her head buzzed like a swarm of bees were inside it. She shook her head, but the sensation continued. Annoyed, she reached for her communicator and switched it off. The moment she did the sensation stopped. Great, now her communicator was malfunctioning. She tossed it on the small table beside the couch. Not to worry, she'd get someone to look at it later.

Chapter 17

Avery couldn't believe it. How could his mother be Moir? Why would an ascended being have a child only to leave it behind? It didn't make any sense. Then again, why would Zarnika lie to him? She wouldn't.

Then there was the fact she'd told him his daughter was more important than he was. He didn't have a daughter, and now Leda was dead, he would never have one. Zinanans didn't remarry.

However, he was only half Zianan. Would he?

Avery didn't want to think about it. He had only two other women in his life, his best friend Sarah, who was happily married, and Yeltzie, who was like a daughter to him. It would be queer indeed if either of them wanted to have his baby.

Damn it. He just wanted to run after Zarnika and make her tell him all she knew. If need be, hold a laser pistol to her head.

Shame overcome him and he rubbed his face in his hands. Avery might be able to do such a despicable thing to an unscrupulous criminal if he had no other choice, but to do it to a Zianan librarian... It was sacrilege to even consider it.

In Zianan she'd said, "Seek and find". The words had a specific meaning in their language. It was the belief that information had to be obtained at the right time by a person seeking it. If potential futures were revealed too early, it could prompt a person to make choices based on what they knew, as opposed to what they would know in time. In other words, Zarnika believed he'd find the answers to his questions when he was mentally and spiritually ready.

He sighed. For the moment it was enough to know who his mother was. Everything else the high archivist had told him would require serious contemplation. At the moment he had a job to do so he did his best to push the conversation from his mind.

Opening the lockbox, Avery took out Leda's medical file, flipped to the last page and began skim reading it in reverse. He frowned as he found dozens of medical appointments made at the Research Centre, he knew nothing about. Complaints of headaches, dizziness, fatigue and a general sense of being unwell. The medical problems dated back twenty years.

Avery couldn't believe it. How could his wife have been unwell without him knowing? He was about to give up when he noticed something odd. A change in the colour of paper that the file was printed on. A small change, cream to white, but a change nonetheless.

Why had the archivists changed the colour of the paper? It could have been as simple as running out of one colour and using what they had, but Avery didn't believe that. The librarians were meticulous people and a change in paper colour meant something.

He continued to skim read the file only to discover it was as if he'd returned to where he'd started. He rolled his eyes when he realised what he was looking at. There'd be no need to cross-reference the Cloudnet with what was printed. When the document had changed, the archivists had noted the anomaly and had printed pages all the way back to where the changes had begun. They'd used a different coloured paper to indicate it was a break in series. Quite clever really.

Zarnika would have been informed and she'd have ordinarily contacted him. However, with her awareness so well developed, she knew he'd come looking. But why delay? Because she knew something he didn't. She'd spoken to him, but unfortunately in a cryptic manner.

Damn, all he could do was continue to seek and find.

For the moment he had what he needed from the library. Avery would get a copy made and have this copy re-archived. It was time to confront the Rian Institute of Health. They had the metadata detailing when the changes were made and by who.

*****

The Rian Institute of Health was located on Ria a year's space flight away. There was, however, a branch office at the Zianan Research Centre, just a kilometre from Port Town. Avery caught the train back and went straight over. He was stopped by security at the gate, but only for the time it took him to show his fleet badge and identification. Then he was escorted by an android directly to the correct place.

Following a wait of thirty-five minutes, which Avery used to obtain a disgusting coffee from a dispenser, he was shown into an office and sat on the opposite side of the desk.

'I'm Amanda. How can I help you Mr. Vander?'

'I have found an anomaly in my late wife's medical records and I'd like to understand why.'

She made a holoscreen appear above her desk in a position that they could both view it. 'Do you have your wife's MIN.'

Avery read her Leda's medical identification number and a moment later her medical records appeared on the screen. Avery produced the original printed report.

'As you can see, the entire report has been altered.'

Amanda made no attempt to look at the details. Instead, she stared wide-eyed at the printed pages themselves.

When she'd regained her voice she said, 'Mr. Vander, what you have is clearly a forgery, because it is impossible to print a medical record. Rian cybersecurity prohibits it.'

Avery smirked. 'The archivists at the Zianan library found a way around that problem. They've been printing key documents since they discovered that e-files can change without explanation. I assure you; these pages are genuine and Leda's medical file has been tampered with.'

Amanda's face reddened. 'That's illegal. I'm going to have to notify fleet police.'

Avery produced his badge and identification. 'I'm a detective with fleet.'

Whether Amanda hadn't been notified of who he was, or whether she'd temporarily forgotten, Avery didn't know or care.

'What you speak of might be illegal on Ria, but this is Ziana and in printing the pages no crime has been committed. Fraud is, however, a crime, but you should know I'm actually investigating a suspected murder.'

Amanda looked visually sick.

'Now, what I need from you is access to the metadata which is not displayed. I want to know the name, medical licence number, and full details of every medic Leda Vander nee Jenner saw in the last twenty years and I want it, as soon as possible.'

She swallowed and looked away. When she looked back, her face had hardened. 'I'm sorry Lieutenant-Commander Vander, but I'm going to need to see a warrant before I can authorise your access to the metadata.'

Avery smiled sarcastically. Leaning forward he said, 'I'll get you a warrant along with one for your arrest.'

She returned a faux inquisitive look. 'And what would I be charged with?'

'Obstructing the course of justice, which is a very serious crime here on Ziana.'

It was her turn to smile sarcastically. Calling his bluff, she said, 'This research centre is also a Rian outpost and as such comes under Rian law. I'm sorry Lieutenant-Commander Vander, but until you can provide a warrant, I'm unable to further assist you with your enquires.' She shut down the hologram and stood up to show him out.

Fuck it. He should have contacted Sarah and Captain Loody before barging in here. He'd get a reprimand over this and breach of procedure was grounds for a court-martial. He could be facing a demotion or worse, a transfer to a remote and desolate rocky moon outpost.

Avery stood up and left without a fuss and walked straight over to the fleet base half expecting to be met by troops who'd escort him to Commodore Venetia Erickson's office. Since the base, unlike most of Port Town, had Rian technology, surely Amanda had telephoned ahead of his arrival and kicked up a stink about his visit and demands.

However, when he arrived at the front gate, no one was waiting and his presence raised no suspicion. Instead, the guards saluted him. He headed straight for his own base apartment, then remembered he'd already let it go. No matter, he had access to Sarah's digs because she trusted him like a brother. Once inside he donned his communicator and switched it on.

Avery created a case number and spent the next few hours completing e-paperwork and filling an official report detailing his investigation, which he forwarded to Sarah and Captain Loody. They were in space on *The Zee*, but the ship was only doing a patrol around Zeus and its moons and thus wasn't far away as space went. Courtesy of satellite relay, they'd receive it directly.

When he finished, he considered contacting Commodore Erickson to see if she'd approve an application for a warrant, but Avery thought better of it. Official tampering of records was a political hand grenade. Even though the library had known about it for years, fleet would deny all knowledge. The Zianan Chief Minister, along with her cabinet, would be outraged and the Admiralty would have to get involved. In short, if it wasn't handled sensitively, all hell could break loose.

The problem was, the Zianan in Avery couldn't abide by corruption and since he didn't care what happened to him, he was prepared to go all in to get justice for Leda. He considered his next move. Since he couldn't continue investigating Leda's medical files, he'd be best off investigating Roger Smith and the company Black and White.

Avery had the communicator's AI run searches across a number of databases on the Cloudnet. Searches of citizen records revealed there was no less than twenty Roger Smiths living on Ria. When cross-referenced with Black and White as a company name, he found no connections. He did discover that Black and White was a newly listed space industry company. The founders were unoriginally listed as Cameron Black and Jason White. Again, common names, if anything a little too common.

He wondered if he were simply chasing ghosts and Avery was about to move his investigation on when he remembered that Yeltzie had mentioned teleportation. Roger had had Yeltzie and Kaylor teleported, so perhaps he'd also travelled here the same way. Avery searched for a teleportation record for Roger Smith and hit pay dirt.

Not only was there a record, but also a full body image. Avery ran it through the identification database and scored a hit. Yeltzie was right, his name wasn't Roger Smith, it was Daniel Sparta. What was more, the man was on the Space Intelligence Agency's watch list. So, what had he done to gain attention from the spooks?

Chapter 18

Avery could not remember the last time he'd attended the sun festival. It wasn't that the officers who ran fleet didn't understand its importance to Zianan culture, it was more that space traffic was always busy when it was on which meant *The Zee* needed to be patrolling.

The festival could be summed up in four words: food, drink, music, and dance. Having eaten, Avery was searching for a beer tent when he did a double take. With sun cloak draped across the back of her chair, Kaylor sat alone, a few stalls down, under the protective canvas of the chanter's tent. He wouldn't have recognised her; except he'd looked up her holo-image after he'd finished investigating Sparta.

Meeting her like this was no coincidence and Avery wandered down to introduce himself. When she glanced up, he said, 'Dr. Kaylor Emmerson.'

She returned an inquisitive look. 'Yes, have we met?'

'No, I'm Avery Vander, I believe you know my honouree daughter Yeltzie.' She took his proffered hand and shook it lightly. 'The chanters are catching their breath and won't begin again for a while. Would you like me to get you a drink?'

She seemed unsure, but then seemed to change her mind. In the drinks tent, they found a vacant table and Avery purchased a beer and a pink wine.

He was keen to talk about Sparta, but Rians insisted on beginning with small talk. 'How are you settling in?'

'Fine, I'm fine.'

Sarah said fine when she was pissed off and spat it out like spoiled food. 'So strange that Rian word because it means the exact opposite of how your dictionaries define it.'

Kaylor glanced at him awkwardly, but slowly a smile formed on her face. 'Yeltzie liked to call bullshit too so I'm guessing it is a Zianan thing. Since I'll be staying a while, I'd best get used to it.'

Avery took a calculated sip of his beer. 'Our culture is very different. We recognise distress even when it's being hidden and we do our best to help.'

'I see. In that case, I'll be direct. I need to find somewhere else to live.'

'You don't want to stay at the Research Centre?'

'No, I can't live in a coffin without windows or real air and don't get me started on the processed food, nor the fact that my communicator keeps malfunctioning. It buzzes like I have a head full of bees.'

Sarah ranted from time to time and Avery had learned to wait quietly until she stopped, which was what he was doing until that last bit. 'Say that again, about the bees.'

She sighed and repeated what she said.

It was odd that her communicator had the same issue his did. 'Have any of your colleagues reported the same problem?'

'No, but I've been indisposed so I wouldn't know if they had.'

'And it doesn't happen all the time, just occasionally?'

'Yes, but It's frightfully annoying, because it's never happened before.'

No one else's, just hers, which meant it was no coincidence. 'When did it begin?'

Kaylor made a face as she racked her brain. 'It didn't start until my new boss Roger Smith got it back for me.' She proceeded to tell him all about how she'd been fired and had to hand in Torri and then how Roger had got her AI back.

Why would Sparta do that? More to the point, why would the Rian Scientific Institute let him have it? Odd.

'Do you know someone who can fix it?'

'I'll make enquires.' He considered her other problem. He should at least offer because Yeltzie would be pissed off if he didn't. 'But I might be able to help you with a place to live. That is, I've got spare rooms, but I live five kilometres from town. Getting to work would be... problematic. '

Kaylor's face brightened. 'I'd like to take a look anyway. When would suit?'

'After the festival.'

'Sounds great. How do I get there?'

'The taxi driver, Quentin, he knows the way.'

A thunder of drums stole Kaylor's attention so there'd be no point asking her anything else. 'That's your cue I believe.'

She picked up her wine glass. 'Thanks for the drink, I'll see you later.'

Avery glass was nearly empty and he was considering another beer when Sarah sat in the seat Kaylor had just vacated. She pushed back the hood of her sun cloak and removed her sunglasses.

'That seat is taken,' he replied gruffly.

'It was. It's not now.'

He drained his beer. 'I'm guessing you got my report.'

'Oh, yeah. I was ordered to come. Flew a shuttle straight here and you know how much I looove piloting. Course you weren't home, so I considered flying out here, but there's nowhere to land in this frigging port except out at the base. But I couldn't take the shuttle there, because that would get people asking questions. So, I had to walk into town because there're no phones on Ziana to call a taxi with.'

'They use two-way radios.'

'Which are not compatible with our communicators. Do you have any idea how hot it is under a sun cloak during long day?'

'No, I've never needed one.'

'Then it cost me good silver to get into the festival...'

'It's a great festival.'

'I'm sure it is, but we need to talk Lieutenant-Commander.' She fixed him with a stare that brokered no negotiation.

'I thought we were talking.'

'No, I'm ranting, we need to talk.'

Thankfully Quentin, Avery's friend, and wheelman, was happy to drive them to Avery's place, and by the time they arrived, Sarah had calmed down. Set bordering a food forest on public land, his new homestead was made of rendered mud bricks with surrounding verandas. Sitting on the front veranda, where there was protection from the sun, was a woman he'd never met before. With short black spiky hair, a muscular physique and tattoos, gender notwithstanding, Avery knew a badarse when he saw one.

Avery approached cautiously. 'I don't believe we've met, so why are you sitting on my deck?'

The woman stood up. Despite her height being below that of his shoulders, she removed her sunglasses and looked him in the eye. 'And here I was led to believe Zianans were friendly.'

Sarah hurried over. 'Agent Dee, this is Avery.'

A spook. Damn it, this was as bad as it gets. They shook hands, but Avery remained cool.

Stepping through the front door, he proceeded through the porch and continued into the open plan lounge, dining room and kitchen. He was about to suggest they sit at the table, but Sarah and Dee had not followed him inside. Instead, they'd continued around to the natural swimming pool and taken a seat at the outdoor setting beneath the shade of a large maccanut tree where the Rians would be protected from the rays of the sun that would burn their skin.

Avery removed a carafe of iced herbal tea from the fridge, grabbed three glasses and followed them. Taking a seat, he poured the drinks.

Sarah adjusted her position so she was completely in the shade.

Addressing Avery, Sarah said, 'The shits hit the fan, but I'm guessing you've figured that part out already.'

'I told you Leda's file had been altered, but you wouldn't listen.'

Sarah looked away. She hated being wrong. When she turned back, she said, 'I'm sorry, I should not have dismissed your concerns so lightly. You didn't tell me you could prove it, detective.'

'Would you have believed me if I had? Or just kept psychoanalysing my "mind state"?' He made air quotes with his fingers for additional emphasis.

Sarah winched. 'Alright, clearly you're angry with me and you've made your point, but I've apologised, so can you forgive me now?'

Avery took a deep breath and exhaled slowly. Sarah was his friend, but also his superior officer. Best if he didn't antagonise her further, now he'd said his piece. 'So, what now?'

'Before Captain Loody and I could even consider what to do, we were contacted by Admiral Cadel.'

Avery spilled his drink. 'Isn't he…'

'The highest-ranking officer in fleet. Yes. Yes, he is.'

Damn. Avery had expected the brass to take an interest, but Commodore Erickson, not Admiral Cadel.

'I don't know how he even knew about the case. I mean you'd just filed it. We hadn't even looked at it properly.'

'He'd have found out through Gorman,' said Dee.

Mark Gorman was the Executive Director of the Space Intelligence Agency or SIA. 'I take it Intelligence has me under surveillance.'

Dee nodded. 'We knew you wouldn't leave the case alone.'

'Then why wasn't I more formally warned off earlier?'

'Because we were told to let it play.'

Avery understood. Intelligence knew that he'd investigate and they were happy to ride his coattails, except, he'd moved faster than they'd anticipated and now they were trying to arrest his momentum. He gritted his teeth. Zarnika had told him to be careful who he trusted, but it would be foolish not to at least try and find out why Intelligence was involved.

He added. 'I'm guessing you know that Roger Smith is really Daniel Sparta and that he's taken an interest in Dr. Kaylor Emmerson.'

'We didn't, but we do now thanks to your superb detective work.'

Sarah piqued up. 'Sparta?'

'You know him?' asked Avery.

Sarah made a face like she'd swallowed something sour. 'Yes. I was assigned to profile him a few years back. He's a fixer.'

'Your assessment?' asked Avery.

'He's charismatic, charming and intelligent, but also selfish, narcissistic and greedy.'

'Violent?' queried Dee.

'No, I don't think so. He's the sort that would contract out violence and murder if it was required.'

'Did the investigators find anything?' asked Avery.

'No, he's squeaky clean. I personally searched for college misdemeanours and police notations by interviewing Rian police officers, but no one could even remember giving him a warning for being a smart arse or nuisance. I dug up nothing; not a damn thing.'

Sarah had been a wild girl in her teenage years and had quite a juvenile record as did many Rians. She didn't trust anyone who didn't have at least a few slights against their name.

Dee nodded agreement. 'The man's slipperier than an eel, but he is an expert at what he does and he knows how to cover his tracks.'

'What's he involved in presently?' asked Avery.

'That's classified,' said Dee. 'Which is why I'm here, to tell you to stand down.'

Anger surged through him. 'The fucking cheek of it.'

'I beg your pardon,' said Dee.

'I found out more in a day than you spooks have in years. Now you want *me*, to stand down.'

'Avery,' cautioned Sarah.

Ignoring her, he leaned forward towards Dee. 'Someone killed my wife in a sadistic fucked up way and I want to know who and why. I want justice.'

Dee took a calculated sip of her drink. 'My condolences for the loss of your wife, but this is far bigger than that.'

He knew that, but that didn't prevent him from being angry. 'What can you tell me?'

Dee considered for a moment. 'Document alteration goes all the way to the top and of course it's denied. The new Rian government is out of control and if the Zianan government calls them out for fraud, which they no doubt will, then the Rian government will react adversely. I won't bullshit you; the new regime wants a reason to pick a fight so they can invade Ziana.'

Avery's anger turned to fear as he suddenly saw things more broadly.

'What we are trying to do, is find the links, if they exist, between Leda's death, document alteration, Kaylor Emmerson and a certain desire for conflict,' said Dee.

Avery smiled wanly. 'And of course, there's something you are not telling me because all those things are fleet's jurisdiction.'

Dee shrugged off Avery's probe. 'I have my orders and so do you.'

Avery sat back and considered the agent. 'Shame I'm being frozen out, because I may have the missing link you're searching for.' He went to stand up.

'Sit down,' hissed Dee with a steel edge to her voice.

Thus far she'd kept the badarse bitch in check, but now she was threatening to make a guest appearance. They eyeballed each other for a good ten seconds.

'Stop it, both of you!' said Sarah.

Dee yielded by glancing away.

'How do you feel about making a deal?' asked Avery.

Dee returned her gaze but refused to commit one way or the other.

Avery continued. 'You give me access to the metadata on Leda's file. I know you Intelligence agents can bypass the legalities to do so. Then I'll tell you what else I know.'

Dee sat fuming in silence until Avery again went to stand up.

'Alright. Deal. But it's totally off the record and just between us three.' She looked him directly in the eye. 'You share everything you know and discover with me and no one else.'

Avery considered the compromise. He wasn't investigating for fame and glory or to further his career. This was purely about justice for his late-wife. 'Deal.'

Sarah exhaled. It occurred to Avery that she hadn't been sent here to tell him to stand down because Dee had done that. She'd been sent here to stop Dee and him killing each other.

'You were saying,' prompted Dee when Avery didn't immediately begin sharing.

'My communicator's been acting weirdly.'

Sarah rolled her eyes. 'It's probably missing key updates because it's always switched off.'

'That was the conclusion I first came to, but I happened to run into Kaylor at the sun festival. Her communicator is behaving exactly the same way and I seriously doubt it's because of a lack of updates.'

Dee narrowed her eyes. 'I admit it's odd but it could be a coincidence.'

Avery looked patiently at Dee as he explained the oddities that Yeltzie had identified. As he did so Dee's began to take him more seriously.

Chapter 19

Thankfully Dee kept her end of the bargain and gave him access to the metadata on Leda's medical files. Most places on Ziana did not have a communicator signal, but Port Town was an exception and Avery's house was located close enough to receive it. Dee sat with him at the kitchen table and they accessed the Cloudnet with her communicator. Once visible, the metadata provided the names and licence numbers of all the medical people Leda was supposed to have seen. Dee instructed her AI to cross-reference the information against databases. Each and every person was revealed to be real.

'It's not that surprising,' said Avery. 'If Sparta was behind the changes, he'd be meticulous and careful about making them look real. We need to verify the appointments actually took place through eyewitness testimonies.'

'Agreed,' Instructing her AI Dee said, 'Requesting confirmation data.'

The android receptionists who'd answer the queries had no human memory; they had hard drives. Those hard drives would have been updated at the same time as Leda's medical file was changed. However, androids also captured video images through their eyes which were actually cameras.

Because of the distance between Ziana and Ria, the lag time was significant, but androids were efficient. They responded to Dee's queries immediately. Appointments were verified, with video.

'He's good,' said Dee, leaning back in her chair and rubbing her face in her hands.

'Everyone makes a mistake,' said Avery refusing to believe the video files were real.

Instructing the AI to play the minute-long videos, Avery watched intently.

'Well, I'm not seeing it if he did.'

'Look closer.'

Dee sighed and resumed watching.

Avery smiled. 'There are six videos that were recorded at genuine appointments. They've been recycled.'

Dee's eyes widened. 'Oh my god. I would have missed that.'

'I told you Avery was good,' said Sarah.

'I'll concede that but all this proves is Leda's medical files were altered and we knew that already.'

'True, but now the Rian Institute of Health can't say the printouts are forged.'

'Which means we need to proceed carefully,' said Dee.

'What we need to know is why Sparta is so interested in Kaylor. What's her claim to fame?'

Dee's AI brought up Kaylor's resume profile.

'She's a sound specialist,' said Sarah.

'Which explains why she so fascinated with Zianan chants and music, but not why Sparta paid a fortune to teleport her here,' said Avery. 'What was her last project?'

'Planetary sound analysis,' said Dee sounding frustrated.

'But she was caught up in the mass layoffs,' said Sarah.

'And there's the bit we all might have overlooked.' Avery stood up and stretched.

'Yeah, you're going to have to explain that,' said Dee.

'Sparta is a fixer who works for money. Not necessary a villain except by association.'

'I'm not following you,' said Sarah.

'It's possible that Sparta was paid to bring Kaylor to Ziana and convince someone at the research centre to continue her work.'

Dee looked at him as if the cheese had slid off his cracker. 'Who cares about the racket that planets make as they move through space?'

'Well, that would depend on what Kaylor has discovered. It's entirely possible that someone tried to kill her as well, but cocked it up.'

'And then Sparta brought her here for safekeeping using the fastest transport available,' said Sarah.

'It's speculation,' said Dee.

'I agree,' replied Avery. 'But it's a lead.'

Dee shut down her communicator and looked out the window. 'Is there no sodding night on this world. What time is it?'

'The middle of the night for us Rians,' said Sarah. 'I'll make some coffee. Do you want some?'

'No.' Dee gestured to one of the couches in Avery's lounge room. 'Do you mind if I take a nap?'

'Not at all,' replied Avery. 'I'll have some coffee, but I'm taking a walk first. I need to clear my head.'

*****

Sarah pottered in the kitchen making coffee. Deep in thought, the flash of laser frightened her so badly she dropped and smashed a glass cafetière.

A microsecond later, her training kicked in and she hit the floor only narrowly avoiding cutting herself on the shards. Across the room, Dee had rolled off the couch she'd been napping on and was also keeping low.

Sarah considered her position. There were windows all around giving the shooter a clear view from ground level, but not from an elevated position. The laser had been fired from up high towards the ground. Meaning the veranda roofs should be obstructing the sniper's line of sight.

Unless of course there was more than one. She couldn't know, but she also couldn't just lay here knowing Avery was in trouble. There was no way to contact him and no way to know if he was dead or alive. The shooter had fired only one shot. Avery might already be dead and his murderer might be beating a retreat.

Sarah began leopard crawling. She'd brought no weapons with her, but inside Avery's closet was a gun safe which housed a projectile rifle. It wasn't fleet issued; the locals used it to hunt the giant birds called *ulso* that roamed the wilds. She had to get to it.

By the time she reached it, she was thankful for the gruelling training she was put through every year. The mandatory week-long torture that saw them running ten miles before breakfast and leopard crawling the length of sports ovals. Not to mention the yelling and screaming from drill masters who had the authority to lord it over officers as high ranking as Admiral Cadel for that short period of time.

She stood up and opened the wooden doors of the closet. The safe was made of steel held fast by a combination lock.

Please be Leda's birthdate. Please be Leda's birthdate. She spun the dial but the safe refused to unlock. She tried again using Avery's birth date, followed by her own and then Yeltzie's. They were all incorrect.

Damn it, Avery wasn't that imaginative. It had to be something memorable.

Sarah grabbed hold of the hair on both sides of her head and yanked. Think woman, think. What date would Avery use? Nothing came to mind. Damn it. They'd have to try and get to the shuttle which had all manner of weapons onboard.

Sarah was considering the best approach when she was struck by a thought. She spun the dial and heard the safe click open. Damn, he'd used the date of Leda's death. Had he been planning to kill her murderer when he discovered who it was? She could well imagine him standing right where she was, cold and calculating as he entered the combination for a date he was about to avenge.

Zianans were peaceful and Avery had no unusual violent inclinations, but Zianas were also deeply loyal and committed to only one mate for life. They'd martyr themselves for justice.

She grabbed the rifle that Avery had trained her to use and noted it was already loaded. Double damn.

Keeping low, Sarah headed back the way she'd come. There'd been no more laser shots meaning the snipper might be done and gone or they could be trying to flush out Dee and her.

Sarah crawled onto the deck and peered through the scope.

With sun cloak on, Dee fell onto her stomach beside her and whispered, 'What's that relic?'

'A projective rifle and don't mock it, it's lethal.'

Sarah searched the surrounding vegetation and caught sight of the sniper in the fork of a dead tree. 'I've sighted him.' She slid back the bolt back chambering a round. 'It's not a clear shot.'

'Has that scope got a camera.'

It was now that Sarah realised that the rifle might be ancient tech, but the scope was state of the art. Gently she used her thumb to take several digital pictures. The snipper was side on and was wearing a combat helmet so she couldn't capture his face. Even though the captured images would be of limited value, all data was useful.

Dee put her sunglasses on and removed a laser pistol from the back waistband of her pants. Military issue, it contained a red dot laser pointer. 'I'll try for a better position, if he moves, shoot him.'

Before Sarah could argue, Dee was across the veranda and making her way down the driveway. Using vegetation as cover, she moved quietly with considerable skill and in short time she'd covered half the distance.

Whether the snipper sensed movement of heard something Sarah wasn't sure, but he broke his focus and turned to face her. Sarah hurriedly took a photo before squeezing the trigger. The rifle roared and kicked her in the shoulder. The projectile missed to the right and cannoned into a branch spraying the snipper with woodchips which bounced harmlessly off his armour.

Before anyone could react, the air became electric. A red stream of laser light struck the dead tree from directly above. An horrendous cracking echoed around them as wood splintered moments before exploding into flames. A fireball rose ten metres in the air with heat so intense that Sarah was forced to turn her head away.

'You alright Dee?' screamed Sarah.

Dee had thrown herself on the ground. Luckily the sun cloak had offered some protection from the laser blast. Seemingly unperturbed, she was climbing to her feet.

'Dee!'

'I'm fine.'

Avery emerged from the nearby forest. He too seemed unhurt as he ran to grab a soundwave fire extinguisher from a nearby shed.

'What the fuck happened?' asked Dee.

Avery was concentrating on putting out the fire.

'How are you not dead,' shrieked Sarah desperately trying to wrap her sun cloak around herself with heart searing her as her hands shook involuntarily.

'I turned my head at the crucial moment and he missed, but I couldn't run because I was pinned down behind a fallen log.'

Sarah looked for a burn mark. His pale green hair was singed, but his gold skin was undamaged. Lucky beyond words, because Zianan's gold skin reflected harmful light. The sun would not tan them, but it also wouldn't cause sunburn. Thankfully, it also offered some protection against laser.

Sarah tapped the side of her head to switch on her communicator. 'Commander Bartell contacting *The Zee*.'

'Receiving, Commander. This is Captain Loody. Can you confirm the target has been neutralised?'

Sarah's eyes widened. *Fuck, had The Zee fired a shot from space?*

'Commander.'

'Yes, confirmed.' She fought the need to freak out. 'Who ordered the laser strike from *The Zee?*'

'Admiral Cadel. You're ordered to clean the site.'

Sarah's mouth fell open as she took in the damage. The tree had been split in half and turned to charcoal. All remanence of the dead tree was gone. The snipper was a burnt corpse and only his armour had prevented his total disintegration.

'How?' she stammered.

'Hide the body.'

Sarah's eyes flicked upwards. The captain was watching her even as she stood here. The viewing optics on *The Zee* were such that they could count the pebbles beneath her feet.

Avery quelled the last flames. The stench of burnt flesh was overwhelming and he waved his hand in front of his nose to try and combat it.

'We need a body bag,' said Sarah still overwhelmed at the task before her.

Dee did not need an explanation as to why and knowing the best place to look for one, she sprinted towards Sarah's shuttle.

Avery, who wasn't privy to the orders she'd received looked at her as if she'd lost her mind. 'This is a crime scene.'

Sarah raised a finger upwards to point at *The Zee*. 'We have orders.'

Clutching a body bag, Dee skidded to a halt. 'Don't suppose you have a hover sled.'

A wave of panic slammed into Sarah as sirens filled the air. 'Double time!'

*****

'Fuck me!'

Sparta slid down the grassy bank and ran as fast as his legs would carry him. Through persuasive means, Sparta had been granted a special licence to bring technology to Ziana. The fleet customs officials had even waved the exorbitant bond that they normally collected. When Avery had barged into the research centre demanding answers, Tank had alerted him.

On Ria, spying was relatively easy if you had the equipment and knowhow. Everyone carried a communicator and they were all linked to the Cloudnet. That wasn't the case on Ziana.

The lack of technology made spying extremely difficult. No one used communicators except fleet personnel and government officials. There was no Cloudnet to link cameras and microphones, but surveillance was still possible. There were low tech gadgets that worked on radio signals. The problem was, they had a limited range which meant Sparta had had to go into the field.

Ziana had no mammals, but it was flush with avian species which the locals loved to observe. For what reason, he didn't know or care. Sparta had dispensed with his suit in favour of some local garb, a good quality sun cloak and sunglasses and had purchased a pair of ancient binoculars and a paperback birdwatching book from Port Town's information centre.

No one had taken the slightest interest in him as he made his way along the vehicle track that led to Avery's homestead. He'd arrived to find Avery was out and Sparta had planted bugs around the house, sat himself down out of sight and waited.

He hadn't even known what he'd garner, but when the two women had turned up Sparta had got his hopes up. Unfortunately, his bugs had provided poor sound quality, but he'd still managed to get the gist of the conversation. They were onto him, but it was no cause for alarm. Someone was always onto to him, but their investigations always proved to be futile because he knew how to cover his tracks.

Was his luck about to run out? If Avery believed Sparta had killed his wife, would the fleetman dispense with a trial and become an executioner? Zianans lived a long time. Serving twenty-five years in prison to exact revenge wouldn't bother Avery. He'd spend the time meditating and reading. Once released, he'd resume his life as if nothing had happened.

Someone had just tried to kill Avery. Why? And more to the point why had a laser shot been fired from space which was an act of war? None of it was his doing.

There was something else. The project was in jeopardy because the persuasive program did not work on Avery or Kaylor. It just created an annoying buzzing sensation which resulted in them taking off their communicators. Why it didn't work on those two he wasn't sure. Perhaps they had some rare and special gene and it was probably the reason the Zetas specifically wanted a child from those two.

Should he cut his losses and run? He should, but Sparta wasn't going to. This current project was the toughest he'd ever had, but of late his jobs had become a little too easy and he'd become bored. It was time to change his approach and use a little old-fashioned means. But he'd have to watch himself because now there were new players in the game.

Chapter 20

Avery had feared the snipper might fall apart like an overcooked fowl. Thankfully his protective suit had acted like a carapace which held him together. Well mostly. The body separated at the major joints like one of those toy robots you could disassemble. Using shovels, they managed to get the limbs and torso into the body bag. This left the head and having extracted a couple of hairs for DNA sampling, Dee kicked the head in like one might a soccer ball before zipping up the body bag.

Straining with all their might, they managed to lift the body bag off the ground and move it three feet before dropping him.

'We can't drag him,' cautioned Avery.

'No, we can't, but why's he so fucking heavy?' asked Dee.

'No idea,' said Sarah wiping her brow.

'Have you got a hover sled?' asked Dee.

Avery ran towards the shed. He didn't have a sled, but he had something that would suffice.

'What the bloody hell is that?' asked Dee when he returned pushing it.

'It's a wheelbarrow. Zianans prefer low tech.'

'Low tech! That's prehistoric! I hate to think how many dinosaurs it's tripped up over the years.'

There was no scientific evidence that Ziana had ever had dinosaurs, but Avery still understood the reference.

They managed to get the sniper into the wheelbarrow. Even moving as fast as they could, there was no chance of getting him on the shuttle before the emergency crews arrived. The closest place was inside the shed and Avery could have lived without the stink that would linger. It couldn't be helped; he'd have to light scented candles later and hope for the best.

They had barely got the door shut when two red hovercars flew in with fire and rescue written on the side of them. One hovered over the burnt area re-bombarding it with sound waves, while the other landed. Sarah was using a digital camera to take holoimages as if she were a tourist admiring an attraction.

Dressed in heavy boots and bright orange fire retardant clothing, two firemen sprang from the hovercar.

'What the fuck's going on!' roared the fire chief.

Avery's mind raced. He'd never been a skilled liar and he'd been raised to always tell the truth regardless of circumstances.

Sarah flashed a cheeky smile. 'Good shot eh? *The Zee's* gunner is the best in the fleet.'

Eyes bulging, they stared at her, but Sarah continued to act like a shameless tourist.

Shaking his heads, the other fireman began to unroll some natural fibered reflective crime scene tape.

'Explain that,' barked the fire chief.

She squatted down to change the viewing angle. 'Avery needed a dead tree removed because he was afraid it might fall across the entrance.'

The fire chief replaced his helmet on his head. 'Didn't want to get a tree feller in for that?'

Sarah looked up. 'No, see, we thought we'd use the laser to turn it to charcoal so it could be used as biochar. Apparently, it's great for the soil. Helps it hold water, so it doesn't evaporate.'

Avery looked away because Ziana's volcanic soil needed no biochar. This region also had frequent rains, so the food forest custodians usually added gravel for better drainage, not biochar to hold water. Sarah clearly didn't know this, but the local firepersons would. He feared they wouldn't buy it.

Thankfully, rather than frown the chief spat, 'Un-fucking-believable.'

A police hovercar flew in and landed. The local sergeant got out, donned his hat and swaggered over.

'Leave the tape lads, stupidity doesn't equal a crime scene.' The fire chief turned to the sergeant. 'Your scene; we're leaving.'

The sergeant, who was joined by a constable, narrowed his eyes.

'Actually, it's fleets scene and Commander Bartell,' she placed a hand on her chest, 'has got it under control.'

The sergeant folded his arms, then seemed to get a thought. 'Right, well I'll leave you all to explain yourselves to the Chief Minister. She's en route with an entourage so have fun with that.'

The colour drained from Sarah's face. The Chief Minister, Renee Hardy, had an extremely low tolerance for bullshit.

There was a slamming of doors and the hovercars departed blowing detritus all over them before they returned to Port Town.

'Biochar,' said Dee incredulously.

Grimacing Sarah said, 'I was winging it, besides where were you?'

'Winging it? I'd say you sunk it.'

It didn't escape Avery's notice that Dee did not respond to where she was. It was Intelligence who were trying to keep things quiet so they ought to be the ones providing the cover story.

Sarah looked like she was about to throttle Dee.

Avery intervened. 'I hate to interrupt a good bitch fight, but there's a chargrilled sniper in my shed and he can't stay there. Furthermore, I'm not having him buried on my property or anywhere nearby.'

'Why not? asked Dee.

'For one, his mangled corpse is wrapped in synthetic which will leach toxins.'

Dee snorted. Even given everything that had happened on Earth, Rians still didn't care about pollution and what it did to the environment.

Sarah folded her arms and stared at Dee. Avery did likewise.

Dee gestured towards Mt Zalaith who was always emitting a thin trail of smoke on the far horizon. 'Dump him in the volcano. Its lava will burn the synthetic.' She began walking away towards Port Town.

'Where are you going?'

'To run some errands.'

Sarah stared after her disbelievingly. Avery kicked at a nearby stone and immediately regretted it because it would have been the perfect thing to throw at Dee's retreating head.

'She wasn't serious, was she?' said Sarah when Dee had rounded the corner.

'I think she was.' Avery didn't like it, but it was a quick and dirty solution. 'Come on. I'll fly.'

*****

The shuttle had a tilt down door at the rear which allowed troops to make a quick exit. Avery loaded up the sniper, or what was left of him, wheelbarrow and all since it was only an old one which needed replacing.

The shuttle took off vertically and Avery followed the food forest until it snaked around to the right following the contours of the land. The food forest was fifteen metres wide and hundreds of kilometres long. Not one continuous swale, but a series of them interconnected with dams and spillways that flowed into creeks and rivers that ran to the giant lakes.

All along the edge of the food forests were houses with outbuildings built every hundred metres or so. This was where most Zianans lived — close to the supply of food and fresh water.

Every five kilometres, was a half-dome tunnel entrance that led down to the train line.

Very different from Ria, where people lived on top of each other and the land was covered in concrete.

Avery made for the volcano — a cone-shaped mountain set amid low lying undulated hills covered in native forest. He wasted no time sightseeing and flew directly over the crater. There was no visible lava, just a plume of rising smoke and ash. Once at the right angle, their payload tumbled out and disappeared into the superheated chasm below.

Avery didn't dally but quickly flew them out of the way.

'Avery.'

Cripes, don't tell me Sarah wants me to say some words for the corpse. 'What?'

'Is there something you withheld from us? Did you piss someone off enough to have them assassinate you?

Avery sighed and told Sarah how he'd tied to get access to the metadata without a warrant.

'Damn it. It's not like you to not do things by the book.'

'Tried to, but no one would listen.'

Sarah winced and looked away. Despite having apologised she was still feeling guilty for not having taken him seriously. When she turned back, she said, 'Right, get us to Port Town proto and let's try and sort out the Chief Minister.'

Avery grinned. Taking the controls, he flew back through a valley low and fast. The scenery whipping past at a blur, he guided the ship with precision narrowly missing trees and rock walls. He'd been the youngest fleetperson ever to earn his platinum wings from advanced flight school, hence his flying skills were infamous.

When he'd graduated after five years of training, he'd had the option of becoming a combat pilot or becoming a detective. He'd chose to become a detective, but it had been a hard decision to make.

Having blown off considerable steam, he sat the shuttle down with well-practiced gentleness.

Sarah didn't move and sat opposite clutching the edge of her seat, her face and knuckles white. Despite a lengthy career in fleet, she'd always hated flying.

*****

'I suppose you thought that was funny.'

He had, but didn't want to risk voicing that aloud. She was after all his superior officer. 'You said to get us back quickly.'

Despite Sarah's earlier unwillingness to land and park the shuttle on the base, there was nowhere else to put it.

Sarah gave him a sideways look as she ground the gears of the fleet jeep they'd commandeered. Despite extensive training in fleet, she'd never mastered driving, let alone a car with manual gears. What few ground vehicles there were on Ria, mainly street sweepers and garbage trucks, were driven by androids. Everyone relied on the trams or caught self-driven hover-taxis.

Pulling up in front of the government and public service building, she reefed on the handbrake. 'Let me do the talking.'

Avery, who was more than happy with that plan, fell into step beside her. Raised voices could be heard inside the boardroom as they approached. Sarah knocked on the door and opened it enough to put her head through. 'May I join you?'

Switching from Zianan to English, the Chief Minister said, 'Commander Bartell. Yes, come in and explain to us what the fuck's going on.'

Avery sheepishly followed Sarah in. The Chief Minister was accompanied by the Zianan police Commissioner, the Chief fire officer, the minister for Defence and Justice and the fleet liaison officer.

'Might I have a private word with the Chief Minister?' asked Sarah.

The Chief Minister returned a stern look and barked one word, 'Out!'

The sound of chairs wheeling on the floor filled the room as people got up and exited.

Sarah stuck with the biochar cover story but added that the shot had been fired as a training exercise for the crew of *The Zee*.

The door opened and Admiral Cadel entered in his immaculate maroon dress uniform.

'That's the worst cover story I've ever heard,' said the Chief Minister.

'Agreed,' replied Cadel. He turned to Avery and Sarah. 'Where's the other one?'

'It accused us of cocking it up and sodded off. I swear I know not where,' said Avery.

Cadel glowered. 'Both of you, out. That's an order.'

*****

Despite being over three-hundred Earth years old, Renee Hardy, The Zianan Chief Minister, was not an old frail woman. Her feminine body was fitter looking than many of fleet's troops male or female, her forest green hair, worn in a single braid, glistened with a sheen and her bright lilac eyes stared intently demanding an explanation and a bloody good one.

'Do you mind if I sit down?' asked Cadel.

'Don't care if you sit or stand as long as you start explaining and skip the bullshit.'

Politics was a new profession on Ziana. Before the arrival of the Rians, Ziana had been governed only by elders who maintained law and lore. Hardy had never wanted to be a politician. However, she'd been asked to become Chief Minister because she was considered the best person for the job and no one else had wanted it. She accepted the call when asked.

As a result, she cared only about doing the job well and not about whether she was considered popular. She didn't have to worry about re-election because presently, no one wanted her job.

Like all Zianans, she had a low tolerance for bullshit. Cadel understood because he too was Zianan, and the only one of his race, to ever become an Admiral.

Cadel remained standing. 'An assassin just tried to kill one of my officers so I authorised an intervention.'

Hardy stared at him unwaveringly. 'Let's be honest, *The Zee* fired a shot from space didn't it?'

Cadel suppressed a wince. 'Yes, it was in the vicinity and available to respond.'

She smiled sarcastically, 'In the vicinity, how serendipitous. Do you think I'm an idiot?'

Cadel rubbed the bridge of his nose. 'No, of course not.'

'I've been in space numerous times and I know how vast it is. I also know, despite awesome technology that allows *The Zee* to cross AUs of distance in a relatively short period, it would take considerable time for *The Zee* to line up for a precision shot on the surface. That means, *The Zee* wasn't where it was by mere chance.'

Cadel nodded ascent. 'That's correct. *The Zee* moved into position on my orders.'

'Which meant you had intelligence about the assassin and was acting on it. However, that doesn't explain why Avery and Sarah, and whoever the other one is, wasn't contacted and warned.'

'Communication wasn't possible.'

Hardy folded her arms. 'Why. They have permits to carry communicators.'

She had him because although they'd all had their communicators off while they'd been talking outside by the natural swimming pool, Dee had turned hers on for a while when they'd come back inside.

'We did not want any of them to risk themselves either in a firefight or by trying to capture the assassin.'

'Which you could have made explicitly clear in orders, which fleet are trained to obey without question. This tells me the other one, isn't fleet, and you couldn't risk orders from the Executive Director of Intelligence countermanding you. Instead, *The Zee* fired a laser shot, after the assassin had taken a shot at Avery. A shot which could have been lethal.'

'The timing was tight.'

'Meaning *The Zee* wasn't quite into position in time and I'm guessing the assassin came down from space in a pod because he wouldn't have been allowed to arrive with synthetic armour and weapons, would he?'

It was an accusation as much as a question. Although Ziana had its own customs officials they worked collaboratively with fleet who were responsible for the security of the space port which includes Ziana's one and only teleporter. 'Correct on both matters, but how'd you know it was Avery?'

'His hair is singed on one side of his head meaning the assassin barely missed.'

Cadel's stomach flip-flopped. Damn, Hardy was right to chew him out. Not informing Avery when Dee's communicator was on was a bad call. Almost fatal.

Having had a rant, Hardy composed herself and took a seat prompting Cadel to do so as well.

'None of this explains why someone tried to kill Avery,' she said.

'That's classified.'

'Of course, it is, but my security clearance is the same as yours.'

Cadel bit his lip. Unlike Earth and Ria, authority was simple on Ziana. Hardy and her government did not have levels of secrecy above them, mainly because Ziana did not have its own intelligence agency or military. It barely had a police force and most of the officers were forest rangers because crime was low and tended to be misdemeanours.

If he did not tell her what he knew, she'd assume there was a conspiracy and start searching for answers by remote viewing — a skill many Zianans were proficient in.

'The situation is difficult to explain.'

Hardy interlaced her fingers, rested them on the desk and gave him a patient look. 'Try me.'

'You and I, we are both old enough to remember first contact.'

She sat back in her chair. 'I was only seven at the time, but yes, I remember. It was both exciting and frightening. Here were these beings who'd crossed the vastness of space — an achievement I had to respect. Yet,' she glanced out the window for a moment. 'Captain Sorensen, he wasn't fourth seal. He wanted more than just land to build a colony. He wanted power and control over everyone and everything on Ziana. Emperor was the word that was used.'

'Yes, he did. Our elders made the right decision refusing his offers. They also made the right decision when they later allowed the colonisers to build the research station and for Ziana to elect a Chief Minister and form a government, small as it is.'

'I agree. Despite cultural differences, knowledge sharing has been incredibly valuable, but I'm unclear how this relates to Avery being almost killed.'

Cadel sighed. 'Ria's new president is a direct descendant of Captain Sorensen. Sorensen's grandson changed his family name to Inglis because the name Sorensen had been tarnished by his grandfather's actions and attitudes.'

Hardy narrowed her eyes. 'Is President Inglis the reincarnation of Captain Sorensen?'

Cadel grimaced. 'Can't know for sure, but I believe so.'

Hardy swore. 'Explains his aggression and ridiculous policies. He's reincarnated to finish what he started.'

'I fear that maybe so.'

She rubbed her face in her hands. 'What's this have to do with Avery?'

'This is the part that is difficult to explain but bear with me. Some time ago, before he was president, Inglis came to Ziana seemingly for a holiday. Whilst he was here, he sought out a seer and whilst I don't know exactly what he was told, I have the gist of part of it. In his future, a woman of extraordinary mind would oppose him and ultimately defeat him.'

'By using the fourth way?' asked Hardy.

'I can only conjecture.' Cadel poured himself a glass of water from a carafe on the table and took a sip. 'However, despite what may or may not be true, Inglis believes the woman of power to be Avery's daughter.'

Hardy rolled her eyes. 'Preposterous. Avery doesn't have a daughter and now his wife is dead he never will have one.'

'That was probably Inglis's thoughts when he arranged Leda's murder.'

Hardy paled.

'Avery has adopted both Zianan and Rian cultures meaning there's a chance he could have a child with another woman. Which is why an assassin just tried to kill him,' said Cadel.

Hardy got up and began to pace. 'Damn it. Why did this have to happen on my watch?'

'Our watch Renee. I'm with you.'

She returned her gaze to him. 'You fired that shot as a warning?'

'Yes, I consider every member of fleet a part of my extended family and no one messes with family.'

Renee again narrowed her eyes. 'Do you now want me to go on the record and say a shot was fired to protect a Zianan citizen? Fuel the fire so to speak?'

'No. We don't play that childish game with Inglis. Instead, we officially pretend nothing is amiss. Ria won't admit they sent an assassin so his death will not be mentioned. If they send more, we'll defend again. Naturally, I've put a gag order on the crew of *The Zee* and those at the base. Officially, the shot was fired as part of a training exercise.'

She smiled, the first since he stepped into the room. 'The worst excuse I've ever heard and a big fuck you to Inglis.'

'An apt way of putting it.'

A thought struck her. 'What do you know about a Dr Kaylor Emerson? She recently arrived at the Research Centre, but no one is sure who she is or why she's come.'

'She's being coerced by a fixer named Daniel Sparta. As such we honestly don't know what he wants from her but we are pretty sure it isn't scientific research, despite the fact that he's funded her position.' Cadel swallowed involuntarily. He hated to lie to Renee. They'd been friends since they were children.

'I want to know why. Can I leave that with you, or do I need to run my own investigation?'

'Trust me, we'll deal with Sparta.'

'Good, in the meantime, since no one knows why she's here, Dr. Emerson will be employed by my Chief Scientist Ethan. She's clearly a threat to Inglis otherwise he wouldn't have retrenched one hundred public servants in order to hide her dismissal.'

'I agree. Inglis also tried to have Emerson murdered on her way home by having an assassin masquerade as a street ruffian during the riot he created.'

Hardy looked thoughtful. 'Interesting. Dr. Emerson's research is clearly very confronting to him and his administration, and by employing her, she'll become our *alligare*.'

152

Hardy used the Zianan word which was also Latin. After colonisation, the Zianans had discovered their language was a derivative of that ancient language.

'Indeed, and you're right, it was a masquerade. Those others who were retrenched have been quietly reinstated. Not all of them, but a fair few. As for Emerson, she died and was sent back from the light.'

Hardy's eyes widened. 'You thinking what I'm thinking?'

'I'm keeping an open mind. In the meantime, we need to protect them both as best we can.'

'Agreed.'

They shook hands and Cadel took his leave pleased to have Hardy onside.

Chapter 21

To avoid being accosted by other members of the Zianan government, Avery and Sarah exited via a seldom-used side door. Avery drove the fleet jeep back to his house and upon arrival, they discovered the lasered tree had been completely removed. Dee had obviously commanded a team of fleet troops to disappear the charcoal remains into the food forest. Comically, Sarah was right, the tree had been turned into biochar of sorts.

Inside, Dee was lying face down on one of Avery's lounge room couches. One foot had slipped off, her mouth was open and she was snoring loudly.

'That can't be comfortable,' said Sarah.

'I agree, but I'm not moving her to a spare bed. She'll probably knife me if I try to.'

'Yes, the Intelligence types are a bit paranoid and highly strung.'

Still hyped up on adrenalin at almost being killed, Avery didn't know whether to sit, stand or lie. He chose to gently pace.

'How are you doing?' asked Sarah with genuine concern in her voice.

'Ironically, feeling better than I was now I know you believe Leda was murdered.'

Sarah walked over to him and they hugged like the life-long friends they were. Avery held her tight and rested his chin on top of her head for a moment.

The sound of gravel crunching under tyres caused them to separate.

Avery half expected it to be Cadel accompanied by a lower ranking fleet person serving as his driver, but it was Kaylor, who was accompanied by the taxi driver Quentin.

Blissfully ignorant of what had just transpired, Kaylor exited the taxi, and carrying a parasol, walked over to the house. 'Is this a good time? You weren't overly specific.'

Not really, but you're here now. 'Yes, come in, I was just about to make a chai. Would you like one?'

Kaylor stepped into the porch and folded her parasol away, placed it in a stand and slipped off her hemp fabric Zianan-style lightweight boots. 'Yes please.'

'Dr. Emerson, this is Dr. Bartell.'

Extending her hand, she said, 'I'm Kaylor.'

'I'm Sarah.'

They shook hands warmly.

Avery led Kaylor across the open plan lounge room taking a wide berth around Dee. 'Don't mind her and don't worry, she doesn't live here. Yeltzie's arriving shortly, but she tends to come and go as she pleases. It's peaceful now, but there'll be lots of tents up in the nearby field when the food forest harvest starts a few weeks from now, but it's a seasonal thing.'

'I like Yeltizie, she really was good to me when I was convalescing and her cooking is divine.'

'Yes, it is. I've known her since birth; she's like a daughter to me.' He led her down a hallway. 'There are four spare bedrooms which are all the same, so you can have whichever one you want.'

Kaylor gasped. 'Wow.' She walked over to more closely inspect the four-poster king-sized bed. The posts were made from a red grained timber, turned on a wood lathe with the ends carved into animals.

'Zianan totem spirits,' said Avery. 'The *aquila*, or great eagle, protects the skies, the *vespertilio*, or bat, protects you during the long night, the *anuilla*, or eel protects you under water, while the *ulso* or emu protects you on land.'

'How wonderful.'

'Yes,' he shrugged. 'It's just children's stories, like the fairy tales on Earth, but craftspeople love to capture the story in artefacts.' He continued the tour. Gesturing to more exquisitely made wooden furniture he said, 'As you can see there is plenty of wardrobe space, chest of draws and bedside table.' He led her along to a bathroom that contained a spa in addition to a shower, before showing her the laundry. They returned to the kitchen, where Sarah, was sweeping up the broken coffee pot with a natural bristled broom.

Avery grabbed a pot with a pourer on the side and turned one of the hotplates on, on his large stove that had six hotplates and three ovens. To the pot, he added a blend of nut milks, some honey and a pre-prepared Zianan chai mix and while it heated, he sliced off slabs of nutmeal and dried fruit loaf.

'How does the electricity get to the house? Is there underground cables?'

'No. It's wireless and there is an aerial on the roof that's connected to a tower that distributes the electricity via frequency.'

'Wow, I never knew that was possible.'

'It's technology from Earth that was supressed. Anyway, there's a natural swimming pool and kilometres of food forest to forage in. So, plenty of space to relax and there's always fresh food except during the long night when we eat the bottled, dried or frozen fair. There's an abundance of filtered water and Ziana has geothermal energy which is cheap so heating during the long night isn't a problem.' Avery took the pot off the heat, strained the contents into a jug and reached for the electric frother. 'Obviously, you need to be careful in the sun during the long day. Use your parasol, sun cloak and sunglasses.'

'Yes, I was briefed, but it's only for a few weeks not all the time right.'

'That's right, just during long day.

Kaylor glanced outside with a look of reverence on her face, 'This planet is a paradise.'

'You don't find Ziana strange?' asked Sarah.

'Well, yes, I do, but in a good way. I mean the constant day thing is affecting my sleep pattern, but I assume I'll adjust to that in due course. But the world is incredible; just so much life and colour and vibrancy. Odd that there's no mammals though.'

'Except people, no. Just birds, fish, reptiles and insects mainly. Earthlings have described Ziana as a warmer New Zealand prior to the introduction of feral species during colonisation, but I haven't been there so I wouldn't know.'

'Are there many volcanic eruptions or earthquakes?' asked Kaylor nervously.

'Yes, but not around here. Our ancestors knew to build on the stable sections of land.' Avery frothed the chai and poured it into clay mugs which he carried over to the table.

Kaylor took a sip which met with her approval before bitting into a slice of the loaf. She made an mmm sound. 'This is really good. Made with nutmeal and dried fruits?'

'Yes, Ziana doesn't have much by way of grains, but we have dozens of different nut and seed trees which we grind up and use in place of flour.'

'Well, it's really good.' Kaylor looked thoughtful. 'How much will the rent be?'

Avery being fleet had never paid rent in his life since his base accommodation on both Ziana and Ria was provided as part of his renumeration. As a fleet officer, he also received a large salery. He shrugged. 'Six silvers a spin.'

'A spin?' queried Kaylor.

'A Zianan year,' replied Sarah. 'One hundred and eighty-one Earth standard days.'

Kaylor's eyes widened. 'You can't be serious. That's less than a third what I'm paying for sixty cubic metres at present.'

Avery frowned as he pictured the dimensions in his mind. 'My kitchen wouldn't fit into that.'

'Exactly.'

Avery shrugged again. 'I don't need the money, but I have to charge rent as *sheesha*.'

Kaylor smiled. 'Sounds too good to be true.'

Sarah grinned. 'Welcome to Ziana.'

'It's a fair way from the Research Centre,' cautioned Avery.

'Only five kilometres. I'll buy a bicycle with an electric motor. When can I move in?'

'When it suits you,' replied Avery.

'That would be straight away.' She glanced outside and realised Quentin had left.

'He told me he had another job radio in.' Sarah glanced at the two-way radio that was mounted on the wall at the end of the island bench that separated the kitchen from the dining room. 'I can give him a call.'

'No need,' said Avery. 'We can give you a lift back in the jeep because I'm heading over to the base to do some things. Which reminds me, I found someone who will look at your communicator.'

'At the base?' Kaylor paled. 'I'm not in trouble, am I? I was supposed to have all the permits and I'm not allowed to take the communicator off the Research Centre.'

'No, you're not in trouble. Mines playing up as well and the tech wanted to compare the two that's all. Don't worry, I'm a fleet officer and I'll sort the forms so I can take legally take it off the base.'

Kaylor exhaled. 'It's at home, but sure, that would be good actually.'

Dee's communicator began to vibrate behind her ear. In a liminal state between sleep and being awake, she tried twice to shoo it away as if it were an insect annoying her. Finally, she woke looking disorientated and confused. When she realised where she was, she got off the couch, and without saying anything, headed for the bathroom.

By the time she returned Avery had made her a coffee.

'Cadel wants a word with us Sarah,' she mumbled.

'Thought he might,' she replied.

Avery handed Dee the caffeinated beverage.

She took a sip and screwed up her nose. 'Don't you have milk?'

'Do you see any cows?'

'No cows. No darkness. Queer, they got that bit right.'

'Zianans are lactose intolerant and it will be dark in a few hours, but only for a few hours,' replied Avery.

'An eclipse,' said Kaylor excitedly.

'Yep, and four of Zeus's other moons will be visible. It will be quite a show, for newcomers at least.'

'Four moons,' hissed Dee. 'That's a bit excessive, isn't it?'

'Well, Zeus has ten moons including Ziana, but the most you'll ever see during an eclipse is six,' replied Avery.

Dee shook her head. 'Too queer for me. People go off when there only one moon if it is full.' She put the coffee down. 'Don't suppose you have any caffeinated soft drink?'

'Nope, we Zianans don't consume chemical cocktails.'

'Course not, and the water tastes funky.'

'The water is so finely filtered and sterilized with ultraviolet light that it's hospital grade.'

'Yeah, whatever.'

Kaylor looked horrified at Dee. Avery was used to Rians finding Ziana strange. He just smiled as he ushered them all out of the house towards the jeep.

Chapter 23

Sarah had never been in Admiral Cadel's office before. Like the base Commodore's, it was on the third floor of the administration building and offered a view of the entire base. Decorated in beautifully varnished wooden décor, it contained a work desk and a large conference table with holocom equipment. The office had its own en suite and in the corner was a small kitchenette with island bench. The centre of the room contained four two-seater couches placed to form a square with narrow walkways between them.

Cadel had taken off his jacket and loosened his tie. He bade them to sit at ease on the couches. Sarah sat beside Dee opposite Cadel and forced her foot to be still. It tended to jiggle when she was nervous.

He looked directly at Sarah. 'Wait until it gets dark from the eclipse and then arrest Daniel Sparta.'

'On what charge?'

'Identification fraud. He's staying at the Port Town hotel. Not in the hotel, but in cabin number eight out the back. Be discrete. I don't want anyone knowing he's been brought in, especially not the Rian journalists who are also staying there. They've been calling incessantly since the laser strike.'

'They're not on Ziana coincidentally,' said Dee. A hologram containing the image of the sniper, which Sarah had taken through the rifle scope, appeared. 'I ran this image through visual recognition software. Using advanced shape modelling, my AI was able to identify him, with a high degree of certainty. He was a member of the elite presidential guard.'

Cadel showed no surprise.

A knot formed in Sarah's stomach. 'Are those journalists just spin doctors for the president?'

'Can't be sure, but like Dee said they're not here by happenstance. Journalists don't teleport to Ziana unless they are expecting a big story.'

'In other words, they were expecting a big reaction from the Chief Minister over the attempted assassination of Avery, a mid-ranking officer?'

'Or there is still more to come,' said Dee.

'Regardless, we can expect fake news and propaganda,' said Cadel. 'The journalists are from the RBC, which is financed by the Rian government. They won't risk their jobs speaking out against President Inglis or his administration, but they will happily publish sensationalist news that isn't true.'

A cold chill filled Sarah with dread. 'Sir, is there going to be a war?'

'Yes, the first shots were fired today.' Cadel looked away as if to gather his thoughts. 'The warmongers think they can take whatever they want.'

Sarah wanted to yell and scream who's going to stop them, but she refrained from doing so. Sensing she was dismissed she went to stand.

'Can I tag along?' asked Dee.

'You may. I'm prepared to work cooperatively with the SIA, even though this is my directive and as such it's fleet's jurisdiction.'

'Understood.'

'Good.' Cadel turned from Dee back to Sarah. 'I've flagged Sparta's DNA so he can't leave through Ziana's only spaceport or teleporter. All he can do is flee by train, but I want him brought in discretely. If it goes pear-shaped, let him go.'

'Can I post a few officers down at the train platform?' asked Sarah.

'No,' said Cadel.

'Okay, discrete, I get it.'

The fourth way

*****

Avery wasn't invited to meet with Cadel so having sorted the e-forms, he dropped his and Kaylor's communicator at the tech building on the base. Remembering that Yeltzie was arriving via train shortly, and that she wanted to go up to the observatory for the eclipse, he slipped back into Port Town and brought provisions for a picnic.

Since Yeltzie hadn't arrived, he went back over to the tech building.

The tech, Hugh, stood before a raised desk peering through his thick glasses. Despite being a career fleetman, Hugh had never quite got the idea of neat dress. His baggy cargo pants were ill-fitting, his t-shirt was not fleet issue and contained an image of a SciFi holo-series, and he wore his shirt like a jacket, unbuttoned and untucked.

As they approached, he ran a hand through his unruly red hair. 'I've worked out what the issue is.'

'Jolly good,' said Avery who was keen to know. When the suspense reached fever pitch Avery prompted him. 'Well.'

'Nothing. Not a damn thing.'

Avery cocked his head. 'Sorry.'

'There's nothing wrong with your communicator, nor the other one. I have run every diagnostic and test there is. They are both working perfectly.'

Avery narrowed his eyes. 'Then explain to me why it acts like a pissed off bee caught in a spider's web.'

Hugh glanced up and pressed his glasses against his nose. 'Nothing to do with your communicator. It's more likely a dodgy incoming signal. Has anyone been trying to contact you from Ria using that new bodgie satellite array that's only half finished?'

Avery's chest tightened and his throat constricted as he thought of Leda who would formerly have called regularly. His voice croaked as he said, 'No.'

Hugh swallowed audibly. 'So sorry to hear about the death of your wife, my sincere condolences.'

Avery's lips pulled into a tight line.

Hugh avoided eye contact. 'As I said, I can't fault it, so unless I catch it in the act, there's nothing more I can do.'

Avery gritted his teeth. 'I don't trust this one. Can I have another one?'

Hugh shrugged. 'If you want. I'll just run one up for you. It will only take a moment.'

Having secured a new communicator, Avery switched it on and headed over to the train station to wait for Yeltzie's who arrived on the next train.

He was just about to hug her when Sarah contacted him.

'What's up,' he said gruffly.

'I'm arresting Sparta. Could you hang around the train station in case he tries to flee?'

Avery gritted his teeth. He'd been looking forward to spending time with Yeltzie, but he also wanted a word with Sparta. If he got away, that wouldn't be possible.

'You still there.'

'Yes, alright, but be quick about it, I promised Yeltzie I'd take her up to the observatory.' He disconnected. 'I'm sorry, I've got to hang around here for a bit.'

Used to him being dragged away for work, she looked nonplussed about it. She pulled him into a hug.

He handed her the picnic. 'Do you want to go on ahead and I'll catch up?'

Yeltzie looked thoughtful. 'Sure, but I might see if I can find Kaylor. Would you mind if she joined us?'

'No, she'd love that.' He went to explain that Kaylor was his new housemate, but Yeltzie gave him a cheeky wink, took the picnic and wandered off.

We're just friends. Was he? Avery had a thing for the scientific types, Kaylor was lovely and despite having only recently met her he couldn't deny the attraction he had for her. He dismissed the idea. He was still grieving for Leda. He mustn't run into the arms of another woman seeking comfort and later regret it.

*****

Kaylor could barely contain her excitement as she was shown around her new laboratory by the Zianan Chief Scientist, Ethan. The lab was in a section dedicated to joint collaboration between Ria and Ziana. State of the art, it was even better equipped than the one she had been forced out of at the Scientific Institute.

'Has Roger Smith been informed that I've been seconded? He went to a lot of expense to transport me to Ziana and I was supposed to be working on the new satellite array.'

Ethan gently laid a hand on her shoulder. 'You have the full support of Chief Minister Renee Hardy, who has authorised me to negotiate with Roger, so just leave it with me.'

'Yes, alright. He did mention you might be interested in employing me.' She bit her lip. 'I'm just worried he might want reimbursement for the teleport.'

'It'll be fine. Don't worry.'

Kaylor wanted to do a little happy dance but stifled herself.

'If there's anything you need just let me know.'

Kaylor smiled and she nodded in response. 'Torri, my AI, has access to my research, so I can pick up where I left off.'

'Excellent.' He took a step towards the door but turned back. 'If you want to go up and take a look from space just let me know. The Zianan government has a spaceship in orbit at its disposal.'

Kaylor's eyes widened. 'Wow. How much funding have I been allocated?'

He smiled. 'I'll take care of that, but I'm sure you'll find it more than adequate.'

She watched him leave, then did her happy dance.

She would have started work straight away, but she'd have to wait until Torri was returned. For now, the eclipse was about to start.

*****

Sparta's heart thudded in his chest. Sarah and another woman were headed towards his cabin. They were coming for him. Should he let them take him in? No. Even though he had a permit for the device, they'd still find a reason to confiscate it. If they broke through the security, he was finished.

Should he hide it somewhere in the cabin?

No. They'd get warrants to search it.

Fuck.

With no time to think, Sparta did the only thing he could do. He fled, out of the door, across the accommodation complex and into a nearby woodland. They didn't call out his name nor the usual, "stop, you're under arrest", but they did chase him.

Trees whipped past. Twice he was almost taken out by a low hanging branch. He stumbled and fell, but managed to get back up again.

With the coming eclipse, the light was fading fast. The wood was open enough to run through, but ahead it turned into the food forest and became much denser.

Should he try and hide in it?

No, they were too close behind. They'd find him.

Spying a tunnel that ramped downward, he veered to his right. Unless he was mistaken, it would lead to the train station. If he boarded a train without them also getting on, he might be able to get away and keep moving.

At the bottom of the ramp was a large puddle. He ran through it without hesitation splashing muddy water everywhere. At the platform, a train was just pulling out. Damn, he'd missed it, but if it ran to schedule, the one that travelled in the opposite direction would arrive shortly. To catch it, he'd have to cross to the other side. He'd have to hurry or he'd miss that one as well.

There was an access tunnel beneath the tracks. Daniel slid down the stairwell banister and executed a good landing. As he turned to run, he ran straight into Avery who wasn't there by chance. The big fleet cop stood two metres tall and weight one hundred and twenty kilograms — all muscle. A well-placed arm thrust coat hangered Sparta.

Daniel was knocked off his feet. He hit the ground hard, but trained in martial arts, he rolled to lessen the impact. His nose hurt and his eyes watered, but fuelled with surging adrenalin, he scrambled forward determined to get away. He ran only two strides when the concrete lurched towards him a second time. Avery had swept his legs causing Sparta to trip.

This time he skated on his stomach grazing his palms and the underside of his body. Ahead of him was Sarah. The women must have split up and she'd circled around to cut him off. He was trapped. They'd caught him.

*****

Avery was about to pin Sparta to the ground with a knee when Dee hastened forward and zapped him with a sparker. The device was designed to stun and Sparta went instantly limp.

Avery rounded on her. 'What did you do that for?'

'Punishment for making me chase after him. Besides, don't accuse me of excessive force, you decked him twice.'

It wasn't about excessive force; Avery would happily beat him to a pulp. The problem was, Sparta would be unconscious for at least half an hour and they couldn't wait for him to come around. He thumbed towards the stairs. 'Now we have to carry him up them.'

Sarah arrived, panting. 'Damn, the little shit can run.' She pulled on a pair of gloves and began patting Sparta down. From the pocket of his pants, she removed an ancient handheld.

'What the hell is that?' asked Dee.

Avery removed a clean handkerchief from his pocket and unfolded it. 'I'll take that and his communicator. I've got a sneaking suspicion about what it does.'

Sarah placed both devices on the unfolded handkerchief and Avery gently wrapped them up and put them in his own pocket. She continued to search him, but aside from a few Zianan coins, Sparta had nothing else.

Sarah produced a set of metal handcuffs and cuffed his hands behind his back.

'I'll go and get a vehicle or something,' said Dee who was already headed up the stairs.

When she'd disappeared, Avery grabbed him under the arms, while Sarah grabbed his legs. Walking up the stairs backward carrying a body was difficult enough, but Sparta kept folding at the hips causing his backside to land on every step.

'For fuck's sake,' panted Sarah, who was a strong woman. 'Why's the little prick so heavy?'

'Deadweight,' replied Avery, resting for a moment.

'Can't we drag him the rest of the way?'

'No, we can't risk hurting him any more than we have. As it is, he'll probably try and do us for excessive force.'

She wrinkled her nose and conceded his point.

Thankfully Dee returned. Grabbing him by the belt, she stopped him from folding whilst taking some of the weight and together, they got him up the stairs. At the top was an electric hover sled which was supporting a one-point-six metre coffin-shaped wooden crate. Wooden crates were used to transport goods on Ziana and were ubiquitous. Along with palates, there was always a stack of them at the train stations.

Sarah's eyes widened. 'We can't just shove him in there.'

'We can't be seen with him,' retorted Dee.

'Is he going to fit?' asked Avery.

'He will if we fold him a bit.'

Sarah was having no part in it and stood to one side with her arms folded. Having removed the lid, Dee and Avery lifted Sparta into the crate so he was sitting in it with his legs outstretched. Thankfully he was short and by bending his knees, they did manage to get him to fit. Having put the lid back on, Avery threaded the wingnuts onto the bolt thread and did them up finger tight.

The hover sled came with a small remote and using antigravity technology, it was designed to float along beside you as you walked. Being Rian tech, Port Town was one of the few places on Ziana that they existed, although Avery suspected they'd soon be readily adopted in place of wheeled trolleys.

They'd crossed the station and were about to head up the ramp into Port Town when a clerk stepped out of an office. He was carrying a metal clipboard and had a pencil stashed behind his ear.

He said, 'Howdy folks. Just one quick question. How is it that I don't know anything about that crate?'

'Because it's none of your business,' snapped Dee.

Avery winced. Zianans didn't tolerate bad manners, especially not from a Rian.

'All packages that come to and from this train stop are my business. If I could see the tracking ticket, please.'

Dee screwed up her face because she had no idea what the clerk was asking for. On Ria, packages were transported with a nano-sized microchips monitored by Ais that were connected to the Cloudnet. The idea of a paper ticket, was a complete anathema to her.

Sarah produced a ticket and handed it over. The clerk smoothed it out and cross-referenced it with what was on his clipboard.

'This is an old ticket for a crate that came in earlier.'

Nice try Sarah.

'Look, this is fleet business and we are in a bit of a hurry. Do you mind?' said Dee.

The clerk returned a stern look. 'If you were in a hurry, you should have had the ticket on hand.'

'We must have dropped it,' hissed Dee, who was rapidly losing patience.

'That does happen. Look, how about you whip the lid off it and I'll check for contraband.'

'Contraband?' asked Dee with a look of disbelief on her face.

'Yes, synthetics which are banned on Ziana except by permit. Fleet's shocking for not having the right permits.'

Dee's eyes bulged. 'You're worried about a bit of plastic.'

'Pollution,' replied the clerk, his voice remaining calm and professional, 'and yes, I am. I've seen the documentaries and read non-fiction books of what humans did to Earth. Wiped out half the species and nearly wiped out themselves.'

The clerk wasn't going to budge. Not a millimetre. Zianans were both stubborn and passionate and they did their job properly regardless of how menial it was.

Obviously, they couldn't open the crate, but the worse thing was that Sparta could wake up at any moment. Avery was wracking his brain for a solution when Admiral Cadel came striding angrily down the ramp and into the train station.

'What's the hold up with my crate?' he barked.

Avery had no idea what had prompted Cadel to come to the train station, but he was resourceful and also aware. He may have been acting on intuition. Avery, having the sense to play along, snapped a salute. 'Sorry sir, but there appears to have been a mix up with the tracking ticket.'

'You lost the ticket!' Cadel rolled his eyes. 'Imbecile.'

Avery stood to attention with eyes forward. Sarah and Dee did likewise.

'I'm sorry Admiral, but I can't let this crate pass without first seeing a tracking ticket or without inspection.'

Looking apologetic Cadel turned to the clerk. 'I completely understand. If I had people who were half as diligent as you, I wouldn't have to come down here to personally sort out this mess. Do you know how busy I am?'

'I can imagine, Sir,' replied the clerk.

Cadel reached into the inside pocket of his jacket and produced a tracking ticket. Stamped across it in bright red letters was classified and urgent.

The clerk took the ticket, logged the tracking number on his clipboard and passed it back. 'Apologies for the delay Admiral, but we take quarantine very seriously.'

'As you must,' said Cadel. He glared at his three subordinates before bringing his attention back to the clerk. 'None of this is your doing. As for these three, they've just nominated themselves for a little remedial training. They appear to have forgotten the definition of fleet efficiency.'

Avery hoped the Admiral was joking.

'Well, don't just stand there, get the crate to the base.'

They sprang into action. Thankfully parked outside the train station was a fleet troop carrier that was being driven by Cadel's personal driver and general assistant. They managed to get the crate into the back. Dee went to return the hover sled, but the clerk was there ready to do it for them.

That was helpful, except Sparta chose that precise moment to come to and let out a groan.

'What was that?' asked the clerk.

Avery rubbed his belly. 'Stomach ache.'

He ushered Sarah and Dee into the back, climbed in and closed the rear doors in the clerk's face.

The driver glanced over his shoulder. 'Is there a person in that box?'

Cadel, who'd climbed into the passenger seat yelled, 'Eyes forward fleetman. No questions'

'But…'

'Shut it!'

Sparta banged on the inside of the box. 'Let me out of here.'

Avery, fearing that Sparta might suffocate, carefully backed off the wingnuts and lifted the lid a little. It would be a disaster if they unwittingly suffocated him.

It was enough for Dee's sparker, which was only the size of a pen, to slip beneath the lid. Without a moment's hesitation, she gave him a second zap causing him to again go limp.

'That was unbelievably cruel,' said Sarah. 'Don't think that I'll cover for you if I'm subpoenaed to give evidence.'

Dee began to casually do up the wingnuts. 'You should have gagged him. How sloppy would it have been if he'd started screaming for help in front of the clerk?'

'I said, shut it!' roared Cadel.

The vehicle fell silent.

'Avery, you were ordered to stand down. Why were you involved?'

'I was at the train station waiting for my honorary daughter when my commanding officer asked me to assist with the arrest.'

Sarah gave him an exacerbated look for dumping her in the shit.

Cadel sighed. 'What does Yeltzie know? Was she present for any of it?'

'No, she had already left to go and watch the eclipse, but she was unwittingly involved earlier. She was Kaylor's career.'

Cadel sighed. 'I'll need to talk to her.' He thumbed towards the box. 'Sort him out and then bring Yeltzie to my office.'

'Yes, Sir.'

With the help of the driver, they managed to get Sparta, crate and all, into the fleet gaol. Having got him out of the box, they laid him on a cot where he could recover from the sparkings.

Once he was secure, Avery left Sarah to sort out the paperwork, while he left to find Yeltzie. As the eclipse was still happening, he thought it wise to wait a bit before bringing her in. Instead, he called by the tech building to give Sparta's devices to Hugh.

Hugh was outside with his staff and they were all looking up admiring the sky.

'Got something for you. You're going to love it.'

'Can it wait?' asked Hugh.

'No.'

Hugh sighed, stood up and followed Avery into his lab.

Avery took the devices out of his pocket and gently unwrapped them. 'Handle this like top secret evidence.'

Hugh stared bewilderedly at the device. 'Yes, Sir, but, was a museum robbed?'

'No. If my hunch is right, this relic may be responsible for the problems I was having with my communicator earlier.'

Hugh pulled on gloves, gently picked it up and placed it in a machine that would search for forensic evidence including fingerprints, DNA and microscopic trace particles.

When it was done, he placed it back on his workshop bench and swiped the screen. 'Hmm, it's protected by a passcode which means it's going to take a while to get past it.'

'We only have twenty-four hours.'

'Okay, so I'll assume whoever you took it from is under arrest but hasn't been formally charged.'

'Correct, but a warrant was issued for his arrest and two communicators acting strangely, that's probable cause, so go ahead and hack the device.'

Hugh pushed his glasses further onto his nose. 'I'll do my best, but this thing is so ancient I'm going to be winging it.'

There was a ping sound and Hugh brought up a hologram that contained images of some random text.

'What's that?' asked Avery.

Hugh held up a finger to indicate he needed a minute. He was cross-checking something. 'Damn, she's good.'

'Who? What?'

'New cadet. We invited her for a drink at the social club, not long after she started. We got talking to her about awareness and she claimed she could remote view. Course we hung shit on her, but now she's making us eat humble pie.'

Avery suppressed a smile. He loved seeing Rians with ignorant attitudes put in their place. 'How are you testing her?'

Hugh waved his hands in the air. Simple random generator. It can produce numbers, words, shapes, and symbols or a combination of the lot. I send her a target with a name, such as target twenty-eight and nothing else. She sends back the results.'

Avery understood how remote viewing worked. The remote viewer received the target, closed their eyes and focused. Then, they simply wrote down or drew what they saw. No guessing or imagining, just a clear stream of information from the quantum field. As long as there was no ambiguity about the target, then through quantum entanglement, the answer received would always be correct.

'How good is she?'

'On average. Ninety-eight percent.'

'Right, so she's still a beginner, but it might be enough.'

Hugh blinked. 'Beginner?'

'Yes. Look send her a new target and with a bit of luck she'll give us the access code to the device.'

Hugh just stood there. It was as if he'd never even considered how he could use the new cadet's skills to do real work.

'Today.'

Hugh sprang into action and sent off the new target. Two minutes later there was a ping. Avery swiped the screen and entered the code they'd received through the remote view. The screen unlocked and Avery punched the air. Damn, I love awareness. 'Where is this girl?'

'She's just down the hall,' replied Hugh.

'Ask her to come up here.'

A moment later a gold-skinned, green haired young woman appeared. Her lilac eyes electric with excitement she asked, 'Was I right?'

'Oh yeah,' replied Hugh.

Avery removed a small silver coin from his pocket. 'I cannot disclose the classified details, but you should know that you've done a great service to fleet just now. This is *sheesha*.'

Smiling, she took the coin and saluted before bobbing her head reverently and seeing herself out.

Chapter 25

Darkness came quickly. The sun never set; it was simply slowly erased from the sky. One quadrant was filled with Zeus, a huge ball of swirling colours, his rings a series of sparkling silver lines strewn across the sky. Four moons were visible, none of them full. They were different colours: lime green, pale pink, yellow, and white, which was really grey.

Kaylor had called Quentin to pick her up at the Research Centre and drive her up the hill behind Port Town to where the observatory was. En route, he'd stopped outside the train station and to Kaylor's shock and delight, Yeltzie had stepped in.

Quentin winked. She telepathed a message to me which I received, and I thought since you were both going the same way, you could travel together.'

Kaylor, had thought the idea wonderful. Zianans were so kind and thoughtful.

The observatory was just a small building that contained a number of telescopes and some star charts. Over the years, the hill had been terraced so that people could set up their own personal viewing optics and observe without obstructing other people's views.

Viewing through the larger communal telescopes was organised in short time slots and priority was given to newcomers who'd never had that experience before. That was how Kaylor found herself looking through the eagle eye, a fifty-centimetre telescope, which provided an incredible view of the neighbouring moons. The experience cost a small fee, but it was worth it.

Zeus was also incredible. As the light changed so did the colours that were seen. As Ziana began to emerge from behind Zeus, the first fingers of light began to appear. It wasn't like watching day turn to dusk followed by dawn, it was more like a dimming of light into darkness and then a re-emerging. It wasn't just pretty, for many Zianans it was a cyclical event of spiritual significance.

They sang as the light dimmed, they sang at the midpoint of darkness and again as the light re-emerged. Different songs, all without words, just pure harmonic voices singing as one. Not just for something to do, but as a powerful blessing and an expression of love. For Zianans thought of the planets, the moons, and stars as living beings who needed to be loved the same as people did. Singing was their thank you for that incredible greatness that was the universe.

Being a part of it took a leap of faith to understand. Kaylor had to incorporate a larger philosophical world view — a view that changed her even more than she'd already been changed through her NDE and journey to Ziana. Her own culture now seemed so superficial and artificial, not to mention childish and petty.

As Yeltzie had tried to explain back in Kaylor's apartment on Ria, the Rian culture was one of drudgery held in place by fear. It forced people to work for a salary for three-quarters of their life so they could enjoy a few years of rest at the end when they were worn out. And to ensure they didn't rebel, people were distracted by sport, or fake emotional dramas on the holovision, or the circus of governments who stood for nothing but power and the hope of re-election.

From an outside perspective, Zianan culture seemed primitive, but it really wasn't. Just because they lived close to nature didn't mean they were simpletons. Through observation of natural world and its cycles, Zianans had acquired a wealth of knowledge and understanding. They incorporated this into their lives and lived in a utopian harmony that neither Rians or Earthlings could possibly understand.

Not quite true. Kaylor was sure the indigenous peoples of Earth would understand for their cultures were similar in many ways. Especially the singing. They'd all sang and danced. Not just for pleasure but for a myriad of reasons that had never been taken seriously by academia or Western culture.

Kaylor was as guilty of that dismissal as other scientists were, but now she had a chance to redeem herself. Her research would not be simply lab based. She needed to learn from the Zianans because this singing had to be connected to the beautiful sound that this planet made. Proving it scientifically would be difficult, but not impossible. She'd find a way; she had to.

Yeltzie came over and flopped down beside Kaylor who was sitting on the highest terrace. 'You enjoyed that. You should see the expression on your face.'

Kaylor was happy. Happier than she'd ever been in her life. It was the anticipation of being on the verge of a monumental discovery coupled with genuine contentment. 'I love this place.'

Yeltzie flashed a grin. 'I do too, but even though I've been off world, I still yearn to go back up. I can't explain why. When I was fifteen, I considered joining fleet and I even did their two-week introductory course, but I just found them too rigid. Plus, fleet was full of ignorant Rians who poked fun at my culture.' She leaned across and gently touched Kaylor's shoulder. 'Sorry, I meant no offense.'

'None taken.' Kaylor suddenly had an incredible idea. 'Yeltzie, I don't want to make any promises, but I've been invited to go up as part of my job. If it were possible, would you like to come with me?'

'I sure would, but I'm not a physicist, my studies have focussed on gastronomy. I'm not sure how much help I'd be.'

'I don't need a lab tech, although there's work, I could train you to do.' Kaylor paused to gather her thoughts. 'The singing, it shapes this world in ways I don't yet understand. I think you could help me with that.'

Yeltzie beamed. 'You have no idea how surreal that sounds coming from a Rian scientist, but yes, I think I can help you.' Yeltzie grabbed a mini quiche from the picnic basket and offered one to Kaylor. 'You should also talk to Avery. I know he comes across as being a bit macho at times, but he understands both cultures which is quite unique.'

'Yes, well, we'll be sharing a house so I'm hoping we'll have time for conversation. He said you might come and stay. He said you were his honorary daughter.'

'Honorary, yes, but not his daughter. He always wanted a daughter or even a son.'

'He has no children?'

'No, his late-wife, Leda, she couldn't have children.'

'They didn't consider other options?'

Yeltzie shook her head. 'Zianan women don't have high fertility and we menstruate only once a spin and we don't get pregnant easily. So, it is quite normal for couples not to have children of their own.'

'I didn't realise that.'

'Yes, it's an evolutionary thing. This world has never known famine, or pandemics or war that would wipe out a chunk of the population in one swoop. Evolution has reduced our fertility as a means of controlling population.'

'I see, but Leda was Rian. Didn't she want children?'

'It didn't seem important to her. She was a crypto-botanist and living on Ziana, I think she saw a lifetime of work before her. Having children would have seriously hindered that.'

As a woman, Kaylor understood.

'Course they used to have me come and stay, which suited my parents because they are very committed to awareness building, which is very demanding. They loved the respite.' Yeltzie took a bite, chewed and swallowed before asking, 'What about you? Do you have children?'

'No. I always wanted them and still do. I was just never in a lasting relationship so there wasn't an opportunity. Plus, like Leda, my work is important to me.'

'Having a child doesn't have to be the end of your career. Not here anyway. Since Zinans don't have a lot of children in their communities, there are heaps of people who love to share the raising of a child. I mean Avery was an orphan, but he has honorary parents. My parents shared the love of raising me,' she flashed a grin, 'and the pain.'

Kaylor considered thoughtfully.

'I'm not trying to persuade you, please don't think that, but your race doesn't live long, well at least not compared to mine. Avery wants a child, but it's not an easy thing to find a woman who also wants one or who can conceive in a timely manner.'

'Zianans are loyal for life, though, aren't they?'

Yeltzie made a face. 'That was true two hundred years ago before first contact. Ria is changing our culture for better or worse. It is just cultural progression. Many widowed Zianas both male and female are now finding love again and I don't see why they shouldn't.'

A sensation of a butterfly tickling her rippled through Kaylor. She did want a child but because she wasn't in a relationship, she hadn't given it a lot of thought. But if Avery also wanted one perhaps, they could have one together. Didn't matter that they weren't in a relationship, they could just come to a mutually beneficial arrangement.

This was something she'd have to contemplate.

Chapter 26

Having taken a nap, showered and changed, Sarah walked back across the base to the gaol. Sparta was awake and laying on his cot. Both of his eyes were black, the result of Avery's coat hanger. He gingerly sat up when she approached. Bloody sore too by the looks of it.

Rather than enter his cell, Sarah found a wooden visitor's chair nearby, spun it around and straddled it.

'I'd like to know why I'm being detained?' asked Sparta.

'Your charge sheet is still being finalised, but for the moment we are looking at charging you with identity fraud and resisting arrest.'

'No one said I was under arrest. I ran because I was late for a train. I was chased and assaulted.'

Sarah admired people like Sparta who always had an excuse for everything. They were quite creative. 'The trains run every hour, and it's strange you didn't take any luggage. Not even a briefcase or kit bag.'

'I didn't need anything. All my work is done digitally.'

'Fair enough, but tell me, why'd you come to Ziana under a false identity?'

Sparta's eyes moved back and forth as he wracked his brain for an excuse. 'I'd like to speak to my lawyer before answering any more questions.'

Sarah nodded theatrically. 'I think that's wise. Identity fraud is a serious crime.' She stood up and reached into her pocket and removed a communicator. Sitting it on the ground, she gave it a flick with her wrist so it slid along the ground, between the bars, and into the cell.

Sparta picked it up. 'This isn't mine.'

'No, it's just a generic one we use for detainees. It will allow you to contact your lawyer.' A slight smile crossed her face. 'I must say,the one you have is impressive. It has the latest AI which I believe are severely restricted. Anyway, we'll check to see if you have the correct permits for it.'

Sparta remained silent as was his right.

'Makes me wonder why you'd need that other ancient handheld.' She rubbed her chin. 'But we've gotten past the passcode, which is completely legal because we have probable cause, so we'll soon know.' She put the chair back against the wall. 'Do you want a coffee?'

He stood frozen like an android that had been switched off.

'I'll give you some privacy for your holocall, but I'll bring you a coffee and something to eat when I come back.'

Sarah whistled a cheerful tune as she ambled out.

*****

Sparta was numb inside and out. His fear visceral. Yet he kept it together. His job ensured that he was always one step away from being arrested, and he had been many times.

He'd learned over the years to remain calm and to be very careful how he answered trick questions. His motto: never give up regardless of how grim things seemed. There were always loopholes in the law which provided a chance to slip through the cracks.

He kept his eyes on Sarah until she was out of sight. Fuck he hated her. She was a master at getting into people's heads whilst acting impeccably polite. She'd been closer at catching him out than she'd realised when she'd investigated him a few years back. When she was around, he'd need to be extra careful because of the way she riled him up.

He took a deep breath and exhaled slowly before switching on the communicator. The generic AI asked him whether he was happy to pay for the call. When he said he was, there was the painstaking process of authorising the payment by providing identifiers and access codes.

When he was finally able to make a call, he had to go through his lawyer's android receptionist, because he couldn't remember her communicator identifier, which would have allowed him to connect directly.

Brooke Madison was a first-rate criminal lawyer who charged extortionist rates. She didn't take on new clients without a referral, because she only defended professional criminals with an excellent track record of avoiding conviction. She'd been Sparta's lawyer since he'd gone into business and she'd gotten him out of tight spots on three separate occasions. Her father was Sparta's father's lawyer and she'd continued the family tradition by becoming one herself.

The holocall connected and a life-sized version of Brooke appeared in his cell. Tall and athletic with dark hair and eyes; she was stunning to look at. She was dressed in designer business clothes, which included a short skirt so she could flaunt her picture-perfect legs. Her ears, neck, and wrists were adorned with gold and jewels; her makeup applied every morning by a professional — the gay guy who was part of Brooke's entourage of staff.

'Danny Sparta, my golden boy, calling from gaol I see.'

Sparta hated to be called Danny because it was a name one would use for a child, and her reference to him being her golden boy did not mean she liked him. She used the term because she considered him to be her next golden payday.

'I'm in the Port Town fleet base gaol on Ziana. I need you to come straight away. I'll pay for the teleport.'

'Ziana, that complicates things.'

Sparta refrained from wincing. "Complicated" translated as expensive. In addition to her fee, not only would he have to pay for her transport, but also the most expensive room that was available in Port Town, plus her sundry expenses which would be considerable.

'When can you come?'

She made a point of glancing at her ladies Rolex. It wouldn't reveal her schedule, but it was just a reminder of how valuable her time was and how much he already owed her. 'Two days is the earliest I can manage.'

Sparta gritted his teeth. He wanted her here now, preferably before Sarah returned.

'Sorry, but it's the best I can do, and even then, it will mean a lot of rescheduling on my part.'

'Fair enough.'

'You don't have to answer their question until I get there, so keep your mouth shut and sit tight Danny boy.'

The holocall disconnected. There were no goodbyes with Brooke. Just e-bills that would be sent to Tank.

He returned to laying on the bed and began to work his cover stories in his mind so he could iron out the flaws.

*****

Avery came to with a jolt. He was being shaken. He'd sat down in Hugh's high back swivel seat and he must have nodded off.

Upon opening his eyes, he discovered the tech's excited face a mere thirty centimetres away.

'Wake up. You're not going to believe this. It's unbelievable.'

Avery's mind returned from some deep place in the land of nod and slowly he remembered where he was and why. He leaned forward so the chair returned to a neutral position. 'What have you discovered?'

Rather than explain, Hugh played with Sparta's ancient handheld. A moment later Avery's head began to buzz as it had previously. Annoyed, Avery removed the communicator from behind his ear and switched it off.

'Great, now this one is playing up.'

A sea of bewildered faces looked at him and Avery realised for the first time that there were other techs in the room. Techs whose names he could not recall.

'He's immune to it,' proclaimed a dark-blonde woman.

In a vain attempt to try and bring clarity to the situation, Avery blinked repeatedly. It didn't work, but he spied a pot of coffee sitting on a nearby hotplate and made his way over to it. Having poured himself a mugful he said, 'Could we rewind a bit?'

Hugh started talking so rapidly that Avery couldn't understand him.

'Okay, I'm guessing you've had a lot of coffee, so I need you to slow down. I bought the handheld in. She,' he pointed to the Zianan cadet also present, 'broke the passcode. Then what?'

'It has a subliminal program on it that can send an encoded message to any communicator and make the person do whatever you want.'

Avery cocked his head in confusion. He knew subliminal messaging worked but only to a limited degree. If the person listening to it didn't want to change a habit, like quitting excessive drinking or buy a product they didn't want, then the effect was cancelled out by the strength of will.

Seeing Avery's sceptical look, Hugh said, 'Watch, I'll demonstrate with Tess.'

'The fuck you will,' hissed the blonde. 'I'm not flashing my tits again, you bloody pervert.'

Hugh turned a shade of red. 'It was for science, I…'

Tess snatched the device from his hands and hastily typed a message on the screen. A moment later, Hugh dropped into a trance and began robotically doing laps of his workbench. Avery attempted to interrupt him, he even stood in Hugh's way, but the tech just went around him.

'He won't stop until he's completed the directive,' said the Zianan tech.

After the tenth lap, Hugh stopped, blinked and said, 'We'll give you a demo.'

'And Hugh doesn't even remember what I just had him do,' said Tess.

'What did you make me do?'

'Let's not worry about that shall we,' said Tess.

Hugh was worried, Avery could see it in his eyes.

'There's more,' said Tess. 'The forensic analysis found faint traces on an unknown DNA on the device. We ran it through every database on the Cloudnet but couldn't match it.'

'So, I sent Kara another remote view target. Blind of course,' said Hugh bringing up a hologram of Kara's reply.

Avery looked at it. She'd drawn a picture of a grey alien and written two words beneath it, Zeta Reticuli.

'I just reported what I saw,' said Kara matter of fact.

Avery rubbed his face in his hands. Parts of it were starting to make sense. Why Sparta was on the spooks watch list and what was so top secret that they couldn't tell him. Had Sparta come here to manipulate the Chief Minister and her government? Was he "fixing" something for President Inglis? Possibly, but if that was the case what did this have to do with Kaylor and himself? Dee knew, but she wasn't saying.

'Okay, I'll take the device…'

'But I'm not done with it,' cried Hugh.

'And we'll keep this just between us.' He took the handheld from Tess and dropped it into his pocket. 'That's an order.'

The room fell silent.

Avery put a hand behind his ear. 'What was that?'

There was a chorus of yes sir, which although necessary, made him cringe. Being humble, he'd never liked being saluted to or being called sir. He made for the door but turned back. 'By the way, sublime work. Absolutely first class. I promise it won't go unnoticed.'

'Yes, sir. Thank you, sir,' they said in unison.

Avery knew he should report straight to Cadel whose involvement now made sense, but his emotions clouded his judgement. Instead, he headed straight for the gaol. When he arrived, he walked straight past Sarah and Dee and went straight for Sparta.

Sparta took one look at Avery and leaped off his cot, his eyes fixed on the door.

Avery stood at the bars because he didn't have the key to let himself in. The barrier was a good thing because it prevented him from hurting or even killing Sparta.

'Did you kill my wife?'

Sparta remained silent.

'Did you kill Leda Vander nee Jenner?'

No answer.

Avery showed him the device. 'I know what this thing does. How about I have you flush your own head down that toilet, or, I know, how about you bash your head against these bars until you split your skull open and your brains spill out.'

Sparta reefed off the generic communicator he was still wearing and dropped it on the floor.

'Did you kill my wife?'

Sparta looked him directly in the eye. 'I swear I did not.'

Avery was so sure Sparta was guilty he was momentarily caught off guard by his response and direct eyes contact. 'Did you make someone else do it using the subliminal program?'

Still looking him in the eye he repeated, 'I swear I did not.'

Damn it. Avery believed him. He closed his eyes. 'Then what were you playing at?'

Sparta returned to being a statue.

'I know you used this to try and influence me and also Kaylor. Why?'

Silence.

'Fine, I'll just grab the key and we'll do this the old-fashioned way.' Avery turned to go and get them only to be confronted with Sarah and Dee.

'As fun as it would be to torture the bastard, we need to report to Cadel,' said Dee.

Avery was torn between reason and anger. It was unlike him. Normally he could work a case and interrogate with a high degree of professionalism. This one, however, was too personal; too close to his heart and emotion was clouding his judgement.

Sarah stepped past carrying a mug of coffee and a plate of food on a tray. She slid open the small service door that allowed her to place the tray on the small table inside the cell.

Dee examined Sparta's meal. 'Smoked salmon, with turkey eggs benedick with nut bread and a side salad!'

Sarah shrugged. 'It could be his last meal.'

She was joking but for affect, Avery glanced at Sparta with false sympathy. He was white and shaking.

Chapter 27

Avery had never seen Dee smile, but right now her face was sourer than usual. 'So, the persuasive program can instantly turn people into zombified slaves who will fulfil their assigned directive without question? And Sparta's been running amok with it for goddness knows how long, having people do fuck knows what.'

'Yes, that's my understanding,' replied Avery.

Dee narrowed her eyes. 'A fucking capitalist's wet dream. One line of code and the entire populace is compulsive shopping and running up unpayable debt.'

'Yes, think of the implications. Women could claim they were being influenced when they weren't and have a shopping spree anyway.'

Dee looked at him blankly. He doubted shopping was her thing. Sarah, however, shot him a look of daggers. He'd pay for that jibe in a not-so-subtle way, sooner rather than later.

'I was thinking more along the lines that people could commit murder or steal State secrets without any moral restraint,' added Dee.

'So true, but my question is, what did Sparta use it for?' asked Sarah.

'Kaylor said Sparta got her communicator back from the Rian Institute of Science after she was laid off. I'm not sure why he'd bother. He was pretending to be a businessman offering her a job. Why not just give her a new one?'

'It has to do with the embedded AI. AIs can be transferred from one communicator to another via a secure storage space on the Cloudnet, but for Rians, AIs tend to be owned by their employer.'

'So, it was about the AI rather than the communicator?' asked Avery.

'We're conjecturing, but maybe. AIs who are working with scientists and other professionals have the ability to organise data in an accessible way, whilst doing their own analysis. A new one would be starting from scratch. It would need to be trained so to speak.'

Which brought Avery back to the notion that Sparta may not be the villain they thought he was. However, it also brought him back to the last question he'd asked Sparta. What was he up to?'

Sarah waved her hands excitedly. 'Think of the positives.'

'Come again!' spat Dee.

'This program could revolutionise trauma treatment. Instead of years of therapy, people could simply be given an instruction telling their brain that they were well. It would be instantaneous.'

It was so like Sarah to find a silver lining to what was otherwise a terrifying piece of equipment.

'I can see your point, but there are larger implications. The technology is unlike anything Ria or Earth has developed and it certainly wasn't created by Ziana. That means its alien technology. Kara, fleet's remote viewer, described it as being from Zeta Reticula. Why does Sparta have their technology? Who gave it to him and why?' asked Avery, slipping into detective mode.

Sarah's eyes widened telling him that Sarah hadn't known that fact. Cadel remained unmoved as did Dee, but their eyes met briefly telling Avery they knew what was going on at least to some degree. It was top secret and had major implications for security.

Cadel adjusted his sitting position. 'The program is a weapon. I can only assume that it was loaded onto outdated technology to restrict its capabilities. However, it is still unbelievably dangerous. In the hands of a despot, worlds could be enslaved faster than they ever have been before without a single shot being fired.'

Inglis. Was Sparta working for or against Inglis, or was he working for some other completely unrelated purpose?

'We need to know what Sparta end game was,' said Avery.

'I agree,' said Sarah, 'but Sparta won't talk and he's a professional. He won't crack easily.'

Again, Dee's eyes flicked to Cadel. This was an Intelligence operation in which fleet had been reduced to pawns.

Ignoring Avery's probe, Cadel addressed Sarah. 'Formally charge Sparta with identity fraud, resisting arrest and use of illegal technology. We can adjust his charge sheet later if we need to. Once he's been charged, Sparta needs to be taken to the union court on Isla for a hearing, and we need to push for the refusal of bail.'

Isla was another of Zeus's moons and thanks to warp drive technology it was only a short flight away relatively speaking. The union court was an independent authority, which was used to trial criminals under union law. It was utilised when a criminal's crimes were committed in space, such as a mining outpost, or where the crimes stretched across multiple worlds.

Right now, refused bail would suit them well. It meant Sparta could be detained until he was trialled in a standard Earth years' time. Longer if the court was backed up, but time enough for the spooks to extract from him everything they wanted to know.

'Do we take him now,' asked Sarah.

'No, get some sleep first. You all look like you are dead on your feet.'

Avery stood up and walked towards the door. He'd opened it and was about to step out when Kaylor and Yeltzie, accompanied by a fleet escort, come walking up the corridor. He made eye contact with Yeltzie who looked concerned. Kaylor showed no concern and acted as if the highest-ranking officer in fleet had invited her around simply for afternoon tea and scones.

Cadel glanced up and realising he had guests said, 'Do come in and have a seat. These three were just leaving.'

'What's this about?' asked Yeltzie, in her usual articulate manner.

'Just wanted to have a quick chat. Don't worry, you're not in trouble.'

Yeltzie entered, her eyes scanning every centimetre of the room. With arms folded, she refused to sit. Glancing again at Avery, she beseeched him to stay.

Cadel gave a little motion with his hands leaving no ambiguity about the fact that he wanted Avery to leave. Reluctantly he obeyed. Yeltzie could take care of herself and Kaylor would no doubt give them valuable intel about Sparta that they could use.

*****

When Avery returned to the base ten hours later, he found it buzzing with activity. People were scurrying around running errands he knew nothing about. Several Rian reporters were gathering near the main gates. He frowned. Had news broken about Sparta's arrest? Had one of the techs leaked news about the subliminal program?

He doubted it. Something else was up and it way bigger than that.

Parking the jeep in front of the gaol he hurried in to find the wardens huddled in the dining room, their attention drawn to a holovision. It was playing news footage that had recently arrived via the satellite array from Ria.

Avery watched intently as the footage showed an explosion tearing a hole in one of Ria's biodomes. The resulting suction from depressurisation, caused objects to fly upwards towards the leak. As they struck the biodome, the hole largened creating enough vacuum to reef a tram full of passengers off its rails.

People screamed and desperately sought something to hold onto — signposts, park benches, anything. Many failed and were lifted upwards careening towards the hole.

The footage cut to a reporter name Mandy Rayella — a pretty brunette with big hazel eyes and a clear voice.

'A terrorist has detonated an IED in Ria's dome number six causing a massive explosion that tore a hole in it so that it is haemorrhaging air. The dome has been sealed off from the rest to prevent any further air loss. Local police and emergency services are scrambling to evacuate people and restore order. It's unclear how fast the air is escaping or how much time people have left. Emergency crews are desperately trying to seal the leak, but it is so large I fear there won't be time before depressurisation in the crippled dome reaches critical levels. At this stage, the dome is maintaining structural integrity but it is feared the vacuum created by the leak will cause it to implode.

'The terrorist attack coincided with a fleet training exercise in which most of fleet's planet-based personnel were off-world. The drill has been cancelled and help is on its way, but it's unknown when it will arrive.'

Mandy reached a hand to her ear. 'Wait, news has just come in. Rian police have made an arrest.' The footage chopped to a dozen local police officers who were bustling a gold-skinned, green haired man along the footpath that led to the main police station. 'His name has not been released, but he is believed to be a Zianan citizen who was teaching at the university.'

The footage chopped back to the segment that showed the explosion and continued until the tram flew upwards. In quick succession that bit was played twenty times. If the media kept true to form, Avery knew that footage would be aired no less than a thousand times over the next twenty-four hours. The sensationalist media, controlled by the new Rian government, wanted to maximise fear and outrage.

Sarah suddenly screamed and fled from the room into the nearby office.

With the voice of a fleet officer, Avery yelled, 'Holovision, freeze footage, rewind, play at ten times reduced speed.'

The AI within the holovision complied and Avery watched closely. 'Freeze footage.'

An image of Sarah's husband Mike holding on to a street sign filled the screen. Avery swore. He glanced at Sarah. Knowing the footage was time delayed, she was desperately trying to contact him or anyone who could tell her he was okay. It was a frantic act, because the communication array would quickly jam as Rians on Ziana tried to contact family on their home world.

'Holovision, play arrest scene at slow speed.'

The image changed. 'Freeze and enhance.'

The image of the arrested man became larger. It was a Zianan who was looking frightened and confused. It wasn't the face of a terrorist or even a hardened criminal capable of mass murder. Avery had seen plenty of those over the course of his career. The entire event seemed fishy, like a false flag operation that had been staged. The classic, problem, reaction, solution. Ria was still in the reaction stage, but the solution would soon be put forth by someone in a high position of power.

Avery left the room and made his way to Sarah who was trying for audio only. Tears were trickling down her cheeks, but for the moment she was still focussed and hopeful.

'Yes, I'm here ... Oh thank God ... Can you patch me through to him? ... I don't care about the cost of teleported communication.' Sarah stared eyes forward but seeing nothing. 'Mike? ... Oh god, are you okay. ... Mike, please listen to me. You need to get off Ria. ... Get on the passenger transport or else use the teleporter ... I don't care about the cost ... Because I know the attack's a farce ... Look, just trust me will you ... Don't go, I ... I love you.'

The call disconnected. Five seconds later Sarah's body shook as she began sobbing in earnest. Avery pulled her into a hug and just held her until she was ready to be let go.

'He's fine,' she reached across and scuffed a handful of tissues from a box on the desk. Having blown her nose, she said. 'He managed to get safely out of the damaged dome. He's a bit battered and bruised, but he's okay.' She sniffed. 'He won't listen to me.'

Avery remained silent. He'd always liked Mike and they'd gotten along well. When Avery was on Ria, they'd always go for a beer and they'd watch a sporting game together. Avery wasn't into sport, but Mike was and so Avery was happy to tag along. Mike, however, had two faults: he was stubborn, and as a result of that, he hated to be told what to do by his wife. 'Give him time to think, then call him back.'

She stood there looking lost, so Avery got her a glass of water from the kitchen and handed it to her. She took a sip and they returned to the holovision.

'It's been confirmed. Eleven hundred people are dead and three thousand are seriously injured. The Rian hospital is exercising triage. Fleet medics have been deployed and are at this very minute setting up an emergency field hospital.'

The camera panned to show a large tent being erected in Foundation Park. The park contained the colonisation memorial. It had been placed on the exact spot where the first One World Earth flag was ever raised on what would become Ria.

'The medical hospital ship, *Caduceus*, is now in orbit.' An image of the circular ship with its enormous red cross painted across its roof was shown. The footage was taken from a neighbouring ship that was also in orbit.

The ship contained a state-of-the-art hospital but its appearance was completely political. People with serious injuries could not endure the g-forces from the acceleration needed to reach space. Those who weren't seriously injured did not need to be taken into space because they could be treated in the fleet hospital tent or one of the other first aid stations that would be erected around the city.

'We cross now live to President Inglis.'

The president was dressed in a navy suit with a rusty red tie, the official Rian colour, which was the same colour as the planet's surface. He stood at the lectern that contained the Rian presidential seal and on each side of him stood five Rian flags. A red background with the planet Ria in the centre.

The flags were a symbol of Rian nationalism and the number of flags was colloquially known as the flagginess. They depicted the seriousness of the announcement. In his twenty-five-year career in fleet, Avery could not recall a national address that required ten flags.

As the camera zoomed in on the president, Avery caught sight of Vice-Admiral Ralph Peterson in full dress uniform. He was Cadel's second in command and fleet's advisor to the president.

President Inglis stared directly into the main camera. His facial expression one of sternness with a hint of grief.

'My fellow Rians. Today, our people and our way of life was brutally attacked by an act of terrorism. The victims were: our brothers, sisters, dads, mothers, aunts, uncles, neighbours and colleagues. This act of mass murder was not just intended to terrify us, but to punish us for our way of life.' He paused for effect, his face now revealing anger.

'I say to you, do not apologise to the Zianan zealots who orchestrated this murderous attack. We will not be persuaded into converting to their religion. We are a strong nation and we will not be bullied by cowards. We will stand strong.

'Our first priority is to restore order and attend to the injured. To protect our people from further attacks, we will be posting guards right across our great nation city. Ships will be stationed in orbit. People are asked to obey instructions from police and emergency workers and to comply with the newly imposed emergency curfew. Together we will get through this.

'Please know, we have apprehended the perpetrators and they will face the full weight of Ria's laws. Know also, we will not stop there. We will take definitive measures to ensure this never happens again.

'For although we walk through the valley of the shadow of death, we will fear no evil. Our losses sustained this day can never be replaced or forgiven.' He raised his finger to emphasise his point. 'But this day, Ria unites as one people. Stand with me strong and together we will defeat this evil for all time.'

The press room, where the President's address took place, exploded into applause. The audience stood and cheered as his fellow ministers jockeyed to get close to him, eager to shake his hand. Others waved mini flags in a sign of patriotism. Some reporters waited eagerly to ask questions but the President was done and could be seen exiting the room.

'Fuck you!' yelled Sarah, her anger directed at the holovision.

Sarah rarely swore and her outburst caused even Avery to raise an eyebrow.

All eyes turned to Sarah who continued her soliloquy with a great many profanities directed at the president.

Avery stood there speechless. Ziana had no religion and it had certainly never pushed onto others the idea of awareness building. All it had done, was send a few teachers to the Rian university in the spirit of knowledge sharing. Imposing martial law was also extreme and a deliberate grab for power. At the same time, pretending the fleet ships in space were there to fight off the coming hordes was ludicrous. As was quoting from the Christian bible to a nation of many faiths.

A bewildered cadet said. 'But if they have caught the perpetrators ...' He swallowed. 'What does this mean?'

Avery assumed the question was directed at either Sarah or himself because they were both officers and the cadet was looking to rank for assurance.

Sarah didn't answer and neither did Avery.

A messenger hurried in. 'Chief Minister Hardy is preparing to respond as is Admiral Cadel.'

Avery hurried from the room. Rather than use the base's small press room, a stage had been erected by fleet on a large section of grass just outside the gates. A public place where everyone within the vicinity could bear witness in person if they so desired.

The were no flags. Ziana had never had a flag and they refused to create one despite being asked by both Earth and Ria to do so. That was because the Chief Minister and her government considered flags to be too corporate and nationalistic. A symbol of ownership that was used to denote possession. An object that was frequently used in war and conflict.

Zianans did not believe they owned the planet for it was no ones to possess. The people were custodians permitted to live there only if they looked after it and agreed to share it with the biodiversity that also lived on it.

Chief Minister Hardy, was dressed in a traditional hip length wrap around green tunic held in place with a mushroom leather belt. Her beige pants were three-quarter length; her arms and feet were bare. She hurried up the three steps onto the stage with determination and grace. Her unfettered green hair flying wildly in the breeze. Unlike most politicians, she wasn't vain or concerned about image and thus wore no makeup.

The fleet liaison officer tried to hand her some pages, no doubt a prepared speech, but she was having none of it. Whatever Renee was about to say would be her own words unfiltered and straight from the heart. As she approached the podium, the still gathering crowd fell silent.

Renee stared straight at the camera. 'My heartfelt condolences to those who were killed or injured, and to those who lost loved ones and are grieving. We send our love and our healing to all those who are affected by this senseless act of violence. Including those who are now homeless and will be forced to seek shelter where ever they can find it. I hope the repairs to the dome and all that is in it are swift and succinct. In the meantime, Ziana will accept refugees but only those who agree to abide by our ethos of non-violence towards our people and our environment.

'I want to say clearly and decisively that neither the Zianan government nor the Zianan people condone this act terror, nor did we orchestrate it.' She paused to gather her thoughts.

'Ziana has no religion and has never had any religion. We do not proselytise or push our beliefs onto others and we certainly do not commit acts of unspeakable violence in the name of ideology.'

There were murmurs of agreement.

'We too stand together as one. Not to inculcate fear through xenophobia and propaganda. We stand as one to forgive the accusations levelled against us. We too do not fear, for we are a world of beings at peace. We want only peace with our neighbours and that is all we have ever wanted.

'I extend my support to fleet police. I have every confidence that those responsible for this act of terror and violence will be brought swiftly to justice.'

Renee walked away from the podium but remained on the stage. She scribed the Zianan symbol for distance healing in the air before closing her eyes to focus on it. Every Zianan present including Avery and Cadel did likewise. The healing lasted two minutes and afterward, Renee quietly left the stage.

She was replaced by Cadel in full dress uniform. He too looked directly into the camera. 'I too wish to extend my condolences to all who are affected by this murderous act of terrorism. Rest assured, fleet will use every resource at its disposal to assist the wounded and the displaced as well as recover the bodies of the deceased with dignity.

'I have already spoken to fleet's Select Oversight Committee and we have called an emergency meeting of the Admiralty which will commence directly after this briefing. In the meantime, let me assure you fleet's investigation will leave no piece of evidence unexamined and no questions unanswered. Fleet will have jurisdiction and it will tolerate no interference in the course of securing justice.

'Rest assured that justice will be done. Those responsible will be caught, arrested and trialled in Isla's union court, and they will be severely punished.

'In the meantime, fleet will use all of its resources to restore order, provide medical assistance and set up a refugee camp. It will make available emergency food rations and warm clothes and blankets. I ask all Rians to please be patient and courteous. Help will be available through this time of crisis and grieving.'

Cadel hurried from the stage and into a jeep where he was whisked away at speed in the direction of his office.

Avery stood for a moment trying to get his bearings. Footage of the two speeches was already being beamed across space at warp speed. The question on his mind was whether they'd be aired uncut or otherwise. Inglis controlled the media and had the power to order the speeches to be censored or altered so they painted both the Chief Minister and the Admiral in a bad light.

There was nothing anyone could do except wait and see what the response would be.

'We had best get Sparta up to Isla,' said Sarah. 'His lawyer was informed that he was being taken there. She's going to teleport to Isla rather than Ziana.'

'Assuming they haven't closed the teleporter down.'

'Ah, yes they may have.' She wrinkled her nose. 'But Sparta's lawyer Brooke is very resourceful. She'll find a way, but I'd hate to be paying Sparta's legal bills.'

Avery winced. No, neither would he, but Sarah was right. If Brooke couldn't use the teleporter in the Rian hospital, then she'd catch a shuttle up to the orbiting space station and use its teleporter.

They began to walk back towards the gaol when Avery caught sight of the Chief Minister. She was quietly talking to a Zianan journalist who was taking notes the old-fashioned way with paper and pencil.

'Yes, my remote viewers have seen the arrival of an armada who have come with hostile intentions,' said Renee.

'When can we expect it to arrive?'

'It is not certain but remote views indicate they will be here in approximately one Earth standard year.'

'That's the time it takes to travel across space from Ria. Do you think this was all pre-planned?'

'I fear that's the case, but fleet is yet to investigate, so let's not jump to conclusions.'

'If they arrive with intentions of invading what will be Ziana's response?'

'We have no weapons of war nor will we be obtaining them. We will defend, as we always have, by using the fourth way.'

'I see. So, *The Zee* will not be firing its lasers?'

'No, not by my orders. *The Zee* is a fleet ship designed and built to administer the law. Although it has lasers on it, it is not a military ship. It was not built to fight a war.'

Renee went to walk off.

'Please, just one last question if I may. What is your message to the Zianan people following this awful event?'

'Don't be drawn into fear and hatred, but do prepare for the possible arrival of an armada. Stay centred and focus on sending love and healing to it. We are not responsible for this mass murder, but we will forgive the accusations and those who have bought into them.'

Renee hurried away, no doubt for her own crisis meeting with the rest of the Zianan government and its advisers which would include elders.

The journalist hurried away to write up his story. It wouldn't just be printed in the local paper. A special insert would be sent via trains all over the planet for everyone to read. Especially for those who lived a traditional Zianan lifestyle close to their local food forest. Those who wouldn't have access to a holovision and wouldn't know what was going on.

Sarah leaned closer to him and whispered, 'Please explain to me what the fourth way is.'

Sarah wouldn't understand. She'd doubt and that would drag her into fear. Still, it wasn't his place to judge so he whispered a reply.

Chapter 28

Sparta was initially shocked. When the news had begun broadcasting through the holovision, Dee, who'd handcuffed him in preparation for his space flight to Isla, had escorted him out of his cell. He'd stood inconspicuously out of the way where he could see the footage.

Initially, he was grief-stricken by the loss of life, but like a lot of other Rians present, he'd turned numb. He disliked Zianans but even he knew they were incapable of such horrendous violence and destruction. So, who had bombed dome six and why?

A sinking feeling in his stomach spread throughout his entire being. Would eyes turn to him? Prior to his arrest, with the aid of the persuasive program, he'd had the means. Finding a motive wouldn't be such a concern to fleet's investigating offices. Sparta was a fixer who worked for money. It was that simple.

Still, without proof, they couldn't convict him of a crime he hadn't committed. He'd been in gaol at the time of the terrorist attack and fleet had confiscated the device. Strong alibis that were enough to create reasonable doubt in the minds of any jury.

Not that he wasn't still in trouble. Even if they couldn't conclusively prove what he'd done with the program, the fact that he had it, was enough for a conviction. There were laws about the possession and use of dangerous technology. The prosecution would argue that he should have turned it in. That the program was dangerous and no one should have it.

Feeling queasy, Sparta clutched his stomach fearing he might vomit. Fuck, had the terrorist used the device and persuasive program for the attack? For all he knew the device could have been teleported to Ria, used to commit an unspeakable act of horror, before being teleported back.

It needed only to be missing for a few hours and no one would even know. That wasn't quite true, there'd be a record of the teleport. Every teleport was logged but those records could be manipulated. Hell, with the program, the teleport operator could be convinced not to log it.

Damn, was this partially on him because he hadn't handed the device in? Sparta's morals might be set at a different level to most peoples but he couldn't condone this. This was utterly despicable. Way beyond anything he would ever consider "fixing".

He glanced at Dee. He knew she was Intelligence rather than fleet. Cold and calculating spooks like her functioned on the razor's edge of mental stability. There was no emotion on her face. No reaction to the news feed. Did she even care?

She glanced back at him expressionless but didn't speak.

Sparta didn't either. He was angry now for a selfish reason. His home on Ria was in dome six. Even if it wasn't damaged by the loss of pressure, the dome was now uninhabitable and would be for months. If by some miracle he made bail, he wouldn't be able to return home. He'd have to return to Ziana, or else remain on Isla and rent a place in the tiny settlement. He didn't like either option.

*****

'You're looking a bit pale Danny. You feeling, alright?' asked Avery.

Dee had had the hotel staff pack up Sparta's room and check him out. His luggage, along with Avery's, Sarah's and Dee's was now stowed onboard. Avery just needed to get his passengers on and they could leave for Isla.

Sparta didn't answer.

'Surprised you care,' said Dee.

'I don't want him puking in the back and stinking out the cabin. Not like we can open a window in space.'

'Good point,' said Sarah. 'Do you want a drink of water Mr Sparta?'

'No thank you. I'm fine.'

He walked up the ramp and onto the shuttle of his own accord. Since his hands were cuffed, Sarah did up his harness for him.

Sparta raised his hands in the air. 'Are these really necessary?'

'Standard procedure,' replied Avery.

'But are they necessary?' asked Sarah.

'I don't trust him so yes they are, and before you try and pull rank, unless you want to pilot, it's my call.'

Sarah sat down and did up her own harness. 'Alright, no need to get cranky.'

'Now you're looking pale Sarah,' said Dee.

'I hate flying in shuttles. I'm fine once I'm up there on the big ships, I just hate the shuttles.'

A look of disbelief crossed Dee's face as she took the front seat beside Avery and belted in. 'A fleet officer who doesn't like flying is like a seaman who doesn't like sailing.'

Avery agreed.

'Anyway, shouldn't she be here in the co-pilot's seat, because I can't fly.'

'The view is less, eh … unsettling, in the back and these shuttles don't need a co-pilot, because they have an AI who can fly.' Avery turned the control switch to manual neutralising the AI.

'Which I take it won't be needed for this flight,' said Dee.

'The only automated feature I use is the cruise control.'

Dee rubbed her chin. 'Word is you're arguably the best pilot in fleet. Is that true?'

Avery shrugged. 'I got good because I actually fly; most just let the computer do it for them.'

'It's more than that though isn't it.'

He glanced at her to see if she was trying to take a rise out of him, but she didn't appear to be. 'Flying is more than just steering.

To fly at the speeds this thing can, you have to be right there in the zone and predicting what you have to do next ahead of time. It takes focus and skill.'

Dee nodded in understanding.

Avery locked the doors and did a pressure test. The shuttle lifted off vertically before thrusting forwards at an upward inclination. Opening the throttle, they were laid back in their seats with increasing pressure on their bodies. The shuttle accelerated steadily to twelve metres per second — the speed needed to breach the atmosphere.

Experiencing three-Gs, they shot through the cloud layer and speed towards space. It was a rush that Avery never got tired of. Having passed through a thin blue-green line, the sky turned black and the stars shone brightly.

Avery took them out past the line of orbiting satellites before course-correcting with a series of burns to line up with Isla. Sightly, smaller in diameter to Ziana, she was a bright white orb in the distance. The closest Isla ever came to Ziana was four-hundred thousand kilometres. However, because the moons orbited Zeus at different speeds, they sometimes found themselves on opposite sides of the gas giant. Luckily, today Isla was on the same side of Zeus as Ziana was.

Unlike Ziana, who very slowly turned on its axis creating the long day and long night cycle, Isla never rotated so the same side always faced the sun.

Avery switched on the warp drive which created an energy field around them. The field cancelled out inertia which allowed them to rapidly accelerate without feeling the effects.

'Why can't we use the warp drive during take-off and eliminate the three-Gs of force?' asked Dee.

'That's, the chest of gold question, isn't it,' replied Avery. 'Fact is, no one really knows. All physicists know is, if you turn on a warp drive inside a planet's atmosphere, you disappear.'

'Disappear?' queried Dee.

'That's right, there's a flash of light and the shuttle disappears. Physicists think they go into alternate space time, but I think they're conjecturing.' Avery shrugged. 'Who knows, the missing shuttles might reappear in a few millennia.'

Dee paled. 'But it never happens out in space, right?'

'No, not to my knowledge.' Avery set the autopilot and floated through into the back of the cabin where he took a seat opposite Sparta. Unlike the larger ships, the shuttles had no artificial gravity.

Dee floated through and joined them. 'How long will it take us to get to Isla?'

'At this speed, an hour of warp and then another thirty minutes or so to taxi in and land. Isla only has a wispy thin atmosphere so there's no burning re-entry. Why do you ask?'

'Just wondering.'

Avery thumbed towards the rear of the shuttle. 'There's a toilet in the back, but going in zero gravity's a bitch.' He retrieved a bottle of water from a storage locker. 'Would you like some water, Danny?'

Sparta kept his eyes lowered. 'No thank you.'

Avery broke the seal. Gently biting the extendable nozzle with his teeth, he pulled it open and took a swig, before closing it again. He managed it without any water bubbles escaping due to an absence of gravity. 'You sure, because this is Zianan water. The water on Isla is artesian and tastes metallic.'

'I'm good thank you.'

'Suit yourself.' Avery gestured towards the side window. 'You ever see anything so beautiful?'

From this position in space, Ziana was a gigantic fluorescent green orb. Across the landmass, you could see the food forests that feed the inhabitants. Long squiggly lines that lay on contour and shaded green from the foliage buffered by cleared strips on either side.

Eighty percent of the planet was untouched wilderness. No open plains because there were no grazing animals to utilise them.

Instead, the land supported great forests except in the mountainous regions where there were towering snow-capped alps.

The planet had no oceans, but it did have enormous freshwater lakes that were feed by an intricate system of rivers. Some of the lakes were nestled in deep valleys surrounded by snow-capped mountains, so deep their depths were measured in kilometres. The lakes hosted some interesting creatures including large water dragons that the Earth scientists had nicknamed Nessies.

'When I was courting Leda, I used to bring her up here to admire the view. Well, I mean the view wasn't the only thing on our minds.'

Sparta didn't react; he just sat there silently looking at the floor.

'Against regulations of course, but I'd do it anyway. As we orbited Ziana, she'd point to a spot on the surface that she wanted to go to and on the way back in we'd do a flyby and note the coordinates. If she liked the spot, she'd mount an expedition and travel there by train. Amazing our ancient train network, we've still got no idea who built it.'

Sparta refused to look at Avery or the view.

'Those were good days.' Avery gestured at Sparta. 'What did you want with Kaylor and me?'

Silence.

'I'll find out Danny, but it would be so much less inconvenient if you just told me.'

Sparta swallowed.

'The right to remain silent eh. Whoever invented that legal shit was clearly a criminal desperate not to have to incriminate themself.'

Dee laughed aloud, strange because Avery would have bet a gold coin that she had no sense of humour. Sarah just rolled her eyes.

Moving at the speed they were, Zeus was rapidly becoming the main feature of observation. The planets equatorial diameter was ten times larger than Ziana, Zeus was the largest planet in this solar system. A gas giant, it was a mass of coloured gas storms with shimmering silver rings. The rings were seventy percent ice, the rest rock, and dust.

Within the rocks were exotic metals not found on Earth. So valuable, that a dozen mining operations had been set up to obtain them.

The mining stations were wild places that kept fleet busy policing them. Violence was normalised and murders were common. In Avery's mind, the cost in human life to extract the metals, was too high. The mines should be shut down, the metals forgotten about. A moot point, because both Earth and Ria wanted the metals so mining would continue. Capitalism didn't care about the human cost.

As they neared Isla, Avery returned to the pilot's seat. Getting ready to come out of warp speed, the shuttle was rapidly slowing down. Isla loomed before them. Once the moon had harboured life. There were fossils in the rocks to prove it and evidence of oceans and great forests of trees. There were also historical accounts from the few who fled to Ziana and recorded written accounts.

Isla had been destroyed by war fought with weapons so destructive they killed everything including the once habitable atmosphere. Irresponsible didn't even begin to describe it, for the war had been fought between two men desiring the right to rule. In the end, everyone lost, including nature.

Now Isla was a lifeless world of rock, dust, and sand with little atmosphere and no air. Dotted with craters the surface had taken a beating and was still susceptible to asteroid strikes. These days collision course asteroids were obliviated with lasers before they could hit.

It was unnecessary because asteroids could easily be bumped onto a different trajectory. Destroying them was simply a continuation of the war that had destroyed the world. Working with nature rather than trying to dominate it was still an anathema to lower seal beings.

The moon would have been left alone to mourn the loss of its habitability except Isla had one last valuable resource. Deep below the surface was fresh water and as scientists were fond of saying, where there was water, life could survive. Now millions of years after the war, humans had returned to Isla. On the surface of the ancient ocean beds under biodomes, they'd built a prison to house convicted criminals, most of which came from the nearby mining colonies.

In the beginning, that's all there was. However, the prison wardens had wanted to move their families closer to them. To facilitate this, more domes were built and beneath them was a town. Large enough for a school, a hospital and a number of shops. Once ruled by the base commodore, the town now had a small governing council. Today, Isla supported four generations of people who considered themselves Islatations.

Avery took the controls and switched the shuttle back over to manual. The control panel beeped telling him a dozen laser cannons had locked onto him — the wardens took security very seriously.

Turning on the communication radio, Avery said, 'This is Lieutenant-Commander Vander approaching in shuttle PSX431, requesting permission to land.'

'Prison control centre, receiving Lieutenant-Commander. Shuttle PSX431 is authorised to land on platform five.'

'Roger that.'

Avery flew them in at a comfortable speed. The settlement looked like an outbreak of giant mutant fungus. In reality, it was dome-shaped buildings constructed on stubby towers set into the ancient seabed. Outside the biodomes was earthmoving equipment that was used to mine the helium-three, a source of fuel for the power plant reactors and the space ships.

On the smoothed stripped mined surface, amid some deliberately scooped out sections, were eighteen little flags.

'Is that a golf course?' asked Dee.

'It is. The inhabitants need something to do or they go stir crazy. Apparently hitting a little coloured ball around is therapeutic.'

The balls had to be fluorescent coloured or they blended with the surface and became impossible to find.

'You ever played?' asked Dee.

'Only once. Some of the crew from *The Zee* dragged me out there for a game, but hitting the ball around just seemed to spoil a good walk.'

Dee laughed again although why Avery couldn't say.

The landing platform looked like a giant spoon without the depression. Avery sat them down right in the middle of the giant five. The platform retracted and they passed through an airlock, followed by a decontamination wash, before arriving inside a giant hangar. Armed wardens stood nearby.

Avery finished powering down and opened the backdoor with a hiss of escaping air.

Sarah unbuckled Sparta and he stood up. 'Take your time and watch your step. The gravity is slightly less than Ziana or Ria. It takes a bit to adjust.'

They walked down the ramp of the shuttle and Avery and Sara shook hands with Commander Wentworth, the shuttle hangar's manager.

Sarah removed Sparta's cuffs

Wentworth then placed a band on Sparta's left wrist. 'Mr Sparta, you've been placed in prison apartment number seven. We've received a meme that your lawyer will be arriving by teleport at twelve o'clock Isla time. That's four hours from now. The apartment is within a containment area which you are free to move around in. There's a cafeteria where you'll be served your meals and also a general store that sells approved items. Questions?'

'When is my hearing?'

'Ten o'clock, two days from now.'

Sparta acknowledged that he understood and walked off with his escort towards his assigned apartment.

'He gets an apartment?' asked Dee incredulously.

'Yes, it's the innocent until proven guilty thing,' replied Sarah. 'Even if he's denied bail until he's been convicted, he's technically a "guest". However, if he's found guilty, the cost of his accommodation and food will be added to his court fees.'

'Sounds fair,' said Avery.

Dee snorted. 'Do we get an apartment? Or do we have to bunk in the barracks?'

'Fleet officers get an apartment, not sure about spooks,' replied Avery.

Sarah fixed him with a steely-eyed look. 'I booked an apartment big enough for the *three* of us.'

Avery was thinking of something cheeky to say when a fleetman came running towards them.

He skidded to a stop and snapped a salute. 'Commander Bartell, Lieutenant-Commander Vander, Agent Dee.' He sucked in a deep breath before continuing. 'There's been an incident. Admiral Cadel has been shot.'

Chapter 29

Kaylor sipped Zianan sparkling wine from a flute glass and helped herself to a canapé. She was pleased she'd purchased an evening dress, in the Zianan equivalent of silk, and new shoes, before coming aboard. That was because the reception room on *The Explorer* was elegant and required formal attire.

The floor was lacquered wood with swirling natural patterns. The lights were dimmed crystal chandeliers. Musicians played traditional wooden flutes on a stage, while wait staff roamed ensuring guests had plenty to eat and drink.

However, all of this paled compared to the *pièce de résistance* — an enormous glass window that provided a spectacular view of space. Having collected its passengers from Ziana's spaceport, the tour spaceship was now warping across to Isla. It would visit all of Zeus's ten moons, and have a close encounter with its rings and the gas giant itself, before returning to orbit Ziana.

The tour was paid for by insanely rich tourists who could afford to teleport from Earth or one of its colonies, such as Mars or Titan. *The Explorer* was the epitome of extravagance; the space equivalent of an Earth cruise ship. The suites were luxurious, while the spaceship housed all forms of entertainment from concerts to formal dining. For those who'd completed the intensive EVA training and held a current certificate, there was also the opportunity to take a ride on a jet pack outside in space or board a shuttle down to the moon's surfaces, where you could take a walk.

Courtesy of the Zianan government, Kaylor and Yeltzie had received free tickets to come aboard. That was because *The Explorer* also doubled as a research vessel. Using equipment mounted to the outside of the ship, Kaylor would be able to record the music of Zeus's moons and the planet itself for analysis. It was also a rare opportunity to see the moons up close.

The expedition was twenty days long, so there was plenty of time to enjoy the endless onboard party as well as work.

Yeltzie, having gotten changed in their twin share suite, glided towards her. She was dressed in a traditional Zianan outfit that bore similarities to a Viking dress, or so historians said. Normally barefoot, she'd conceded to wear a pair of elf-like shoes that were adorned with tiny gemstones. Her long green hair, normally unfettered, was done up in a bun.

She'd caught a shuttle up from Ziana. Kaylor, who was still recovering from an injury that refused to completely heal, had had to teleported aboard.

Smiling, Kaylor said, 'How about this?'

Yeltzie returned the smile. 'I can't tell you how grateful I am for this opportunity.' She glanced around nervously while smoothing her outfit.

'You seem apprehensive, is it being in space that's concerning you?'

'No,' Yeltzie lowered her voice to a whisper. 'It's the company, they seem …' she searched for the right word in English, 'spurious.'

Kaylor laughed softly while casting her eye over the guests who were dressed in tuxedos or evening dresses and dripping with gold and jewels. 'Pretentious is the word you're looking for my dear. Rich and vain they are mostly concerned about how they are perceived while their primary focus is on whether their family's wealth, is continuing to accumulate while they live a life of leisure.'

Kaylor leaned closer to whisper in her ear. 'Keep your wits about you. To Earthlings, you're beautiful and exotic and young rich men are used to getting whatever they want whenever they want it.'

Yeltizie screwed up her nose and replied, 'Lower sealers.'

'Quite so, but also influential. I'm going to mingle and network, but feel free to slip away if you want. I'll change and head to the lab once we reach Isla.'

Yeltzie lips pulled into a tight line and she hurried away.

Kaylor helped herself to more finger food while looking for an opportunity to introduce herself. She'd been briefed about the situation on Ria, but she hadn't watched the holo-footage of the explosion nor the responding speeches. She was thankful that she was no longer on Ria and that her research now had the opportunity to progress.

*****

The Explorer was now orbiting Isla and Kaylor had a live feed of the sound the moon was making. Torri had graphed the frequency which was continuously updating.

'Nowhere near as bad as I've seen, but far from harmonious,' said Kaylor.

Yeltzie was looking out the lab's porthole window. 'I wouldn't expect it to be any different. The moon has never recovered from the laser wars that destroyed it. The inhabitants can't help but be affected by the lingering evil that occurred there.'

Yes, that made sense. Old building, particularly those that had had bad things happen within them, felt eerie to enter.

'The frequency will remain while Isla mourns and she'll continue to mourn until she feels loved again. Being loved was never going to happen whilst the place was just a prison, but now there is a community, the dynamic of people will hopefully expand.'

Kaylor rubbed her chin. 'So, you are saying the planet, or in this case, moon, takes on the frequency of the inhabitants, and those inhabitants are directly affected by past events.'

'Yes. Reality is shaped by consciousness which is a resonance. Just standing here, I can feel Isla's sorrow, feel her pain and suffering.' Tears trickled down Yeltzie's face. 'Even after everything she's been through, she still has weapons of war on her surface. It's so wrong.'

Kaylor wrapped her arms around Yeltzie.

'Islatations don't know how to tune into their mother world. Don't know how to intuit the songs they need to sing to heal her. And worst of all, they are too lower seal to understand why they need to.'

A lump formed in Kaylor's throat. Rians didn't know either and they'd laugh at anyone who tried to explain it to them. Without Zianan wisdom, they could not possibly know what had happened previously on their planet. Had Ria also been destroyed by a war? Perhaps not, but it could easily have been destroyed by mass pollution that had poisoned the atmosphere.

Now Ria was imploding. Fuelled by unknown past events and exacerbated by colonists who were conquers rather than gentle folk who would love and respect their world. Ria also lay directly in the path of discordant frequency that was coming from Zeta Reticuli. To make matters worse, Ria was now ruled by a despotic president. In summary, the denizens didn't stand a chance.

Could Zianan wisdom and love put an end to this? Could it stand against such discordance and ill will? What about Zeta Reticuli? What had happened on that world to create such a force of darkness? Kaylor didn't know, but to heal something so massive would take an extraordinary mind.

Someone like the ascended master Moir, or perhaps her son or a daughter. Shivers run down her spine. That was it. They needed Moir's help.

Chapter 30

Avery hurried towards Commodore Keenan's office. His door was open and he was pacing back and forth. All three of them came to a halt; the two fleet officers snapped a salute.

'As you were,' said Keenan.

'What's happened?' asked Sarah.

'We don't know the exact details. All we know is Admiral Cadel was in a holo meeting with the Admiralty and the Select Oversight Committee in base Commodore, Venetia Erikson's, office. He'd hurried from the room to retrieve something. When he failed to return, Venetia went to check on him. She found him dead on his office floor, shot by a laser pistol.'

Sarah gasped and covered her mouth.

'Do we know who shot him?' asked Avery.

'No, we don't, but we fear we may have a traitor in our midst. Venetia has ordered the base into complete lockdown.'

'Do we know what the motive was?' asked Dee.

'Yes, we're assuming the shooter was caught in the midst of a heist. Cadel's safe was found unlocked and the door open. We don't know what was taken.'

Avery did and he should have been more circumspect getting the device investigated. Not that he was blaming the techs for leaking information, but security should have been tighter and more secret. Damn it.

'Any ideas?' asked Keenan.

Should he tell the commodore? Zarnika, the high archivist, had told him to be careful who he trusted. Still, they'd brought Sparta here for a hearing in relation to the device. If Keenan did not already know about the persuasive program, he soon would.

'Yes Sir. Daniel Sparta was arrested for possession of an ancient device that has a dangerous mind control program on it. It allows the operator to persuade people to do anything they want. The device was given to Admiral Cadel for safe keeping. If it is no longer in his safe, then it's a fair guess, that that's what the thief was prepared to kill for, in order to steal it,' said Avery.

Keenan growled. 'God damn it! The device should have been brought straight to Isla and locked in our deep unground vault.'

'Yes, I agree Sir. The device was to be brought here. Cadel was going to deliver it personally. He intended to teleport here with it as soon as his meeting was over.'

Keenan took a seat and drummed his fingers on the desk. 'Shut the door.'

Sarah did as he asked.

From his desk drawer, Keenan removed a communication jammer and switched it on. 'I won't lie. The situation is bad.' He looked at the ceiling. 'What I'm about to tell you is off the record and between us. I shouldn't be saying this, but Cadel trusted you three and I trusted Cadel.'

Avery knew what was coming. He'd known for a while now and so had Sarah.

'Vice-Admiral Peterson has assumed command of fleet. As you know he's in collusion with President Inglis. If they have the device, they'll use it as a means to an end. I believe that end is to invade Ziana in order to steal her natural resources and enslave her people.'

Sarah closed her eyes. 'Is there anything we can do Sir?'

'For the moment, no. All we can do is wait and see what orders Peterson issues before deciding if we are going to comply or refuse and risk court-martial. If we refuse to comply with orders then we become criminals, enemies of Ria and fleet and essentially rebels.'

The room fell silent.

'Sir, I need to speak with Director Gorman. He's in the loop, which is why I'm involved. The SIA don't take orders from fleet except when it's a collaborative operation. I assure you, the SIA will do everything it can to recover that device and if need be, bring down the Inglis government.'

Keenan looked Dee in the eye and indicated she was dismissed to contact her boss. She hurried from the room closing the door behind her.

'What's Sparta's involvement in all of this?' asked Keenan.

'We don't know for sure. He's exercising the right to remain silent and acting like a mute,' replied Avery.

'I've been monitoring his psychological state since his arrest. He's very afraid and he was genuinely upset about the terrorist attack,' added Sarah.

'Little fucker has gotten himself in over his head this time. Now he's scared he's going to burn for it and sickened by what he's done,' said Keenan.

'Can we use the *Interrogation Act* to force him to talk?' asked Avery.

The Act could only be enacted when there was a serious threat to national or intergalactic security and was used only as a last resort. Avery though the situation complied.

Keenan rubbed his chin. 'I'm loathed to do so at this stage because if he still refuses to talk, we'll be forced to torture him. If things go as pear-shaped as I'm predicting, then he may decide to talk on his own.'

'I agree,' replied Sarah.

'Alright, we'll wait,' said Keenan.

'With all due respect Sir, I'm not convinced it's wise to wait. Sparta's lawyer is arriving shortly. She's very skilled and we can be sure she'll do her best to get bail for Sparta. If that happens, we'll lose our chance.'

'Point taken, but we've got two days and a lot can happen between now and then.'

'Fair enough, but one other thing Sir. The device works by sending messages through communicators. You may want to consider having your personnel remove them from their person and handing them in. Once someone is under the influence of the persuasive program, they lose their sense of self and become zombies.'

Keenan's eyes widened. 'Damn it, this is worse than I thought.'

Ordering people to hand in their communicators would cause a serious ruckus. Vice-Admiral Peterson would be notified and he'd countermand the order and relieve Keenan of his duties. However, not doing so might result in the program being used to permanently relieve Keenan of his duty and take over Isla. It was check. Keenan was damned if he did, damned if he didn't.

'Leave me for the minute, I need to think on this.'

Sarah and Avery snapped a salute and filed out.

*****

When Avery and Sarah arrived at their apartment, they found Dee sitting on the couch watching the holovision. The reporter, Mandy, was talking and Avery paused to listen.

'Thus far there has been no response from either Chief Minister Hardy or Admiral Cadel following the terrorist attack and President Inglis's response speech. We have, however, received word that Admiral Cadel has been shot and killed. We cross live now to Vice-Admiral Peterson.'

The image chopped to Peterson who was standing in the press room where President Inglis had made his speech a few hours ago. Avery did a double take as he noted the Rian flags had increased from ten to twelve. It wasn't just the increase of flags that got Avery's attention but the fact that a fleet officer was making a speech in their presence. Fleet was independent of Ria and therefore a fleet officer should not be associating with the Rian flags. It spoke volumes about Peterson's collusion with President Inglis although most Rians would not make this connection.

'It is with a heavy heart that I officially inform you that Admiral Cadel has been shot and killed with a fleet issued laser pistol. Zianan fleet base commander, Commodore Venetia Erikson, has confessed to his murder. She has been arrested and detained and will be court-martialled directly.

'I have assumed command of fleet and following this tragic loss of life I will be asking all fleet personnel from cadets to ranking officers to submit to a new psychological evaluation. I want to stress that this is a precautionary measure only to ensure an incident like this does not happen again.' Peterson neatened his notes on the lectern. 'I'll now take some questions from the floor.'

The room erupted in chatter until Peterson pointed to someone.

'During her confession, did Commodore Erikson provide an explanation as to why she murdered Admiral Cadel?'

'I'm not able to provide comment on that until after Commodore Erikson's court-martial.'

'Who will be in command of Ziana's fleet base now that Commodore Erikson has been relieved of command?'

'I intend to teleport Commodore Grieves to Ziana to assume command of the fleet base, but presently Chief Minister Hardy is denying that form of transport.'

'By denying, what do you mean exactly?'

'The teleporter in Port Town is not responding and neither is the one on *The Zee*. I have received word that those two teleporters have been deactivated by order of the Chief Minister.'

'Are you suggesting that Chief Minister Hardy is now interfering in fleet's operations?'

'Yes I am.'

'How do you intend to respond to that?'

'Fleet is, and always has been, an independent institution answerable to the Select Oversight Committee. Ziana is a signatory to the accords that grant fleet authority to police Ziana and the space around it. By interfering in fleet operations, she has committed a serious crime which she will be charged for.'

'Have you issued a warrant for her arrest?'

'Yes, I have.'

The room erupted into chaotic chatter until Peterson brought it to order.

'Do you expect any resistance to Chief Minister Hardy's arrest?'

Peterson stared straight into the camera. 'If fleet officers refuse to arrest Chief Minister Hardy, then that will be taken as refusing orders and the offending officers will be relieved of duty and court-martialled. A mass refusal, or denied access for fleet officers to the planet will be seen as a rebellion. One last question.'

'And how will you respond to a rebellion?'

'The same way fleet responds to all riots and rebellions. By sending sufficient officers to put it down and restore law and order.'

Peterson walked away from the lectern leaving journalists still shouting out questions.

Sarah's face reddened and for a moment Avery feared there'd be a repeat of her outburst following the President's speech but she hissed, 'That lying bastard.'

Avery asked the holovision to mute before saying. 'That about sums it up. They refused to screen Cadel and Hardy's speeches, murdered Cadel, framed Venetia, they've ordered a purging of fleet personnel to weed out Zianan sympathisers and tried to teleport over that brown-nosing puppet, Commodore Grieves. Renee Hardy has refused to play ball and so Peterson has issued a warrant for her arrest.'

'Do you think anyone will try and arrest her?' asked Dee.

'Not likely, unless someone has used the device to mind control someone into doing it,' replied Sarah.

Avery wondered what Captain Loody was doing following the orders he'd have received from Vice-Admiral Peterson. Was *The Zee* in chaos? No Loody would order them to stand down on that matter. He'd also order base personnel to reopen the investigation into Cadel's shooting.

'No one is going to arrest Hardy,' said Avery. 'Peterson and Inglis are banking on it because they want a so-called rebellion in order to justify an invasion.'

'Then Captain Loody played right into their hands,' said Dee.

'In a way, but he was left with no choice. What he and Hardy are doing, is saying, I won't play your games or accept your lies. No one comes or goes from Ziana without ministerial approval,' said Avery.

'Then fleet will come in force.'

'Renee has the option to withdraw permission for fleet to operate on Ziana and the space around it. The fleet officers at the base and on *The Zee* will then be asked to leave, or stay and pledge allegiance to Ziana effectively making them rebels.'

'Does *The Zee* not belong to fleet?' asked Dee.

'No, *The Zee* was paid for with Zianan gold and is owned by Ziana. It's on permanent loan to fleet, but no, fleet don't own it.'

Not quite true. There'd be some tight contracts between Ziana and fleet. Still, in the face of an invasion, Hardy would ignore them.

Sarah sat down and rubbed her face in her hands. 'So, I have two options. Follow orders and arrest Hardy, or become a rebel and a traitor to my own planet.'

Avery wrapped his arms around Sarah and just held her. 'Or we can rally behind Loody and ask him to issue arrest warrants for Inglis and Peterson on the grounds that they have in their possession an illegal device that they are using to commit acts of terror.'

'If the SIA can retrieve the device, that would work,' said Dee.

Sarah sighed. 'It's a long shot, but I agree, it's the best we have.'

*****

Since his arrival, Sparta had sat on the couch in his apartment glued to the holovision. He'd listened to Peterson's speech with interest. He wasn't stupid and neither was Venetia. If she was going to murder Cadel, she wouldn't moments later confess to it. She'd have had an exit strategy and several backup plans in place. If she had confessed, then there was no doubt in his mind, that it was because she was under the influence of the persuasive program.

Few knew about it and the little band that had arrested him would know better than to talk about it or even list its functions in his arrest report. Would the techs analysing it have said something? Perhaps, but it was doubtful. They too would understand how dangerous it was.

That narrowed things down. The base could be bugged, but bugging required a lot of effort and resources to constantly monitor them even with androids. Bugging was also risky. AIs like Tank could hack into feeds and electronic storage, and the last thing they'd want was hardened criminals finding out what was really going on.

No, it was more likely someone had informed Inglis or Peterson about the device. Cadel would not have done so nor would Director Gorman. That narrowed it down to two people: Black and White, whatever the hell their real names were. How or why, they'd leaked the information, Sparta didn't know.

Fuck it. He shouldn't have taken the job. Still, he had no way of knowing at the time that the job would entwine him with a despotic president and a rogue vice-admiral. In any case, how did any of this connect to the desire for a child from Avery and Kaylor, little grey aliens and a freaky extra-terrestrial vehicle that could cross galaxies in a second?

He didn't know, but he did know it equated to a whole lot of trouble for him. He wished there was a bottle of strong liquor here. There wasn't, and in any case, he needed to stay sober to talk to his lawyer who'd be arriving shortly.

Mandy was talking again.

'I can confirm that Commander-in-chief Inglis, has been in a meeting with Ria's cabinet ministers and advisers since he delivered his speech following the terrorist attack. We have received word that he will be making another statement shortly and we will be crossing live.'

Whoa, when had the president become the commander-in-chief? The title gave him command of Ria's fleet ships and it could only be bestowed if an act of war had been committed. Was the terrorist attack now being considered an act of war?

Inglis now stood behind the lectern in the press hall and the camera zoomed in.

'My fellow Rians. I am happy to report that the terrorists behind the bombing of dome six have been apprehended. Following their arrest, they confessed to heinous crimes committed. In light of this good news, I'm happy to say that there will be no need for a long and expensive investigation. The terrorists will face the full weight of the law. Justice to date has been swift and decisive.'

The crowd applauded. Inglis held up a hand to silence them.

'However, I have grave news. During the confessions, the terrorists implicated a number of key Zianan officials including the Chief Minister and the Minister for law and justice.' He sighed theatrically. 'They have been given twenty-four hours to reply. Given we are still waiting for a response to the terrorist attack, we do not expect one will be forthcoming. If that is indeed the case, given the grave nature of the accusations, I will have no choice but to declare the act of terror an act of war.

'It is a grave decision and not one that was arrived at lightly. However, I cannot and will not stand idle. Not while an outside threat attacks our planet, attempts to destroy our way of life, murders our people and destroys our property. I must respond.'

There was another applause. 'I have been in conference with Vice-Admiral Peterson. He agrees with my decision and the decision of the Rian Cabinet. He has agreed that the situation warrants the enacting of emergency clauses within the fleet accords. These clauses permit fleet to act in a military capacity in response to an act of war. As a result of this, fleet ships will be readied to depart for Ziana the moment the deadline ends.'

He paused for effect and the room fell silent.

'I ask all Rians to pray for a peaceful solution but to prepare for the worst. May God be with you all in this grave hour.'

Sparta sat there and watched incredulously. What the fuck. Hardy had responded and so had Cadel. He'd watched the live feed from the recordings. Denying that there'd been a response meant Ria was being dragged into a war under false pretences. That was treason.

Sparta sat there powerless to act as the world spiralled out of control. What should he do? Confess and accept the consequences of that? Or wait and see how things played out?

A knock at the door interrupted his musings. He got up and noted it was his lawyer; Brooke Madison and he opened the door for her. Wafting fragrant perfume, she glided into the room in her trademark high heel boots and black skirt suit. She was accompanied by two fleet escorts, who remained outside. There was also a gender-neutral android who was controlling a hover sled laden with baggage.

'Jamie, I'll need my briefcase and handbag,' said Brooke addressing the android. 'Have the rest of my luggage delivered to my suite in the Premier Hotel.' She glanced around the one-bedroom apartment with bemusement. Having considered the couch, her attention moved to the dining table. 'We'll work here.'

The android removed the items she requested from the sled.

'Advise the concierge that I'll require room service and you're to deliver it here.' Her attention moved to Sparta who she gave a once over, 'And shut the door on your way out.'

When the android had left with the sled and they were alone in the apartment, Brooke asked, 'Danny boy, are you responsible for the mess that Ria is in?'

He swallowed, his throat drier than the rusty red sands of Ria. How should he answer that question?

Chapter 31

Four standard Earth hours later, *The Zee* arrived in the orbit of Isla and Avery flew a shuttle up to it. Avery, Sarah, Dee, and Commodore Keenan, now sat in the spaceship's briefing room which overlooked the bridge.

Grim-faced Captain Loody interlaced his fingers. 'Commodore Venetia has a major gap in her memory. She remembers ordering the base to be locked down, but nothing between doing that and coming to in a gaol cell.'

'Gaps in memory are quite common for anyone who has been under the influence of hypnosis,' said Sarah.

'Which means we can be confident that the persuasive program was used on her,' said Keenan.

'That's a reasonable assumption,' said Sarah. 'Using hypnotherapy, I may be able to recover her memories. They'd allow us to know what she did whilst under the influence, but unfortunately, any information recovered is not admissible in court.'

'Do we have a copy of the recording of her so-called confession?' asked Avery.

'No, Peterson has secured the evidence which will be presented at her court-martial. It's scheduled to take place on Ria, but Renee has ordered that no one enter or leave Ziana without her permission. Needless to say, permission has not been granted,' said Loody. He paused to gather his thoughts. 'Unfortunately, someone left Ziana via teleport soon after Cadel was shot and whoever it was convinced the operator to not record their identity.'

Damn it. 'Do we have a suspect?'

'Yes, one of the Rian reporters is missing, but my guess is he was actually another one of President Inglis's special guard.'

Double damn it. They'd been caught asleep at the wheel.

'Can I assume that the Chief Minister has not been arrested?' asked Dee.

'According to the law, the Head of Government, has the authority to lock down their planet during a crisis. Which means in point of fact, Renee has not committed any crime. I advised Peterson of this and shortly after, Inglis declared the terrorist attack an act of war.'

'Has Renee responded to this?' asked Avery.

'Yes, she gave another address, this time from her office, reiterating that Ziana was not involved in the bombing,' said Loody.

'She says she wasn't involved, Inglis says she was. This is madness. Can't somebody put a stop to it?' hissed Dee.

'Admiral Cadel would have intervened and forced them to the negotiation table,' said Keenan. 'Unfortunately, he is no longer with us and his second-in-command has declared that fleet will respond to the declared act of war.'

'What orders have been received?' asked Avery.

'A new warrant has been issued for Renee's arrest. This time she is being charged with aiding and abetting war criminals.' Loody drew a circle in the air with his finger. 'Which means we are right back where we started.'

'And back to my first question. Has she been arrested?' asked Dee.

A slight smile crossed Keenan's face. 'She was temporarily detained and brought before an emergency holo-hearing held in the Zianan Council boardroom. In more elegant words, Judge MacGregor said the entire situation is ludicrous. He granted Renee bail but ordered she be fitted with a tracking bracelet and she's to remain in Port Town.'

'Which wouldn't overly trouble her,' replied Avery.

'I agree,' added Loody. 'Barsha might be the official capital, but Port Town is the real centre of power on Ziana.'

'What about Venetia?' asked Dee.

'She's been suspended pending her court-martial,' said Keenan. 'Renee has provided permission for Venetia to be taken to Isla to the intergalactic court, but not to Ria. Renee has also suggested that Inglis and Peterson teleport to Isla to present their evidence against Venetia and herself.'

'Can we expect their arrival then?' asked Dee.

'We've received no word as such,' replied Keenan.

Avery smiled. 'That was nicely played.'

'I didn't quite follow that,' said Sarah.

'The device is dangerous, but it only has a short range relatively speaking. If either of them tries to bring it with them, the teleporter's AI will detect its presence. If it does, we can arrest them the moment they arrive. If they leave it behind, they effectively cut themselves off from the source of their power,' replied Avery.

'Well put,' said Loody. 'Both Inglis and Peterson know the evidence they have in the form of confessions is flimsy. If we put forth the notion that the confessors were not in their right mind at the time, then reasonable doubt is established. Without hard evidence, both cases will collapse like a house of cards.'

Sarah's eyes lit up. 'Then Inglis's actions will seem rash and there'll be grounds for his impeachment.'

'True, which means he's in danger of overplaying his hand,' said Dee.

'Yes and no,' said Avery. 'The problem is the media are not fulfilling the role of the Fourth Estate and broadcasting Renee's responses. The failure to do so is no doubt due to an edict issued by Inglis. However, the media are supposed to be an independent insistution separate from government.'

'And whilst he has control of the media, Inglis will continue to pretend Renee's responses don't exist,' said Sarah.

'That's the sum of it, and Inglis's actions are riling up the populace of Ria who will soon be baying for blood if they aren't already,' said Avery.

'In other words, the war will go ahead unless Inglis and Peterson are removed from power,' said Dee.

'Yes, and assuming they're victorious, it won't matter what laws have been broken,' said Sarah, 'because victors write their own laws and histories.'

'Oh, it still matters,' said Keenan. 'It just means we have to work out a way to arrest both Inglis and Peterson before they assume power of Ziana and Isla. That won't be easy, but it's all we have.'

'Do we have a plan?' asked Sarah.

'We only have one frigate, *The Zee,* and I believe it is too dangerous to fly her towards the approaching fleet. All we can do is wait until they arrive in a year's time and try and find a way to sneak aboard and apprehend Inglis and Peterson.'

'That won't be easy,' said Avery. There's no way to avoid radar contact. Inglis is likely to laser approaching shuttles, but even if he permits a boarding party, he'll be heavily guarded.'

'Plus, he has the device,' said Dee.

Avery nodded agreement. 'Once the fleet is in range, we won't be able to use communicators. We'll need to revert to scrambled radios frequencies and talk in code.'

Sarah rubbed the bridge of her nose. 'We are going to need to train for that.'

'Yes, and not just in the different style of communication, shuttles will have to be flown without AI, because pilots can't instruct them with them without communicators.'

Sarah paled. 'How many pilots can fly a shuttle without an AI?'

'You're looking at him,' replied Loody gesturing towards Avery.

Sarah swore. 'Can we at least ask Earth for help?'

'We have sent a message to Earth, but the reality is they have no spaceships that can arrive before Ria's fleet does. I'm afraid we're on our own.'

The room fell silent.

Keenan broke the silence. 'Until we receive additional orders from Peterson, we prepare as best we can. Otherwise, we carry on as normal. I've ordered Venetia to also be confined to Port Town. Captain Loody will act in her stead and Sarah will act as the commanding officer of *The Zee*.'

'What about Sparta?' asked Avery. 'Have you considered my suggestion?'

'I did. Interrogation through force can only be undertaken with approval from the head of fleet. Peterson denied the request,' said Keenan.

'Which means Sparta was likely working for him and Inglis,' said Dee.

'No, it means Peterson is shit scared Sparta will squeal about the device,' said Avery. 'He doesn't want that for obvious reasons.'

'It will come out at the hearing anyway,' said an exacerbated Dee.

'We'll see,' said Avery looking her in the eye. 'So why don't you tell us, what did Sparta wanted with Kaylor and me?'

Dee's face became deadpan. Despite all that was going on, that was a secret she wasn't going to reveal.

Keenan broke the tension by clearing his throat. 'Despite the tenaciousness of the situation, I'm loathed to break the law. We mustn't give Peterson anything to use against us. Sparta's arraignment will go ahead as planned. Let's see what Brooke's play is.'

Avery didn't like it, but he could understand the Commodore's reasoning.

*****

Avery would have like nothing more than to have tortured the information out of either Sparta or Dee. Sparta was with his lawyer and off limits. He was sure Dee knew the answer to his question, which was why she continued to be involved. The problem was, as big as he was, he wasn't sure he could best her in a fair fight and he was loathed to play dirty.

Frustrated, he tossed aside the pad and pencil he'd been using. He'd never been particularly good at remote viewing. It was a skill that required active synapses between the midbrain and the neocortex. The midbrain could process higher frequencies in the quantum field allowing it to receive information for remote views and various forms of telepathy.

Anyone could activate the midbrain and its neural connections. Some were even born with it active. Most, however, had to spend years doing single point focus. The most common method was to focus on a candle flame, although there were other methods.

Avery had just never set aside the time to do it and he hadn't been born with any natural talent. Sighing, he created a target which he emailed to Kara, the young female cadet who successfully supplied the code for the troublesome device.

The response was prompt. He wondered if she didn't have enough work to do. However, he concluded, Kara would have assumed a remote view sent by a fleet officer was urgent.

Avery's heart fell when he opened the holographic image. It was a picture of a shining star. Damn it, she must have gotten it wrong. That happened occasionally.

He sent her a new target, received the same result, before trying a third time. Now he had three images of the same star. Not helpful. What the fuck did a star have to do with Kaylor and himself?

That was the question, time to use his detective brain to work the problem.

Avery was trained in navigation and he'd studied star charts in detail. Despite the clarity of the images, he did not recognise the star, nor could he find it in any chart. Had Sparta been trying to give them information about the star? Did this star somehow relate to Kaylor's work? Or was the star a metaphor for something else?

Avery was reaching, which as a detective he sometimes needed to do. On this occasion, it just didn't feel right. If it was just about a star, then why would Sparta refuse to tell him?

It didn't make sense. No, Sparta had gone to a lot of effort and expense to bring Kaylor to Ziana. Why? It made sense that it was for her protection, but again, why withhold that?

What was his connection to Kaylor? Did she simply need a pilot to take her to this star? Avery was a good pilot, but there were hundreds of skilled pilots, so why specifically him?

Nothing was making sense.

Chapter 32

The more excited she got, the more Kaylor waved her arms in the air. Her holo-presentation was filled with graphs and charts that provided evidence for her conclusion.

'Discordant energy has made its way across lightyears of space from Zeta Reticuli. Based on the distance from here to there and the speed at which information travels on light, the events that caused the discordance happened centuries ago. But time is relative.'

Both the Chief Minister and her boss the Minister for Science simply sat there unmoved. Damn it, had she lost them in the detail or were they simply processing?

She pushed on. 'I'm hypothesising that this discordant energy is what is causing Ria to be so lower seal and chaotic. Ziana isn't affected because the inhabitants create harmony by singing and raising the frequency of the planet above the discordance. What is needed on Ria, is a mass intervention.'

Renee finally spoke. 'We know this already.'

Kaylor's cheeks flushed red. Of course, they did. How stupid of her to assume otherwise.

'You have more to add?' asked her boss Ethan.

'Yes.' She swallowed. 'I don't think sending a choir to Ria would be enough, and given the current situation, not possible anyway. I think what is needed is a higher form of intervention.'

For the first time in this meeting, Renee looked interested.

'I think we need to collectively ask the ascended master Moir for help. I know masters are not supposed to help, but what if we asked?'

Clearly amused, Renee began to chuckle. 'Dr Emerson, you've come a long way since coming to Ziana, but you still lack basic knowledge taught to our children.'

Kaylor wanted the floor to open up and swallow her. She had a PhD and yet they were saying her knowledge was that of a kindergartener.

'Ascended masters can offer advice, some even have their own schools, but they cannot intervene,' said Renee. 'It's cosmic law.'

'Sure, but can't we ask her superior? Does she answer to God?'

Renee's amusement seemed to deepen. 'My dear, God, as you were raised to believe in him, is a myth made up to frighten children into behaving. Regrettably, some men and women, remain child-like their entire lives looking to a great Papa or Mama to take care of them. God is not a man or even a being, God is a great mind that is connected to everything.'

Confused, Kaylor sought clarification. 'Then who or what stops Moir from helping us?'

'It is neither a who, nor a what, but a why. What you have to understand, is not all-powerful beings are good. Some have posed as gods and enslaved worlds in order to be worshiped. Their slaves have then slain others for blasphemy when those others accused their gods as being false.'

Kaylor could see the logic in that.

'If you study Earth history you will discover that many of the wars fought on that planet had religion. Or, the war mongers hid their real agenda behind religion.'

'Isn't that what President Inglis is doing?'

Ethan slow clapped while smiling.

'Anyway, back to your question, said Renee. 'If Moir appeared and reined fiery meteors down upon the fleet ships, she'd be hailed as a goddess. Thousands would fall upon their knees and proclaim them loyal to her. Even if she was to tell them she wasn't a goddess, how many would believe her? Worse still, how many would go on worshiping her as an idle even after she left? Would her followers create another religion in her name that would provide neither knowledge or truth? Do you understand?'

'Yes.'

'Good and now you can understand that every generation must develop the skills to deal with its own problems. Adversity is what drives people to become aware and without it, they become lazy and dependent on higher beings to rescue them from their problems.'

Kaylor switched off the holo-presentation. 'I'm sorry, I didn't mean to waste your time.'

Renee softened her expression. 'Forgive me, I should not have laughed at you. Your work is sublime, but it is not for us. It's scientific evidence to convince Rians that our singing is not merely entertaining or in their words: queer. It's purposeful on a very meaningful level.'

'Oh, I see.' It made sense, but it was ironic that her people with all their technology still needed to listen to and understand simple wisdom. A connection to the natural world was critical to maintaining balance and harmony. It wasn't just about singing; it was about mutual respect for all life that made existence possible. Without this connection, there was nothing to bring chaos to order.

'I won't take up any more of your time.' Kaylor made for the door as fast as her short legs would carry her.

'Kaylor.'

Kaylor turned to look back at Renee.

'You have a question that remains unanswered.'

Of course, a Zianan would know that.

'It's regarding events in history.'

'Yes, but I'm sure the library has the answers.'

Renee smiled, 'My dear, I'm two-hundred and twenty-seven years old. I do not simply know history; I've lived through it.'

Kaylor blinked. 'You don't look a day over forty.'

Renee laughed with deep mirth. 'Flattery is wasted on my ilk, but do come and have a seat.' The Chief Minister got up and walked to a cabinet in the corner of her office. From it she retrieved three wine glasses and a bottle of deep purple-coloured wine. Inside it was a wine rack.

'I'm afraid I don't do formal as well as Rians. We Zianas prefer to, what's the expression in English, break bread.'

Kaylor sighed, took a seat and accepted the proffered wine.

Renee made a point of showing Kaylor the tracking bracelet on her arm. 'As you can see, presently I have all the time in the world. So, what was your question?'

Kaylor took a nervous sip. The purple wine was deeply flavoursome with a hint of spice and aged wood, yet smooth and soft with no sharp aftertaste. An expensive vintage suitable for the Chief Minister of Ziana, who was a queen in all but name. 'I wanted to know what really happened when first contact was made. I have trouble envisioning why the colonists simply flew away to colonise a lifeless world.'

Renee glanced at Ethan with a deep sense of approval in her eyes. The question had struck at the heart of the current issue of the looming conflict.

'They did not simply fly away. We used the fourth way to convince them to.'

Kaylor put down her glass. 'You sang with intent.'

Renee stared deep into her eyes. 'You've used your time with Yeltzie well and you've listened to her.'

Kaylor slowly nodded. 'You intend to sing again.'

'Yes, but this time we are at a disadvantage. Last time it was one ship, this time it's an armada and the President's resolve is firm. Last time we also had a master singer who was extraordinarily telepathic. Using her mind and intent, she was able to coordinate our efforts into singularity. To create a gestalt, which led to a unified moment, or put another way, an observed moment which created reality.'

Kaylor understood. In quantum physics, there was a simple principle that reality is shaped by observation.

'What happened to her?' asked Kaylor.

Renee fixed her with intense eyes. 'What makes you think it was a she?'

'I,' Kaylor swallowed, 'I assumed.'

'No, you didn't.'

'No, you're right, a picture of her just flashed through my mind, then she became a bright star. Did she ascend?'

Renee took a sip of her own wine. 'No, she was very old even for a Zianan. She died soon after the intervention, but she was often referred to as the bright star.'

Kaylor paused to consider. 'I don't understand. She was so powerful. Why didn't she ascend?'

Ethan raised an eyebrow. 'You ask very pointed questions.'

Kaylor glanced first at Ethan and then at Renee. 'I'm trying to understand.'

'This is the bit that takes faith and it's why I gave you some wine. It doesn't just help you to relax, but allows your acceptance to be more pliant.' Renee topped up their glasses. 'A being who ascends leaves behind those they love and is limited in how they can help for the reasons I just explained. One who chooses reincarnation, has the power to do as they will, once they are reborn.'

Kaylor knitted her brows. 'But rebirth wipes your memory, so a reincarnated person wouldn't remember why they came back.'

'A common misconception. Upon death, one does not have to give up one's memories. Lower seal beings choose to because it erases trauma played out through that life.'

'So Starliah could be reborn with her memories intact?'

Both of the Zianans stared at her.

'You even know her name,' said Ethan after an intense pause.

'I… it just, come into my head, coincidentally of course.'

'There are no coincidences,' said Ethan. 'Everything happens for a reason.'

Kaylor bit her lip.

'Before she died, Starliah wrote something in her journal. A promise to return at Ziana's darkest hour.'

'I see. Has she been reborn then?'

'No, I don't believe so,' said Renee.

Kaylor frowned. 'Pity, we could really use her help about now.'

'Yes, we could and it is something you should consider deeply.'

'I don't understand.'

'Starliah needs to be born. I'm not giving you a mandate; I'm simply asking you to consider what's at stake.'

Kaylor's wine sloshed in her glass and she was forced to set it down. 'Are you suggesting that I could give birth to her?'

Renee simply raised an eyebrow.

'No. No, she'd chose a great sage as a mother, not me.'

'You belittle yourself. Your understanding of the sound issue is greater than anyone alive,' said Ethan. 'Your knowledge will pass into your child's DNA.'

A tingle ran down her spine. Was this the real reason she'd been sent back from death?

'Daniel Sparta, the man who presented himself to you as Roger Smith, do you know what he really wanted?' asked Renee.

Kaylor's mind raced. He'd gone to a lot of expense to bring her to Ziana and then seemed completely disinterested in the offer the Zianan government had made her. Now she thought about it, it was all very odd. 'No, I don't.'

'He's not a nice man. Not someone I'd normally let teleport to Ziana, but sometimes malevolence has to be fought by deviance. It wasn't my place to interfere even though I had the authority to do so.' She paused. 'Stephen Cadel acted rashly when he had Sparta arrested. He also lied to me, because I'd withheld from him. It didn't matter; I worked it all out in the end.'

'I didn't understand that riddle.'

Renee winced, 'Pity, there're things I can't directly tell you because they are classified.'

A picture of Dee flashed through Kaylor's mind. The woman wasn't fleet, which meant she was an SIA agent and not in the fringes of her life by chance.

'Alright, but let's say I did have a baby and by some miracle, it does turn out to be Starliah. The armada is already on its way. She'll be a newborn when it gets here. Powerless to do anything.'

Renee again fixed her with a deep penetrating stare. 'Is that so? You said yourself just moments ago, time is relative.'

Kaylor closed her eyes. How was it possible for a child to be conceived, born and grown up inside of a year? The rational scientist screamed it wasn't possible. The post-NDE scientist knew quantum physics allowed for the seemingly impossible as defined by classical physics. Was it her place to deny the possibility of a miracle?

'Alright, I'll have a child. It's no burden because I want one anyway. The problem is that I don't have a lover to get me pregnant, so I'll have to be artificially inseminated. I don't suppose you have a man in mind whose sperm I should ask for.'

Both of them looked at her bewilderedly.

'Artificial insemination? We don't approve of that,' said Ethan.

Kaylor rolled her eyes. Of course, they wouldn't, it went against the natural order. It would have to be natural conception or Starliah mightn't return. Not so bad, it would be a shame to go through all the stress of pregnancy and the pain of birth and not have had the sexual pleasure of conceiving the child.

'The man, well, Sparta went to some effort with him as well. He got you both living together, although I'm not convinced it's altogether his doing.'

Kaylor's heart fluttered. 'Avery?' She wouldn't deny she was attracted to him. 'But he's mourning his wife.'

'Yes, the timing is frightfully inconvenient, and he'll likely tell you that he intends to remain a widower for life. You'll need to be convincing.'

Anxiety gripped her. Kaylor's flirting skills were rusty and she'd never been skilled in that area even in her teens. Kaylor drank some more wine. 'Why him?'

Renee leaned forward, 'He has a secret that even he didn't know until recently. He's Moir's son.'

And suddenly things began to make sense to Kaylor.

Chapter 33

Cast from pure nickel mined on Isla, Lady Justice stood proudly in the Intergalactic Court's enormous foyer facing the entrance. Dressed in a toga and sandals, her long hair unfettered; her eyes unbound, she's free to see all and seek truth from all quarters. Her left hand holds a broad sword, the tip resting on the podium she stands upon. Her sword promising justice will be swift and stern. Yet her right hand, holds balancing scales also promising justice will be fair with all opinions taken into account.

Avery never walked past without pausing to admire her. It wasn't just that she stood for the allegorical personification of the moral force of the independent judicial system. Or in simpler terms, law and justice. What he found most interesting, was that Lady Justice existed on Ziana prior to Earthlings arrival. She was further proof that Earth and Ziana had ties to the same ancient ancestors and their belief in justice through law.

Avery crossed the marble-floored foyer held up by elegantly carved sandstone pillars. Quarried locally, the building was the epitome of Zianan architecture and stone masonry. It had taken ten years to build. Too long for the impatient Rians who sought fast gratification, but their opinions didn't matter to the builders. Zianans were long-sighted and ten years was a mere blink in time, when the building would stand for a thousand year or more.

The arched doorways supported solid wooden doors milled from Zianan hardwood finished with clear natural resins. The handles cast from silver and polished daily.

Presently, the double doors were open and having crossed the threshold, Avery looked up. The high ceiling was made from hardened glass, kept spotlessly clean by cleaning bots who did likewise for the dome. The courtrooms were the only ones in known existence which offered a breathtaking view of the stars. With little atmosphere to hide their appearance, they twinkled at all times despite the world being bathed in constant sunlight.

Avery paused in front of the plush bench seats upholstered with fine velvet coloured in stripes of blue, red and green — blue for Earth, red for Ria and green for Ziana. Unconsciously he smoothed his dress uniform jacket and checked his tie. He'd spent last evening polishing his brass buttons, not because they needed it, but because it gave him something to do.

It had been a long wait. Despite his promise to himself to never play golf again, Dee had dragged both him and Sarah out for a game. Afterward, he'd found a physical book in the library to borrow. He didn't care how far away the mind control device was assumed to be; he wasn't using a communicator until the device was destroyed or placed in a faraday cage.

Sarah smoothed the back of her dress uniform skirt and sat down beside him. Unable to control her nervous tick, her right foot jiggled. Dressed in a black pants suit with a white shirt, Dee continuously cast her eye around the court noting all of the exits.

The prosecutor sat behind his desk going over documents using a holo-reader. Appointed by the Select Oversight Committee, the prosecutor was an impartial representative of the union that was made up of Earth, Ria, and Ziana.

A click-clacking sounded across the court as Brooke Madison entered. Her painted face was a work of art. She wore a dark green skirt suit which matched her eyes. Eyes that revealed a depth of intelligence and a willingness to use it. Her long chestnut hair hung loosely around her shoulders, while her gold adornments provided evidence of her wealth and the measure of her success, along with an outward display of pretentiousness. She stood tall and walked with enviable confidence.

Dee did a double take before watching her intently.

'Your type,' whispered Sarah cheekily.

Dee broke her gaze and avoided eye contact. 'Only in appearance.'

Avery agreed Brooke was physically stunning, but also not his type. Brooke was fleet's most despised lawyer due to her uncanny ability to get criminals off on legal loopholes.

Daniel Sparta walked beside her. Dressed in an expensive navy suit with his good looks, Sparta himself cut a handsome figure. There was neither a smirk nor a shifty look upon his face. Instead, Sparta walled himself behind a deadpan expression that revealed nothing. An emotional state that had no doubt been practiced for years, until it was ingrained.

There was no jury and the bailiffs were appointed officers of the court who resided on Isla. They took up their positions around the courtroom.

The court clerk, stood beside the judge's bench and noisily cleared his throat. 'All rise. Court is now in session. In the matter of fleet versus Mr. Daniel Sparta, Justice Ninh presiding.'

Dressed in black judge's robes, Justice Ninh entered and took the high seat. Judges no longer wore ceremonial wigs, but her wild silver hair was an ample substitute. Having served twenty-five years in fleet as a lawyer, fifteen years as an impartial prosecutor and ten years as a judge, she was the most experienced in her profession. Coolly composed she took a moment to examine her notes on a holo-reader before moving her attention to the clerk. 'Please read the charges.'

'Teleporting to Ziana under a false identity, failure to respond to pursuing fleet officers during his arrest and possession of an electronic device installed with a mind control program.'

Ninh, stared unblinkingly at Daniel. 'Mr. Sparta, do you wish to enter into a plea?'

Sparta and Brooke both stood up. He replied, 'I do your honour. I plead not guilty.'

Of course, the little fucker did and it meant having found a loophole Brooke was about to work her magic again.

'Evidence,' asked Ninh.

Sarah stood and gave a lengthy spiel; which Avery thought could have been presented in half as many words.

'Please present the device to the court,' said Ninh.

Sarah swallowed. 'Unfortunately, fleet is no longer in possession of the device. It was given to Admiral Cadel for safe keeping. As you would be aware, he was recently murdered. The device was stolen during that altercation.'

Ninh shifted in her seat, her eyes darkening. She'd have a great deal to say after the hearing about the heist, but right now she was only interested in material evidence relevant to the hearing. 'What evidence of the device's existence can be presented?'

Sarah's face reddened. 'The evidence collected by fleet IT technicians has disappeared. It has been erased from hard drive storage.'

'So, you have no evidence to present to the court of the device's existence.'

'Only testimony, Your Honour.'

Ninh made another trademark gesture with her hand indicating for them to continue.

Avery stood up and explained the sensation of having a head full of bees followed by his experiences in the tech lab.

'Is there testimony from the techs?'

Sarah made a hologram appear. A lifelike image of Hugh appeared and for the next ten minutes, the tech explained the intricacies of the device's persuasive program. Then to Avery's shock, the footage switched to Hugh doing laps of his workbench. It was the very demonstration that convinced Avery of the device's authenticity.

As the hologram disappeared the court fell silent. Even Brooke seemed perturbed — an anomaly Avery thought he'd never live to see.

In time, Ninh gestured to Brooke to present her defence.

She took a moment to steady herself before standing up. 'Your Honour, as you would be aware, it is not illegal to have an alias per se.'

Avery conceded her point. That rule was in place to stop newlywed women, who'd assumed their husband's family name, from being arrested during the time it took to legally change her name. It was, however, illegal to assume identity under an alias if intent to commit a crime could be proven.

Brooke continued, 'I put forth the notion that my client fled Ria under an alias because he was afraid for his life. He had circumstantial evidence that a terrorist attack was going to occur and teleported to Ziana.'

Avery raised his hand indicating he wanted to interject and Ninh gave him the floor. 'If Mr. Sparta was fleeing as you suggest, why was it that he was able to bring two people with him, and why didn't he report this information to fleet upon arrival on Ziana?'

Brooke flashed him a look of daggers. 'My client did not wish to alarm his fellow travellers, and he did not wish to present hearsay evidence to fleet and be accused of wasting time.'

Ninh nodded slowly, evidently thinking there was some merit to Brooke's argument.

'In regards to the second charge. My client was not aware he was being pursued by fleet. He was racing to catch a train and thought the others, who identities he wasn't aware of at the time, were doing likewise.'

Dee waved her arm in the air and was given leave to ask a question. 'Mr. Sparta, why did you run out and leave your cabin door wide open and unlocked?'

'My client...'

'I was asking Mr. Sparta,' said Dee with steel in her voice.

Brooke gritted her teeth. At a hearing, the person the question was directed to, had to answer the answer. Under union law, the right to remain silent in court no longer applied.

Sparta returned his best surprised look. 'Did I leave my door open? I was in a terrible hurry.'

'Yes, I'm aware of that, I was one of your pursuers,' said Sarah. 'But let me ask you, after you ran smack bang into Lieutenant-Commander Vander, why did you attempt to run away?'

'At that point in time, I was still not aware that fleet was attempting to arrest me. No one said I was under arrest and I was still hoping to catch my train.'

It was true no one had said he was under arrest. An oversight they were now paying for.

'Where were you going in such a hurry Mr. Sparta?' asked Avery.

'Objection, that's not relevant to this hearing,' said Brooke.

'Sustained, replied Ninh. 'Mr Sparta's travel plans are his own business unless it can be proven relevant to this hearing. Can I confirm that no one told Mr Sparta that he was under arrest?'

'That's correct,' said Sarah. 'We were under orders from Admiral Cadel to bring him in quietly.'

A slight smirk crossed Brooke's face. Sarah had just buried the second charge.

'In regards to the third charge, no material evidence has been brought forward to prove the device's existence.' Brooke sat down.

Avery stood up. 'Mr. Sparta, do you deny you were in possession of a device with a mind control program on it?'

Sparta's face paled. He stood and said, 'I was in possession of a device, but I know nothing about a mind control program.'

Avery raised an eyebrow. That was a lie and contempt of court, but without the device they could prove nothing. 'One last question Mr. Sparta. Both Dr. Kaylor Emerson and I experience a sensation, which was later proven by techs to have been the result of the mind control program. My question is, what did you want with Kaylor and me?'

Sparta closed his eyes but remained silent even though he was compelled to answer the question.

Dee interjected. 'Mr. Sparta is exempt from answering that question because he been advised by an agent of the SIA because it is matter of union security.'

Avery balled his right hand into a fist. So, Dee had been holding out on him.

'If there are no further questions, court is adjourned for a short recess,' said Ninh.

Dee fled from the room. Avery didn't bother to pursue her; he just sat back down. Sarah went out and returned with two cups of coffee from the court's café. Glum-faced, she handed one to him and sat down without saying anything.

Ninh returned in fifteen minutes and court resumed.

'Having considered the evidence, I find insufficient grounds for the charges of teleporting to Ziana under false identity and failure to respond to pursuing fleet officers during arrest.'

Avery wasn't surprised and it was no great loss. Neither charge on their own was sufficient for a gaol sentence.

'I do, however, find sufficient ground for possession of an electronic device installed with a mind control program. Due to the serious nature of the crime, and the evidence presented of its potential applications, I am unwilling to proceed to a trial until such times as the device has been recovered. As a result of this, I am granting fleet fifteen standard months to recover the device and present it at an additional hearing.

'I am prepared to grant conditional bail on the condition that Mr. Sparta's tracking bracelet remain on his arm and he stays on Isla or resides in the region of Barsha on Ziana. Bail price is ten grams of gold. If he wishes to return to Ria, then bail is set at one kilogram of gold.'

Avery knew the difference in bail price was to pay for the cost of a teleport.

'Point of clarification Your Honour. Why is my client unable to pay in payment units?'

'Excellent question Ms. Madison. President Inglis has declared an act of war was committed. Should the confrontation escalate into an actual war, then there is a high probability that Ria's fiat currency will lose its value as a result of hyper-inflation.'

'Your Honour, that's grossly unfair. I've received notification that the Zianan government is no longer exchanging payment units for gold, silver or copper. With this in mind, how is my client supposed to obtain a kilogram of gold?'

Ninh's eyes flared. 'How your client acquires the bond is of no concern to this court. The orders are final.' She brought her gavel down with finality.

Brooke's face soured, but she decided against further outbursts least she be held in contempt of court.

Avery and Sarah returned to their apartment. Dee was gone, disappeared back into the shadows where the SIA lived. For the moment, Avery wasn't sorry to see the back of her. He knew she was only doing her job, but withholding from him didn't lessen his angst.

'Can I go on holidays now?'

Sarah pulled him into a hug. 'Yes but no more private investigations and you're to leave Sparta alone, that's an order. And you're forbidden from retiring, such a stupid concept to Zianans who live for hundreds of years, and no resigning. I need you to help me captain *The Zee* in due course.'

'I won't resign. Not until I have justice for Leda.'

Sarah held him tighter, but remained silent.

Chapter 34

Avery was locating his camping gear and making a pile on the floor outside his bedroom door. Yeltzie was putting together some food for him and in doing so was also adding to the pile.

'Where are you going and when will you be back?' she asked.

She wasn't being nosy; it was a matter of safety. If he failed to return at the appointed time she'd know where to send people to look for him. 'Catching the train to Harts Lake, walking up The Needle, across Navi Gorge swing bridge and back to here. Should be gone about ten days.'

Yeltzie flashed a smile. 'Nice. Should be lovely this time of the spin.' She dashed to the kitchen and returned with homemade fruit and nut bars wrapped in waxed cloth. 'When you get back the harvest will be in full swing so expect chaos.'

Harvest was the crazy season when every able body was needed to help gather and preserve food to sustain people through the long night. He'd arrive back to find people and tents everywhere, but it was only temporary. Harvest lasted about fourteen standard Earth days and ended with a feast and ball.

'By the way, Kaylor wants to talk to you privately before you go and she's a bit shy so be patient with her.'

What did she want that she was too shy to ask about?

Avery finished packing. The sun was now low in the sky but there wouldn't be any darkness on this expedition. He decided he could manage without a tent; he'd just take a bivouac. He considered his boots. Zianans traditionally went barefoot, which helped them to ground as well as feel the subtle changes of energy through their feet. Being fleet, he wore boots and had consequently become a bit soft-footed of late. Time to toughen up.

Dumping his pack on the veranda he headed for Kaylor, who was seated and reading a book. She glanced up and stiffened when she realised it was him. Damn what was this about? He casually took a seat beside her.

She took her time marking the page and putting it aside. 'I'm wondering if you know who Starliah is?'

'Do you mean the Starliah? Of course, every Zianan is taught about her as part of first contact history.'

She glanced away for a moment before beginning a discussion about her work of investigating the discordant sound frequencies affecting Ria. Avery waited patiently for a question to appear.

'We could really use Starliah about now.'

Avery closed his eyes seeking clarity. He'd always had difficulty with women who multi-tracked their topics of conversation. Starliah was no longer living so why make such a statement? 'There's no point dwelling on such things. We have to work with what we have. If you're worried about the coming fleet then that's understandable. Yeltizie can teach you how to sing. She's far better at it than me.'

'Yes of course, but what I mean is, did you ever want to have children?'

Avery blinked, thrown by yet another topic with no apparent connection. 'Once upon a time I think I did, but I put that behind me when I realised Leda couldn't have them. It was just the way it was. I mean we sort of had Yeltzie so it was fine really.'

'Sure, but I mean you are still young for a Zianan. Would you consider remarrying or just fathering a child?'

What the fuck? That was personal. Stay calm. 'I haven't thought about it. It only seems like yesterday that I lit the rocket under Leda's ashes. Why are you asking me this?'

Kaylor's face reddened and she picked up her book. 'This book talks about how and why Zianans have only one partner for life. It's incredible how deep love can be and it's so far removed from Rian culture.'

Keen to get going, Avery was losing patience.

Noting his response, she added, 'The book goes on to talk about how and why people make exceptions. Particularly young women whose partners died young and left them childless. I just …'

Having read the book, which she'd borrowed from his own library, he did not need to be told the gist of it. 'Yes, it's a fascinating read, but like all Zianan philosophy longwinded and dry. I believe there was something you wanted to ask me.'

Kaylor found a spot on the deck to look at.

Yeltzie, who'd been eavesdropping, bustled out the door and approached before stating in her customary no-nonsense way, 'This isn't going well.'

'Yes, Kaylor's concerns are alluding me,' replied Avery.

Yeltzie, who was constantly frustrated at Avery's inability to understand women, rolled her eyes. 'She wants to have a baby. You always wanted a child. She's asking you if you would consider fathering her child.'

Stunned, Avery's capacity to speak deserted him. His mouth opened and closed, but nothing comprehensible came out. His first thoughts were to say no, but feelings buried deep within stopped him from voicing this. He needed time to think it over, but there was also something else. 'What does this have to do with Starliah?'

'She needs to be reborn,' said Yeltzie matter-of-fact.

Avery waved his hand back and forth between Kaylor and himself. Surely, she wasn't implying.

'Yes,' said Yeltzie.

Avery cocked his head. 'Have you been smoking wacky weed again.'

Yeltzie's hands flew to her hips. 'No! Not since I was a teenager, and then it was only once.'

Despite the situation, Avery couldn't help but smile. He loved Yeltzie's wild forthrightness. To his knowledge, she'd never lied to him. Withheld, but never lied. 'Alright, no need to get uptight. Clearly, I've missed some vital detail.'

Yeltize relaxed her hands. 'Think detective. Roger Smith, I mean Daniel Sparta, he wanted something from Kaylor and you. He was desperate enough to bring her here via teleport so you were both in close proximity to each other.'

A chill ran down Avery's back. Why does Sparta want us to have a child?

'I know it sounds bizarre. I refuted the idea myself when I first heard it, but Renee was insistent that our child would bring back Starlia,' said Kaylor.

'Renee? As in the Chief Minister?'

'Yes, I work for Ethan, but I was briefing them both.' Kaylor swallowed.

'Briefing them on what?'

'My work. The discordant sound frequencies coming from Zeta Reticula.'

Avery sought to arrange the facts in his mind. There were plenty of dots but no clear links. 'What did that have to do with Sparta?'

'Renee wouldn't tell me directly, only cryptically. I asked for clarification, but she said it was classified.'

Something major was being withheld from him by the highest level of authority which included Dee. In his mind a dotted line connected to several dots as he theorised. Was Sparta's purpose to try and get the two of them to have a baby? Was he himself trying to bring back Starliah? It made no sense. He doubted Sparta would even know who Starliah was, but did Black and White?

Pain erupted in his shin because Yeltzie had kicked him.

'Well?'

One of them had asked him a question, but deep in thought, he'd missed it. It didn't matter, he now knew what Kaylor wanted. 'Look, it is not the best time to be having a baby.'

'Did you listen to a word that was said?' hissed Yeltzie. 'Starliah needs to be reborn. Ziana needs her. You need to consider our people. Our world.'

Avery's expression hardened. 'Even assuming conception readily occurs, babies take nine standard Earth months to gestate. If by some miracle it is Starliah, it will be years before she has the mind and voice to help us.'

'That's what I said to Renee,' replied Kaylor, 'but she dismissed that as trivial.'

'Which means Renee knows something we don't,' added Yeltzie. 'Has it occurred to you that you are both thinking too ...' she paused to consider the right word in English. 'Too rigidly. Reality can be shaped by the will of the observer and it's quite malleable.'

Avery considered this. He'd been taught to simply focus on what he wanted and not get caught up in the how. Just let forces external to him be ordered by his observer who could manifest in the quantum field beyond the control of the physical world. 'Yes, you're right Yeltzie.'

She flashed her cheeky smile. 'So that's a yes then.'

'That's, I'll think about it seriously and let Kaylor know when I get back from my trek.' He picked up his pack and put it on before giving Yeltzie a goodbye hug and cheek kiss. He turned to Kaylor, but she was hiding behind her book.

He was ten steps down the drive when he realised the women had been playing nice girl, bad arse bitch. Yeltizie wanted a baby that wasn't her own to dote on. Kaylor was being coerced, but despite this, she really did want to have a baby. It didn't matter whether it was Starliah. The notion of her needing to be reborn was just a selling point.

He sighed. He liked Kaylor, but he was still mourning Leda and would be until he let her go. In time, he could consider courting Kaylor. The problem was there just wasn't time. Such a Rian thing, because Zianans always had time. They lived for hundreds of years.

*****

Sarah starred incredulously out of the windows of the bridge of *The Zee,* which was in orbit of Ziana. Four huge cargo freighters were headed back towards them still fully loaded. She knew this because Acting Commodore Loody, had cleared them to depart for Ria three days ago.

Despite all that had happened — the lies, the accusations, and deceit — Chief Minister Hardy still refused to impose trade sanctions on Ria. Her reasoning was simple. More than half the food consumed on Ria was imported from Ziana. If the supply ships stop arriving, the populace would suffer a famine. Hardy refused to be held responsible for creating such suffering simply because a dictator was in power.

Sarah pointed at the cargo ship and directed a question to Ralph, her communications officer. 'Why are they back?'

His own bewildered stare told her he knew no more than she did. Shaking his head to cast of the daze he opened a line of communication with the biggest of the freighters.

The captain appeared on a holoscreen and acknowledged Sarah. 'The quick answer is pirates have set up a blockade. They are refusing to let us pass unless we agree to pay an extortionist toll. When I refused, they attempted to board. We were able to prevent that from occurring, but there's no way we are getting through.'

Sarah gritted her teeth. Without fleet's protection, there was nothing to stop the merchant fleet from being attacked and pillaged. Admiral Peterson must have recalled the patrol ships that were scattered across space from Ziana to Ria. It was madness, but Sarah knew that somehow Inglis and Peterson would find a way to blame this on Hardy and Ziana more generally.

Ideally, *The Zee* should fly out and deal with the pirates, but if she did that, then Ziana would be left open to attack. In effect, Hardy had play right into the pirate's hands.

The merchant ships could also not fly around the blockade. Freighters were slow and highly visible to radar. They were not built to move incognito and pirates would be able to find and track them where ever they went. They'd also be able to out run them.

'Understood. You will have to park in orbit while we try to find a solution.' There wasn't one. Sarah knew the ships would be parked until the conflict was resolved.

The captain growled something incomprehensible before the holoscreen flickered off.

Ralph caught her attention. 'Sorry to add to the woes, Commander, but Inglis has recorded an interview on RBC. You might want to view it.'

Yes, she might as well get an update on the fake narrative.

A holovision came on and Sarah sat down in the captain's chair to watch it. An image of Inglis appeared seated in a studio. He was dressed in a suit, but had lost his tie and his top buttons were undone. An attempt to look more casual in order to connect with the common populace. He was accompanied by RBC reporter Mandy Rayella, who'd become a familiar face and household name since the crisis had begun. Sarah had little doubt she was on Inglis's payroll.

'Welcome Commander and Chief, I'm so glad you could take this time out of your busy schedule for this interview.'

Inglis returned a charming smile. 'My pleasure Mandy.'

'We'll jump straight to it. It's my understanding that not only did Zianan terrorists bomb dome six, but their actions were sanctioned by Ziana's Chief Minister, Renee Hardy.'

'That's correct. While those directly responsible for the bombing have been caught, they themselves are only a small part of the terrorist problem. The Zianan government, not just the Chief Minister, but the entire cabinet, must be held to account.'

'Correct me if I'm wrong, but to date, there's been no response from the Chief Minister or her government.'

'That's also correct. I assure you that I personally, along with all of my communication staff, have worked tirelessly to negotiate with any and all representatives of Ziana to find a peaceful resolution to this conflict. Regrettably, it has fallen on deaf ears and I have had no choice but to respond.'

'You have been working with Admiral Peterson since the beginning and fleet have responded by sending police ships to Ziana. Tell us, what is the best we can expect from this show of police force?'

'Great question Mandy. The best we can expect is that all those responsible for these horrendous acts of terror not only resign but hand themselves over to the judicial system for trial.'

'And the likelihood of that happening?'

'One can always pray and hope, but let me say this. Not only have those responsible refused to negotiate, but I have just learned that they have imposed trade restrictions on Ria.'

Despite her heavily caked on makeup, Mandy paled. 'Can you be more specific about those restrictions?'

Inglis turned serious and now stared directly at the camera that zeroed in on his face. 'All imports from Ziana, including food and much needed bottled oxygen have been suspended. Effective immediately, the Rian government will have no choice but to impose food and air rationing. This means not only will people have limited amounts to eat, but they will not be able to exercise or otherwise exert themselves.'

Ria could generate oxygen from the underground water it pumped to the surface and extract nitrogen from the atmosphere and together the gasses would make air. However, having lost all the air from dome six, it would take considerable time to replace what was lost. In the meantime, refugees from dome six, who were consuming air, were placing a strain on the life support systems.

Anger flashed in Mandy's eyes. She didn't maintain her athletic figure by skipping gym. 'Can I have your assurance that that responsible will be brought to justice?'

Inglis relaxed his posture and now looked at Mandy again as if she were his bestie. 'Most certainly and I want to add that while there will be hardships in the days to come, there is light at the end of the tunnel. Once the Zianan government has been removed from power fleet will supervise the implementation of an interim government. I'm confident that will open up all manner of changes for the better.'

'Can you outline your hopes for the future?'

'Yes of course. What you have to understand Mandy, is that Zianans have lived under religious oppression for eons. The result has been severe poverty because there is no economic system to speak of on Ziana. The denizens basically live as peasants who are expected to farm the land without modern farming practices and without expectations of fair pay. Heck, they can't even afford shoes.

'The new government will be liberators in every sense of the word. People will be given access to technology. Decent towns and cities will be built so people don't have to live in the forest like savages. Furthermore, we will also offer real employment opportunities by allowing companies to invest in industries such as logging, mining, and fishing.

'I mean can you believe Ziana's rivers and streams are full of gold and gems, yet the people are not allowed to extract this wealth. It's because the current regime is desperate to keep everyone in abject poverty as a means of enslavement. It is just wrong, and I will personally see an end to it.'

'Sounds wonderful. Unfortunately, we are out of time, but thank you once again for joining me Commander in Chief.'

'My pleasure Mandy.'

The holoscreen winked out and the bridge remained silent. There was nothing to be said but the agenda was clear.

Inglis wanted control of Ziana's natural resources and he was prepared to use force to remove the current administration and replace them with puppets. Such actions had been common practice on Earth prior to the formation of the one world government. The military had been used to ensure a coup and then the puppet government would go after the natural resources such as old growth forests, minerals and oil. It was exactly what the Captain Sorensen had wanted when his colonising ship had first arrived.

Everything suddenly fell into place for Sarah and she now had no doubts which side she was on, even though that made her a traitor to Ria.

*****

Lake Hart was truly beautiful. Blue-green water that stretched to the horizon. Avery emerged from the underground train platform to see it in all its magnificence. Caught in a wave of nostalgia, Avery sat on a bench seat that had been carved from a fallen tree.

A few kilometres around the lakeshore a village of master boat builders lived. They carved from timber splendid yachts with hemp sails that that could be purchased or hired. Avery and Leda had hired one and spent their honeymoon here.

Hugging the shore, they'd sailed until Leda cried out, 'shore leave!' Then they'd anchor, climb into a little coracle and rowed ashore. Whereupon Leda had marched them into the forest in search of plants that captured her fascination. They'd return with holoimages and a basket of plant matter that Leda insisted was edible.

It was just as well that Avery was in love because there was a chasm between edible and palatable. Thankfully, he insisted they balance their diet with fish, which included giant lobster, salmon and shellfish, fresh caught and smoked the traditional Zianan way.

It was a wonderful time, but it turned truly magical during an eclipse. As darkness fell, the Nessies appeared. Gentle when left to make contact on their own terms, several had swum up to the yacht and stuck their heads over the side. Bribing them with fish heads, they'd both managed to get a brief head pat before the Nessies went on their way.

Tears leaked from Avery's eyes as he made his way up the steep track dubbed the staircase, which led to the top of The Needle. Because of work, they'd spent too many years apart. Avery in fleet amid the stars hunting down criminals; Leda as a botanist tramping through Ziana's forests chasing plants so she could study and document them in English.In the last ten years, they'd spent less than a third of that time together.

It had never crossed Avery's mind that Leda would suddenly die. If it had, he'd have resigned from fleet and joined her expeditions to be with her like a husband should. Why had he never considered it?

The track became even stepper and now Avery was obliged to use his hands as much as his feet. Climbing hills or mountains in Zianan culture was a symbolic way of overcoming unresolved emotions. Every step upwards brought you to the pinnacle. When Avery's muscle screamed at him to stop and he thought he couldn't go on, he sighted the end. A tall lean spire of rock that stood like an ancient and natural tower of power.

Avery dug deep and used all of his will, refusing to quit until his hand touched The Needle. Afterward, he lowered himself to the ground and sat with his back resting against it and just admired the view. The Zianan wilds that were capable of sustaining life, including people, forever. Why anyone would want to rip it apart for its natural resources was beyond him.

The forest would give you everything. Trees could be harvested sustainably. Chop one down and four more would fight to replace it. Minerals could be extracted without open pit mines. When he first got engaged Avery had trekked along a river stopping in a shallow bend to pan for gold to use to make their wedding rings. On Ziana, it was a tradition that only virgin gold could be used to make rings and if the groom was worthy, he'd be blessed with a find. Such was his focus that Avery not only found sufficient gold but also a beautiful pink diamond.

Leda had squealed and jumped up and down like a child when he'd showed her. When she calmed down, she asked why he hadn't kept panning. There'd been no need. Panning for gold wasn't about extracting wealth for neither of them were going to give up their life's work — their purpose in life. Unlike Ria and Earth, on Ziana, no one worked in a job they disliked. People worked for knowledge and fulfilment which led to awareness.

Thousands had tried to come from Ria and Earth to mine the gold and gems but Ziana didn't allow it. At least not en mass. Tourist were allowed to keep a small nugget or a gemstone they might find while holidaying, but no more. Of course, it created resentment, but humans had to learn the true value of nature and until they did, they'd forever be destructive.

Having munched down a hunk of Yeltzie's honey, fruit and nutmeal loaf, washed down with a flask of chai tea, Avery felt replete and ready to go again. Half a kilometre on was the rope bridge that spanned Navi Gorge. The crossing wasn't for the faint-hearted. Ten metres across, but twelve-hundred metres straight down.

The bridge was thousands of years old, but well-maintained the thick hemp ropes frequently replaced. It was only in recent times that a safety line had been strewn above which, lanyards, attached to harnesses, could be clipped onto. Sure-footed Zianans, unafraid of death, never used it and Avery had never heard of anyone dying. The safety line was for tourists.

Avery stood staring at it. Both Leda and he had crossed dozens of times never bothering to wriggle into a harness and clip on. On that fateful day, his intuition had clicked in and he'd insisted Leda wear a harness. She'd argued, but he'd stood firm, and in the end, she'd humoured him.

Distracted by a plant growing from the sheer rock face, Leda had reached for her binoculars. Her heavy pack had shifted on her back causing her to stumble, slip and then fall. Without the harness, she'd have kept falling dying when her body impacted the ground.

She'd dangled like a spider more frustrated than frightened because she couldn't get herself back onto the bridge. Not with the weight of her pack holding her down. All the while, she'd screamed at him to help her. He'd taken his time putting on a harness, whilst asking her repeatedly to marry him.

At the time, Avery had thought it was a divine sign. She was meant to live in order to become his wife. Now he wasn't so sure.

In all the times he'd crossed he'd never seen any plant growing on the cliff. They weren't there today. Was their appearance meant to distract Leda and cause her to fall? Was she meant to die that day? If she had, would Avery have met Kaylor earlier, got married and had Starliah?

Such painful speculation would never give him answers. All he knew was that if he had the time to do over again, he'd make the same choices. Such was his love for Leda.

Still, Avery knew he had to make a choice, right here in the place where his marriage had officially begun. Would he stay loyal to Leda for life and forever be a widower or would he love again?

He needed a sign. Something that would unequivocally tell him that it was okay to love again. Standing at the centre of the rope bridge he closed his eyes and waited. There was nothing. Not a gust of wind on his face or even the cry of a bird.

He snorted. What had he expected? An apparition to appear and mollycoddle him. His eyes flew open, widened and then widened some more. From a tiny crack in the stone wall, three leaves from a plant were gently swaying in the breeze.

He looked away, but when he looked back the plant was still there. How he hadn't seen it before he didn't know. A lump formed in his throat and he made his choice.

Slowly he wriggled his wedding ring from his finger, held it one last time before letting it fall. The gold returned to the river from whence it had come. Not in its original form, but given back just the same. From his pocket, he also removed a small pouch that contained Leda's engagement and wedding rings. He watched them fall.

Now all that remained were his memories and they could never be taken from him.

A torrent of tears fell and Avery let them. On cue, a gentle rain began to fall. Not cold but refreshing. Avery raised his head and let the falling water wash away his grief. He would never stop seeking justice, but at least now he was free to love again if he chose to.

Chapter 35

Amid the food forests hundreds, of Zianans were busy harvesting. Not just fruit and nuts from the trees, but all manner of foods. The produce would be snap frozen, dried or bottled. Fowl, who wouldn't survive the long night in such numbers, were being slaughtered. Their flesh, along with that of fish, was being persevered through freezing, smoking or salting. Even certain types of bark were being stripped from trees to be used to make rope, while reeds were being cut and made into mats and baskets.

Children, whose parents were distracted by their work, ran riot climbing trees. Some would get hurt. They'd be patched up, dusted off and told to go and play again. Zianans called it tough love, but really it was just letting the little ones learn through experience.

Avery made his way through tent city, past the queue for the composting toilets and the other one for the makeshift showers. Young mothers with babies too small to be left to fend for themselves sat around methine fuel stoves nursing caldrons in which bubbled thick soups and stews prepared to feed the hungry workers.

The food Yeltzie had given him had run out six days in and for the last four days Avery had lived by foraging. He hadn't starved, but his belly now rumbled. He exchanged a copper coin for a wooden cup full of soup which he drank as he walked the last bit to his home.

Having dumped his pack on the veranda he headed in to find Yeltzie busy as always in the kitchen. Every single oven and hotplate were being utilized, yet Yeltzie, a skilled multitasker, was fully in control. She acknowledged him with a flash of teeth and Avery slipped away for a shower.

When he returned dressed in clean clothes she moved in for a quick hug, her hawk-like eyes noticing the absence of his wedding ring.

'You made the right choice,' she said.

'I still haven't decided yet.'

She winked at him. 'If you say so.'

Avery opened the fridge to grab a cold beer and ran smack into Sarah.

'What are you doing here?'

'Nice to see you too,' she replied. 'What haven't you decided?'

Avery busied himself removing the top of his beer bottle. 'It's a personal matter.'

Sarah, who hated to be out of the loop on any sort of news or gossip, deliberately stepped in his way. 'Of course, but you'd tell your best friend wouldn't you, because she wouldn't want to hear it from a third party.'

Handing her the beer that he'd just opened he grabbed a second one for himself before leading her to the small study that adjoined his bedroom. Seated he filled her in on Kaylor's offer to have his child but withheld the bit about Starliah.

Being a psychiatrist Sarah had the ability to sit and listen attentively without interruption. Today, however, she seemed anxious and her leg jiggled.

He ended by saying, 'What do think?'

Sarah sat back as if to consider the question seriously. 'Let me put this to you another way. When a woman offers to be the father of your child that's a big deal to her.' She took a swig of her beer. 'I'm mean I'm not talking about getting pregnant by accident or getting pregnant through a sense of marital obligation. I'm talking about a genuine offer.'

Avery nodded thoughtfully.

'I'm serious. Kaylor could choose another man, so choosing you, that's not something she made a decision on lightly.'

'I'm of the understanding that someone told her to choose me.'

Sarah shook her head. 'Might be so, but if Kaylor didn't think you could give her quality sperm, she wouldn't even give you a second glance.'

Avery sighed.

'Look there's something you're not telling me. Something that's got Yeltzie riled up.'

'She hasn't told you?'

'No.'

Avery told Sarah about Starliah.

Sarah squinted at him. 'What's the discussion Avery?'

Avery frowned. Her reaction was unexpected.

'This is Ziana where spirituality and science meet and become one. A world where ESP isn't just theorised by kooks, but openly practiced with startling accuracy. I'm sorry but there is no discussion. The fate of this world could rest upon you and you're hesitating. Don't be so fucking selfish!'

'But...'

'No. No buts. If the child isn't Starliah it will still be raised in love. Hell, if Kaylor's disappointed and decides to give it up for adoption, I'll take it and raise it as my own. I'll give you that in writing if you want.'

Avery sat there stunned. 'Okay fine that's sorted.'

'It, fucking better be!'

Avery gently leaned forward. 'Sarah, are you okay?'

'I'm fine.'

Fine, a word that was used when the exact opposite was meant. 'So, nothing you want to talk about?'

She looked away and then looked back at him. 'It's Mike.'

Oh, right. With his own woes, Avery had neglected to ask after Sarah's husband who'd almost died during the false flag operation.

'At first, I thought that communications were down and that was why he wasn't getting back to me. Yesterday, I finally received an abusive email. According to him, I'm a treasons traitor and a slut to boot, and our marriage of twenty years is done.' Sarah wiped her eyes with the palm of her hands and sniffed. 'But that's not the worst of it. Six months ago, I'd made a decision that I was going to take maternity leave and have a baby. Now I'm forty and told my marriage is done and I'll likely never have children.' She cried into her palms.

Avery wheeled his office chair closer and gently rubbed her back.

'Loody suspended me. Told me I wasn't fit for duty. That's why I'm here.'

Avery knew Loody. He would have suggested a few days off. Sarah would have refused, so he'd have made it an order. It wasn't serious, just a few days off, go and talk to Avery, have a good cry and get it together. No big deal. Fleet troops might be hardened, but they were still human.

'I'm so sorry Sarah. I feel like a complete arsehole now.'

She pressed her head against his chest. 'I'm fine. Really, I am.'

'You will be. We'll stay here until the harvest is done, which should only be a few more days and then we'll attend the ball and feast. Afterward, we'll both go back up to *The Zee* together.'

'After you've made a baby with Kaylor.'

'Sure, since you put it that way. I mean there's nothing to it really. We'll just rent a hotel room, grab some room service and have a dirty night together. By dirty, I mean absolutely filthy. I mean it's only the fate of the world at stake if she fails to conceive or if she births the wrong child. What could possibly be stressful about that?'

She smacked him playfully and started giggling. 'Stop being such a drama king.'

He mocked a salute. 'Yes Ma'am.'

She smacked him again. 'Do you have any more beer?'

'Are you kidding? It's harvest time. There'll be barrels of the stuff lying around. Come on, let's go and pilfer some and get inebriated.'

*****

For the next three days, Avery and Sarah helped out with the harvest. Being fleet officers, they were assigned co-ordination roles responsible for organising teams and making sure tasks were complete.

'Is it just me, or are the harvesters bringing in more this year than in previous years?' asked Sarah who was sprawled out in an armchair after a sixteen-hour shift. 'Normally they only bring in the best of the crops.'

'No, you're right, they're bringing in as much as they can.'

'Why?' asked Sarah.

'Well, the entire population of fleet is headed this way. When the ships arrive, their larders will be empty and Ziana will need food to offer them.'

Sarah sat bolt upright. 'You mean to say, even though they come to rape and pillage, Ziana is going to offer them food.'

'Yes, and water and oxygen.'

'Why?' she repeated.

'Because regardless of their intentions, they are still our brothers and sisters and Zianans don't understand any other way except to love unconditionally.'

Sarah sighed. 'I don't get it, but at least I know I picked the right side.'

'That's where you are wrong,' said Yeltzie who'd wandered in from the kitchen. 'We don't see things in terms of opposites, so there are no sides.'

'And so those ships that are coming?' asked Sarah.

'It's just a misunderstanding. We'll clear that up when they get here, we'll have the biggest feast ever held in living memory. Speaking of which, the harvest feast and ball begins in twelve standard hours, so you two should go and get some rest.'

Good advice. When this was over, Avery would need a holiday from his holiday.

*****

'Wow! You look absolutely stunning,' Avery proclaimed, 'silver really is your colour.'

Kaylor blushed and smoothed her silk ball gown. 'Well thank you.'

She wasn't just rosy, since arriving on Ziana, Kaylor had lost considerable weight and had a smile permanently etched on her face.

Avery adjusted the cloth waist belt on his traditional Zianan robe, which according to Earth historians bore similarities to druid robes. They came in all different colours, but Avery's was dark green.

'Thank you so much for your offer to accompany me to the ball. I'm learning as fast as I can, but I still don't quite understand every facet of Zianan culture.'

'My pleasure.' Avery had agreed to father her baby, but now Kaylor was having doubts. She said she needed time to think it over. Still, that didn't mean they couldn't go to the ball together.

Sarah emerged dressed in a blue silk gown, smiled and then winked at Kaylor. 'So, you want the left or the right arm?'

Kaylor's eyes sparkled and she stepped closer, 'The right.'

Sarah positioned himself on his left.

Avery looked around, but couldn't see her. 'Where's Yeltzie?'

'Left with her boyfriend a good while back,' said Sarah.

'Boyfriend? She kept that quiet.'

'Nope, it's been out in the open for several days now, you've just been preoccupied.'

He sighed. He got that Yeltzie didn't need his permission to court, but it irked him that her potential lover hadn't been introduced, but maybe it wasn't serious. With a gorgeous woman on each arm, Avery made for the door.

The festivities weren't a single event, but a series of parties spread out along the edge of the food forests. The Chief Minister, as was expected of her, always held her party in Port Town's town hall. Quentin, the taxi driver, gave them a lift in, before hurrying off to collect someone else.

The sun had begun the long sunset painting the sky shades or orange and crimson. The town hall was decorated in twinkling fairy lights, while its courtyard was full of revellers enjoying food and drink amid fire fuelled cookers.

Marching up the road side by side, accompanied by members of their families, was Renee Hardy, the Chief Minister, and Venetia Erikson, the suspended base commodore. People cheered and raised their glasses in a show of support. With heads held high they continued up the steps and into the hall. The actions spoke volumes about their resilience, while the reaction of the crowd demonstrated they were still loved and supported despite the fraudulent accusations that no one had bought into.

Kaylor and Sarah resumed their hold on him and he proceeded up the stairs. Security asked to see their invitations, but relaxed when Kaylor handed over three VIP passes. Normally, attendance inside the town hall cost a gold sovereign, which was collected to offset the costs associated with the Zianan government. Expensive, but the price did include unlimited food and drink. Inside, Renee caught his eye and beckoned him over.

Avery bobbed his head to Renee, but both him and Sarah made a point of snapping a salute to Venetia.

'At ease,' she whispered, but her eyes were brimming with tears which caused her to look away. Venetia had been the base commander for twenty years and her service record was impeccable. Rumour had it, that if she didn't keep banging her head against the glass ceiling, her lapels would be decorated with more than just one star.

'Would you do me the honour of sitting at my table?' asked Renee.

Avery wasn't stupid, Renee would have an agenda, but it was still an honour. 'Are the seats not already taken by your family?'

Renee waved his query away. 'They can sit elsewhere. In any case, they're all outside.'

'In that case, we'd be delighted Ma'am,' replied Avery.

'We're honoured by your display of loyalty and support, but for this evening please dispense with the formalities,' said Renee.

Avery pulled out a chair and sat down; Kaylor and Sarah sat nervously on either side of him.

Renee poured herself a drink from a bottle of red liquid before offering it around.

Avery refused and reached for a bottle of beer, which he poured into a glass. As he did so he leaned closer to Kaylor's ear. 'Be careful with the liqueurs, they're akin to rocket fuel.'

She acknowledged him with a knowing look.

'So nice of you to help with the harvest Sarah,' said Renee.

Sarah's face reddened and she replied by saying, 'I intend to return to *The Zee* tomorrow.'

Renee fixed her with a look. 'You misunderstood. I made no accusation. What I mean is, you made an effort to understand our ways and for that I am truly grateful.'

Sarah shifted to a more relaxed posture. 'I try to. I love this planet even though it is still an enigma to me.'

'It's an enigma to everyone, even Zianans as old as me, but it's meant to be. We are supposed to search for deeper meaning within ourselves and Ziana is meant to foster a safe environment for people to do that.'

'Yes, I see that.'

Renee softened her gaze. 'You do a little bit, but what I'm saying is your efforts help bridge cultural differences and in doing so foster peace.' She sipped her drink. 'There are many races of people throughout the galaxy, but we are all made from the same essence. Our differences are trivial because we are not really separate on a spiritual level.'

Sarah returned a blank stare.

Renee smiled. 'When coming events are over and peace is restored, if you want to stay here, you need only ask me and I'll grant you citizenship. I've already granted yours, Kaylor.'

Both Kaylor and Sarah were spared having to reply by loud applause. Four chefs had appeared carrying a roasted *ulso* on a litter. They sat the enormous bird down on a table and paused to offer half bows. One of them then produced a wicked looking fork and a long razor sharp knife and proceeded to carve.

'Time to feast,' said Renee smiling.

'That was a bit deep wasn't it,' whispered Sarah when they had gotten up to get food and were out of earshot.

'Not really, you're just shallow,' replied Avery.

She smacked him playfully. 'Her offer is a golden boon, because I always thought she didn't like me.'

'She doesn't like you, but you're one of Ziana's great defenders. Trust me, every one of fleet who fights for Ziana will be made the same offer.'

Sarah pretended to be miffed and wandered off to seek food from one of the other tables. In typical Sarah fashion, she bypassed the mains and started on desserts.

'You two are so cute,' said Kaylor. 'How long have you known each other?'

'Since cadet school when we were fifteen — twenty-five years.'

'No romance?'

'No. It was never that kind of love. More of a bond of mateship. I mean don't get me wrong, we've got each other's back and damn we've been through some shit together, but no, we're not lovers.'

'That's what I thought.'

'Sarah's always been my anchor to my Rian heritage. She loves Ziana but rather than trying to understand too deeply, she just rolls with it. Leda, my late-wife, she got it. That is, that science and spirituality are one and the same. She was invited into the fold and studied under all manner of Zianan teachers. That's when she fell in love with the forest. She'd have married it if I hadn't have got in first.'

Kaylor, rather than going for the roast *ulso* and baked vegetables, helped herself to a bit of smoked fish along with an egg and lettuce salad.

'So, what's your story?'

'Me, hmm. I was a hard-core scientist who believed in only the physical world. I mean I hated Ziana and its queerness. Loved AI technology so much that I became dependant on in it. I hated my appearance and believed I was unlovable, so I walled myself in my lab and shut out the world with sound.'

'Far out. What happened?'

'I had a bad day, which ended up being the best day of my life.'

'How so?'

'I got fired, my AI, who was really my pretend friend, got taken away from me and I was killed trying to get back to my apartment.'

'How was that good?'

'I had an NDE where I met your mother Moir. She sent me back and told me I had an important job to do.'

Avery blinked and tried to cut in, but Kaylor was in full flight.

'I met Yeltzie and Sparta offered me a job here. The rest has been like a dream I can't wake from which doesn't matter because I don't want to.'

Avery stopped placing things on his plate. 'Back up to the bit where you met Moir.'

Sarah came bustling over. 'Oh my god, you have to try the fruit thing with the chocolate sauce and honey syrup.'

'Lovely, why don't you run along and get yourself seconds.'

'Oh, right, sorry.' She scuttled away.

Kaylor whispered remind me later and they sat back down and ate.

'You alright Venetia?' asked Avery when he'd finished eating.

'I'm fine.'

Avery rolled his eyes. 'Are little girls taken aside and taught that word.'

She rounded on him. 'I just feel like I let everyone down. Now I'm on the sidelines while a small crew of heroes is gearing up for the fight of a lifetime. It's bad enough being on the edge of a battle we can't win, but to be told you're not allowed to even fight. You don't know what that feels like.'

Avery reached a hand across to her.

'I'm sorry, I shouldn't have said that,' Venita replied.

'You definitely needed to say that,' said Renee, offering her some tissues, 'but I wouldn't worry. When the time comes, we'll slip these bracelets off and stand side by side. That's a promise. And don't worry, we will win this fight and Ria will be sorry it ever picked it.'

Venita dabbed her eyes.

Renee concentrated for a moment and Avery knew she was communicating telepathically with someone. On cue, the music changed to a faster rhythm.

'Venetia, you really should have a dance with Avery before he's swamped with offers.'

Avery glanced at Kaylor but she was clearly in agreement with Renee. He led Venita onto the dance floor for the first dance.

Chapter 36

Kaylor could never remember having fun at a social gathering before. She'd always been the shy girl who did everything to avoid being noticed. During her university days, she'd learned to network, but that wasn't fun it was work.

Tonight, however, for the first time ever, she felt a genuine sense of joy. That was when she was tapped on the shoulder by a young Zianan man.

'No, I don't dance.'

He stood firm, 'Tradition.'

Kaylor found herself standing up. 'I've got no rhythm.'

'You're frightened that people will laugh at you, but no one is watching. It's just you and me. There's not another soul here.'

She wished that were true. Kaylor tried to step, but it felt like her feet were wearing lead shoes.

'Cast them off and break free.'

Damn it, why not. What did she care if she was laughed at? She stepped and kept stepping and a burden fell away from her that she'd carried for a long time. She didn't have to be the tough girl who just kept her head down so she could make it. On this world, happiness and spiritual growth meant more than work performance and management approval. More than the opinions of her neighbours who feared being cast from the herd. Now she was free to be whoever she wanted to be. Free to dance. Not just physically, but also emotionally and spiritually.

Then she was dancing with someone else and then someone else and finally, she was in Avery's arms, her head resting on his shoulder.

'Sorry, I didn't mean to abandon you. I just needed to help Venita lay aside her woes.'

'I understand, I really do. That's what friends are for.'

The music stopped and they sat down for a rest.

Sarah had her eyes fixed on a young Islatation woman. 'She's a swindler.'

'Goes by the name of Claire,' said Avery. 'She works the room doing party tricks whilst placing bets. Swindles enough copper and silver to feed her family for a year.'

'I think I might have a word with her,' said Sarah fumbling in her clutch bag for her badge.

'Let her be,' said Renee sternly.

'Why?' asked Sarah.

'I invited her here for a purpose.'

By invited, Renee meant Claire had been given a free VIP pass.

'What purpose?'

'Just watch, you'll see.'

Sarah wrinkled her nose but stopped searching for her badge.

'Evening Claire,' said Avery when she went to stroll casually past whilst avoiding eye contact.

She froze as if caught in the act of mischief, but then seemed to recover. 'Lieutenant-Commander Vander.'

'We're not doing the formal thing tonight, Claire, so you can call me Avery.'

Her eyes moved cautiously as she took in the table. She knew who was who.

'Rumour has it you can lindy,' said Renee casually.

'Used to, but no one can keep up with me.'

'Really,' Renee magicked a gold sovereign, held it in her fingers and let Claire get a real good look at it. 'I bet you this coin that you can't keep up with Avery.'

Claire hesitated. If she lost, it would cost her everything she'd won tonight. If she won, the gold would be more money than she'd ever had in her life at one time.

'What if we're equals?'

'Then it's a draw. No winners or losers.'

Claire swallowed. Took another look at the coin and nodded.

Avery stood and slipped off his robe so he was dressed in black trousers and a white shirt. Knowing no one would steal it, Claire sat her handbag on the table and slipped off her high heel shoes.

Sarah scrambled to her feet. 'Come on! We need to get a good spot. This will be classic.'

The music changed because Renee asked it to. No one else got up to dance, it was just Claire and Avery. They worked the floor as if it was an exhibition. Avery didn't just flip Claire over; they tumbled and twisted as if they were playing a game of leapfrog. It wasn't just two dancers practicing choreographed moves; they were improvising. Pushing and probing to test each other's mettle.

It became something even deeper. A trust had formed and they saw each other as something more than people. They were now spiritual beings in physical form with the highest respect for each other.

Mutual respect. That was what the Zianans called it. A bond so strong that a merging of their energy field had begun to occur. They danced as one not because they knew each other's moves, but because they could intuit them. In sporting terms, they were completely in the zone.

Singularity. Two minds functioning as one connected to the ultimate power of the universe called the Mind of God. And now they were beyond the physical dancing in no time.

A single tear, leaked from each of Kaylor's eyes. This was the man who'd father their child. What genetics would he provide? Way beyond the norm that was for sure. That was why Starliah had chosen him. Until this moment she hadn't been sure he was the right choice. His hesitancy had led her to question. Now all doubt faded from her mind.

The music stopped suddenly and Claire ended with the splits. The room exploded in cheers and wolf-whistles. Avery helped

Claire up and they bowed before embracing each other. Two people who couldn't be more different if they tried, yet they'd found a common denominator.

Kaylor felt a hand on her shoulder and looked up to see a concerned Sarah.

'You okay?'

She sniffed and wiped her cheeks with the back of her palms. 'I'm so ashamed. I thought she was just a thief and I judged her harshly. Now I see the light in her; in both of them. I've never seen anything so beautiful.'

Renee now stood beside her. 'I sense you no longer doubt. Good, when the moment comes, don't hold back. Accept it all.'

Kaylor blinked unsure what Renee meant, but the Chief Minister's attention had turned to Claire.

Renee handed Claire her handbag and shoes along with the gold coin. 'Enough games for tonight, agreed?'

'Yes.'

'Good. Now go and enjoy the party.' Renee slipped away; her work done for the night.

*****

Avery sidled up to Kaylor. 'So sorry, I feel as if I have been coerced into doing everyone else's bidding tonight and that I've neglected you.'

'I couldn't agree more. I suggest you pay a girl a bit more attention before she loses interest.'

Avery gestured towards the buffet. 'Can I get you anything?'

'Nope. I've had too much food and way too much drink already.'

'A dance then.'

'Absolutely, but I'm thinking of a very different style to what you were just doing. No less vigorous mind you.'

Avery found himself bustled out the door and along the street. It wasn't until they'd stepped into the atrium of Port Town's hotel, did he realise what she'd meant. Apparently, she'd changed her mind but women did that, often spontaneously. He might have slipped an arm around her shoulder or waist, but she had hold of his hand with no intent to let it go.

The room she'd rented was on the top floor. They'd no sooner stepped through the door when Kaylor shoved him against the wall and began to kiss him manically.

'Calm down,' he whispered as he kissed her neck.

She backed off a little. 'Sorry, it's just been a while is all.' She kissed him again and fumbled with the button of his shirt.

Avery pushed her towards the huge bed. They toppled in a tangle of silk and Avery landed on top of her. She winced in pain and he recoiled.

'It okay, it wasn't your fault. It's just this stupid bolt wound. It won't heal.'

Avery pulled her back onto her feet and slipped the thin straps off her shoulders. The dress fell away and gathered at her feet. Avery squatted down to inspect the wound. It looked nasty. A crater of unhealed tissue that threatened to infect.

'That needs Zianan healing.'

'What now!'

'No, we're a bit busy at present.' He turned her attention to her breasts. His tongue gentler than his fingers he used it to good effect and she moaned.

Her hands returned to the buttons of his shirt and this time she managed to get them undone. Now her mouth took an interest in his chest. Being able to multitask she removed his trousers at the same time followed by his underwear.

Having removed her own underwear, she lay back on the bed in an expectant position. Avery kissed his way down her bare legs.

'I'm ready, we can dance now,' she said.

'With all due respect, you're far from ready my dear.'

She moaned as his tongue licked a sensitive spot between her legs. 'You, see many Zianan women spent years trying to get pregnant and then someone came up with a theory.'

'And,' gasp, 'what's,' gasp, 'that?'

'The more intense the orgasm the better the chance of conception.'

She moaned again.

'But to invoke such a reaction, you really have to get her, wet and steamy and hmm, noisy.'

Kaylor arched and moaned, but Avery refused to let up. Finally, she let out a scream of ecstasy as she orgasmed.

'Hmm, I think you're ready.'

'Stop teasing me.'

Avery rolled over onto his back. 'Nope. You see the other part of the theory is men tend to rush and thrust away without concern for her pleasure. So, the pace needs to be set by the woman.'

Kaylor scrambled to straddle him. She shuddered as she impaled herself. Having savoured the moment, she began rocking back and forth, building to a smooth even tempo. Avery yearned for release but held back.

It built and built until he couldn't control himself. He flung her onto her back and pinned her wrists to the bed. She arched her back and moaned, but Avery held on. Now he set the pace, while she bucked and moaned. Pressure building like a volcano about to erupt.

Then finally with one final thrust, he let go. Kaylor screamed as her body convulsed and for a moment it was so intense, he thought he was going to pass out. He rolled off of her and fought to catch his breath.

Kaylor rolled towards him and rested her chin on his chest. His hands gently caressed her hair.

She stared into his eyes. 'I want you to know that was the best I've ever had.'

Avery knew it meant something special to Kaylor. They weren't lovers, but he hadn't just had intercourse as a means to an end, he'd made love to her. He doubted her lovers had sincerely done that with her.

Her lips sought his and he kissed her back with genuine affection. Rolling away from him she said, 'Let me know when you're ready to go again.'

Avery was keen, but his body was done. He was already being pulled into the depths of sleep.

Chapter 37

It was three weeks later that Avery got the message he'd been expecting. He was back on *The Zee* and it was a yellow dot. Avery opened it on the observation deck. Kaylor was pregnant, and the Zianan healer who'd confirmed conception, had also proclaimed she was carrying a girl. Not through scanning technology, but by psychometry.

The sex of the child was not proof that the foetus would grow to become a new body for Starliah, but it seemed more than just a coincidence.

Avery was able to have a holocall with Kaylor as the persuasive program did not work on Kaylor. He'd tried his best to be loving and reassuring. She'd been cheerful, but she'd also told him that he needn't burden himself with responsibility. She could take care of herself and the baby; all she wanted from him was to be friends. When the call disconnected, he was filled with a sense of emptiness. The sort that might have driven him to look for a stiff drink except Yeltzie, who was still working with Kaylor, called back using non-AI technology with video capability.

She smiled at him. 'Congratulations. I trust it was not so hard and no burden. Certainly, Kaylor didn't find your performance lacking.'

Avery blushed. Why women found it necessary to discuss private matters he didn't know. 'I love her, but it'll take time to win her over. Right now, she thinks my affections are just because she's carrying our child.'

'I wouldn't worry. All she talks about is you. It's annoying when her research is so much more interesting.' Yeltzie looked thoughtful. 'Anyway, have you given any thought to what gift you'll give her?'

He hadn't because he'd clean forgotten the tradition. In Zianan culture, when a woman got pregnant and would in due course deliver the gift of a baby, a man was expected to give her a gift of thank you. A difficult thing to decide on, because he still didn't know much about her. 'I'm still contemplating what to give her.'

'May I make a suggestion?'

'Please do.'

'Take her to the concert held in the extinct volcanic crater of Mount Tallis.'

Avery could do nothing but nod. A natural sound shell, the volcanic crater amplified music in a way that no other place could. Plus, the setting was truly beautiful.

'If you like, I could procure tickets. They're limited and difficult to get, but my boyfriend is a new player in the band.'

Avery's expression became sterner. 'I'm looking forward to meeting him.'

Her eyes revealed coyness. 'You've met him before; he's an old friend.'

Yeltizie had never lacked potential suitors. He wondered which boy she was referring to.

'Is that a yes?'

'Yes, there's gold in my beside drawer. Take what you need to buy the tickets.'

She blew him a kiss and the transmission ended before he could ask her his name.

Sarah, who'd been hovering out of earshot, now sidled up to him. 'Good news?'

'Yes.' He gazed at the view of Ziana through the observation window. 'I want to ask you something important, but you should know it's okay to say no. I mean I'll totally understand if you do.'

Sarah turned serious. 'What is it?'

'I was wondering if you'd consent to be my daughter's godmother?'

Sarah squealed with delight and jumped up and down on the spot like a four-year-old. 'Oh Avery, that's wonderful and of course, I will be.'

He put his arm around her shoulder. 'Thank you. It's not just because we're lifelong friends. As much as you hate it, you can pilot, and if she should need to be taken off world and away from here. I mean, I'm talking worst case scenario.'

Sarah's lips pulled into a tight line. 'Yes, I understand.'

*****

There was an issue with attending a concern in a volcano. Volcanoes were mountains and that meant an exhausting climb to get to the crater.

'You alright Kaylor?'

She was red-faced and breathing hard. 'I'm fine, I'm just not very fit.'

'I'm sorry, I should have transported you there in a shuttle. There's nowhere to land, but you could have parachuted out.'

Kaylor paled. 'Jump out of a shuttle? Not likely. No walking's good. The ground's my friend.' She continued at a slow but steady pace.

Burdened with a heavy pack containing ground mats, pillows, sleeping bags, down jackets and a picnic, Avery lumbered along beside her. It was twilight now, the beginnings of the long night. It wasn't yet cold, but the temperature was dropping. Attendees usually had a sleep on the ground under the stars after the concert and Avery wanted to make sure Kaylor was warm and comfortable.

At the top, the crater was a lake the size of a Rian sports oval and surrounded by five metre stone walls. Floating on the lake was a series of rafts that were roped together. The rafts had been transported here on a carry line beneath a shuttle. They'd be taken away again once the concert was over.

When they reached their raft at the centre of the lake, Avery found a young Zianan man called Kanchan sitting in their spot.

'Mr. Vander,' he said politely. 'Yeltzie's just dashed off to use the facilities, she'll be back directly.'

Avery slid the heavy pack off his back.

'Did she tell you we are together?'

'No, she never said a word.'

He looked concerned until Avery grinned at him. Of all the young men that he'd seen Yeltzie kiss, Kanchan was the one Avery approved of the most. He wasn't just an incredibly talented musician; he was also studying sound and frequency healing. Avery truly hoped it worked out for there was no one finer that he'd want for an honorary son-in-law.

'How'd you manage to win her over?'

'I serenaded her. Extreme I know, but love makes us do crazy things.'

Avery suppressed a smile.

Yeltzie came skipping across the rafts. Their bobbing under her feet didn't bother her in the least. 'Toilets are over there Kaylor.'

Kaylor nodded. 'Good, I'll head straight over before I settle in.'

Kanchan stood up, wrapped his arms around Yeltzie and kissed her passionately. When they parted, he said, 'Good to see you Mr. Vander, but I've got to go. I'm playing this year.' He glanced at Yeltzie, 'You coming.'

'Yes, I'll just be a moment.'

Avery watched Kanchan walk off across the rafts. He was as unperturbed as Yeltzie that they moved underfoot. Avery turned back to her. 'Good choice sweetheart, but how'd you managed to win him over?'

She grinned. 'I served him slow cooked quail in orange sauce with fresh bread and a crisp green salad. Extreme I know, but love makes us do crazy things.'

Avery laughed.

'You can laugh. At least I didn't push my sweetheart off a rope bridge and force her to marry me.'

'I never pushed her, she slipped.'

'So, you say. Anyway, I've got other news. I've decided to go to Shenrai this long night and take up studies as a chef. I think it's what I'm meant to be.'

You're already a chef you twit and you are the only one who can't see that. 'Agreed and I'm so happy for you.' He pulled her into a hug.

'One other thing. I booked Kaylor in for a healing session with Kanchan and some others which you paid for. I really think she'll respond to it.'

'I think she will too and thanks for organising all of this.'

Kaylor could be heard approaching. Every time a raft moved under her foot she giggled.

Yeltzie kissed both his cheeks before winking. 'Have fun.' She danced away before he could reprimand her for being cheeky.

Kaylor took a seat on the mat and cushions Avery had laid out. 'Oh Avery, this is the best gift I've ever been given. Thank you so much.'

'You're welcome.'

She reached out for his hand which he let her take. On the horizon, Isla was emerging as a full moon.

'Come on Issie, up you come. I know you need some healing as well. I haven't forgotten you.' She turned to Avery. 'I not turning mad am I.'

He kissed her hand. 'No but you should know, you're turning Zianan, which is kind of the same thing.'

*****

Kaylor wept the entire concert. The music could not just be heard but felt as vibration that spiralled around them. So, electrifying that Kaylor felt it as a pressure in her chest right near her heart sending love throughout her entire body.

The music emanated from a variety of instruments including wooden flutes, stringed instruments including harps, violins and cellos along with huge drums, followed by chants that the audience participated in.

The musicians, dressed in fine robes of silk, didn't just play, they became at one with their instruments and having done so became a channel for the cosmos. The created music so divine it was fit not just for royalty, but for deities.

Between acts, Avery fed her roast pheasant and a Zianan coleslaw that was nothing short of delicious. This was washed down with a fizzy elderflower beverage that he assured her contained no alcohol. It was crisp and sweet and danced on her tongue. Not just thirst quenching, but revitalizing.

And then it was quiet. Comfortably full and tingling with energy, Kaylor lay down and snuggled beside Avery gazing up at the stars. The rafts bobbed gently on the water and in time her eyelids felt heavy. And then she slept more peacefully than she ever had in her life.

*****

Kaylor woke to discover Kanchan and Yeltzie had returned. They were sitting on the raft beside Avery talking quietly in Zianan.

She sat up and stretched. 'Sorry, you should have woken me.'

Yeltzie poured chai from a thermos into a mug and handed it to her. 'No, you needed to sleep.'

'Did you enjoy the concert?' asked Kanchan.

'Words cannot describe it.'

'Yes, English is… limited. You should learn Zianan, it's much more expressive.'

'Oh, I intend to.' She glanced at Avery. 'Thank you so much.'

'I must confess, it was Yeltzie's idea and now we have another gift for you. Kanchan is a sound frequency healer and he wants to do a private session with you.'

'What, right here?'

'No, there's a dry cave nearby.'

Avery helped her to her feet and she followed Kanchan across the rafts and into a cave the size of a small bedroom. Inside she could feel the sacredness of the place — a place where many had come before her to be healed.

Kanchan gestured for her to lay down on a portable stretcher bed and took a moment to arrange pillows to make her comfortable. 'I want you to do more than listen to the sounds we're about to play. Let your entire body feel it. Don't resist. Let it take you on a journey deep within.'

'I will,' she whispered gently cupping her hand over her wound. 'I want to be well again.'

Her words were genuine and heartfelt and they made her cry again. Speaking truth did that, it released pent up emotions through tears. She didn't try to stop them; she just let them fall.

Kanchan began to play a wooden flute. He was joined by other musicians with a variety of instruments and now Kaylor was being treated to her own private concert. The sound was all around her and she began to drift out of consciousness into a deep state of relaxation.

Her body began to vibrate and then her breathing synced and fell into a pulsing rhythm. Kaylor's mind began to travel. Tumbling through space she passed stars, planets, moons, and nebula. Each with its own unique sound and frequency.

The joy that spread through her was intense. A sense of connectedness that revealed that even in separateness we were all one. One mind. One collective consciousness.

It was love. Not love that Kaylor had known formerly. This was a love like a glue that held everything together. Made everything beautiful and sparkly.

But there was an exception. When beings fell into fear and forgot their connectedness to the one, it created discordance.

Kaylor brought her attention back to herself. To where the bolt had penetrated her belly. The cells had been torn apart and thrown asunder. They now acted separately because they'd lost their connectedness to the whole. They were sick and dying.

Spontaneously she began to cry out. Sound flying from her and taking fear and darkness created by the separateness with it. A vacuum was forming and making room for the harmony to return. And when the cells understood they were a part of the whole again, they begin to repair the damage that was done. Returning her to wellness.

And now she moved back into her consciousness and slowly brought her awareness back to the cave and the reality she was in. She went to sit up but she felt light as if she weren't really physical.

'Take your time, there's no rush,' whispered Kanchan.

Slowly she returned to the present. 'I get it now. I understand it all.'

'All? No, my dear, this is just the beginning.'

Chapter 38

<u>Eight months later</u>

The hair on the back of Avery's neck stood up. In one smooth move, he drew his laser pistol and spun around. Dee was in the shadows. Her hair was now long enough to tie back into a short ponytail and had been dyed a reddish-brown. She looked intentionally different, but it was definitely her. Sitting on a wooden crate by the side of the base hangar she wore a fleet shirt she'd stolen from somewhere. He wondered how many fleetman had walked past and failed to even notice her or just thought she was with fleet.

He lowered the pistol and put it back in its holster. 'What do you want?'

'I need your help.'

Avery snorted. 'I'm not going to help you so fuck off.'

She sat calmly. No reaction. Not even a flicker in her eyes. 'Will you at least hear me out?'

'Why should I?'

She shrugged. 'We're not friends, but I'm not your enemy.'

Avery conceded her point. He moved closer and sat down on her crate, but with a good distance between them.

She moved into a cross-legged position and turned ninety degrees so she could look at him even if it was side on. He did her the courtesy of twisting towards her slightly.

'I went to Ria to search for Black and White. Found them. White was killed during the terrorist attack on dome six that was orchestrated by Inglis. Not by the attack itself, he was assassinated by a knife wielder. All hushed up of course.'

Avery wondered how she'd been to Ria and back but concluded she'd have teleported from some secret spook base nearby.

'Black is alive. He's in the ICE unit of Ria's psychiatric hospital. A complete mental case. I had to pose as a shrink to get into see him. Not that he said much. He just kept repeating "the stork will deliver". I didn't know what a stork was until I looked it up.'

Avery knew a stork was a long-legged bird. There were birds similar on Ziana but to his knowledge they never delivered anything.

'I tried, we tried, to get aboard the ships in the armada. Fifteen in all, steaming this way at beyond light speed. Couldn't do it. Lost six agents trying.'

She looked away. 'Figured there wasn't much I could do except come back here. I know we can't stop what's coming, but I fight from the shadows. Thought I might as well slip back into them and wait until there's an opportunity.'

She fell silent.

'What do you want?' asked Avery when she failed to resume talking.

'I told you; I need your help.'

'To do what?'

'To talk to Sparta. I know he won't talk to me, but he might talk to you, now he's fulfilled his mission.'

'He would have told me earlier if it wasn't for you holding a gun to his head so to speak.'

'True, but you should know I wasn't told the full story. It was need to know, and I wasn't fully in the loop. I swear if I'd known even half of the truth, I'd have made different choices.'

Avery narrowed his eyes. 'So, what, you've grown a conscience have you?'

'Look, I know you think I'm a piece of shit. I know that. I won't deny I've done despicable things in the name of union security, but Inglis is out of control. My world, as I knew it, is gone. This world is about to fall. Before I die, I'll do everything I can to stop it, but I need your help. Kaylor's baby is a week from being due and we need to find out what stork delivery is.'

Avery thought it through. 'So, you need me to talk to Sparta, but why do I need you?'

She lowered her eyes. 'You don't.'

'Right, glad we got that cleared up. I'll go and talk to Sparta.'

'You mind if I tag along?'

He shrugged. 'If you think you've got something to contribute.' He meant what he said, but in a strange way it felt good to know Dee had his back.

She jumped off the box.

'Love your hair-do by the way.'

She gave him a look that said you're an idiot and they headed into Port Town to catch the train to Barsha.

'One other thing.'

'What?'

'Could you buy me lunch? The Zianan government is no longer exchanging payment units for coins and I'm starving.'

He narrowed his eyes. 'What, you want charity now?'

'Well no. If I save your life, it would be *sheesha*.'

He snorted. 'Big if.' But he relented and handed her a silver coin. No one went hungry on Ziana and as much as he disliked her, he was pretty sure, if it came to it, she would have his six.

*****

They did not speak the entire train journey to Barsha, mostly because having pigged out on roasted chicken sandwiches and fruit pies, Dee folded herself into the foetal position on the seat opposite and went to sleep. Avery wondered if she ever slept in a bed. He had to admit, having become a spook, she'd lived a hard life.

He woke her five minutes before they arrived so she could wake up. At Barsha's train station he stopped at a café and bought them both a coffee and a piece of nutmeal loaf.

'Do you know where Sparta is?' asked Dee.

'Without turning on a communicator and using it to tune into his tracking bracelet, no I don't. I'm not going to do that, but it doesn't matter, because I can deduce where he is.'

'How so?'

'A white man on Ziana sticks out, and Sparta's like you' doesn't like to be noticed. The only place he can blend in is where there are other foreigners.'

'An interplanetary hotel.'

'Right.'

'But that would cost gold.'

'Yes, but Ziana is very cheap compared to Ria and since he raised no stake about being made to stay here, I'm guessing he had enough stashed somewhere to see him through.'

'No doubt in several train lockers and that made sense because people like Sparta always had contingency plans.' She brushed crumbs off her shirt and drained her coffee. 'Let's go and see if you're right.'

*****

Barsha had three hotels. They tried the biggest one first and found Sparta in the smaller of its bars sitting in a booth in the corner. Nursing a high strength liqueur, he was playing with a deck of cards. Cards had been introduced from Earth, but they'd long ago disappeared from Rian culture. The game was called solitaire and it was one of the few card games that required only one player.

Fear flickered in his eyes when he saw Avery approach. He thought to run, but Dee had his exit covered.

'Lieutenant-Commander Vander, have I violated my parole orders.'

'Not to my knowledge.'

His eyes flicked to Dee who was edging closer. 'What can I do for you then?'

Avery slid onto the bench seat opposite. 'I thought since we hit it off so well, that we might enjoy having a chat.' He leaned forward and made a hand gesture. 'Just the two of us.'

'Just the two of us eh, what about her?'

'Her? No, she's not with me, never was.'

'Right.' Sparta continued playing.

'See, what we were wondering is, what's stork delivery?'

Sparta raised an eyebrow. 'You don't know.'

Avery gritted his teeth. 'No, but I bet a smug little cunt like you does, and I bet he takes pride in fucking others over.'

'Nope, you got that last bit wrong. I got fucked over as bad as the rest of you. I mean, put on a leash and made to live on this shithole of a planet for nearly a year now. I wasn't even offered a deal.'

'Fancy that huh. I tell you what Danny, I'll make a deal with you.'

'I'm listening.'

'How about you tell me what stork delivery is and I'll put in a good word for you at your trial.'

'Really, and why should I believe you?'

''Cause we're friends.'

Sparta smiled quaintly.

'Yeah, I didn't buy that either,' said Dee, 'but here's my deal. 'You tell us what we want to know and we'll let you live.'

Sparta, having decided he'd lost the game he was playing, picked up his cards and started shuffling them. 'How do I know you won't kill me anyway?'

'Good point,' said Dee.

Avery stared at Sparta intently. 'What do you want Danny?'

'Me, oh I want a time machine, so I can go back and change the past, or is it the future. Whichever.'

Aver sighed. 'One last chance. What's stork delivery?'

'Seriously, you don't know? I mean, obviously she wouldn't, but I thought you, having immersed yourself in Earth's children's stories, might know.'

Avery now had a point of reference and sometimes that was all it took to start thinking in a different direction. 'Hang on a bit. Wasn't there some stupid reference to storks delivering babies in children's cartoons?' A chill ran through him as if someone had emptied a bucket of ice water over his head. 'They're going to steal the baby.'

'Who is?' asked Dee.

'The Zeta's.'

Sparta clapped his hands slowly. 'Well done.'

'Why?' asked Dee.

'I don't know, that bit always bothered me,' replied Sparta.

'Then why take the contract?'

Sparta sighed. 'What can I say, I'm a capitalist, but they weren't offering just money.'

'Then what?'

'A fucking time machine or something similar,' replied Avery.

Sparta smirked in response.

'Oh, fuck,' said Dee.

Avery was already leaving.

'Best of luck trying to stop them Lieutenant-Commander.'

Avery would have turned around and threatened him or even assaulted him, but Sparta was such small fry that he no longer mattered. Avery had to get back to Kaylor as fast as he could. Damn it. He should have flown a shuttle here.

The train journey was agonisingly slow. When it finally arrived in Port Town, he bolted from the station and literally ran home, thankful for the fact that fleet's ongoing training kept him fit.

'Where's Kaylor?' he said as he burst through the door.

Yeltzie looked anxious. 'She was napping in her room, but when I checked on her an hour ago, she was gone. I never saw her leave and I can't locate her.

'Fuck.'

Chapter 39

Kaylor woke with an insatiable thirst. Her throat so dry and swollen she had difficulty swallowing. She reached for the glass of water she always kept on her bedside table, but it was gone.

'Damn it, Yeltzie,' she grumbled. The young woman was exceedingly helpful, but she tended to be a little too efficient at cleaning up. Zianans were pedantic about cleanliness. Removing half drank cups of tea she hadn't finished because she'd nodded off in a layback chair. Now she'd removed her water glass.

Kaylor padded across to the bathroom, turned on the tap and drank water from her cupped hands. Despite drinking until her belly felt sloshy, she was still thirsty. Straightening up, her hands went instinctively to her belly.

No longer ballooned, it was flat. Kaylor's heart thumped wildly in her chest as her hands sought to find the baby that should be in her womb.

It was gone. She had to be dreaming, except pinching herself didn't wake her.

'Where's my baby?'

Had she had it and didn't realise. Perhaps it had been a complicated birth and the healers had put her to sleep with herbal tinctures that had messed with her memory.

'Yeltizie.'

Footsteps sounded towards her and an exacerbated Yeltzie appear staring at her wide-eyed. 'She's in here!'

Avery appeared followed by another woman. The short stocky one who'd been rude. Kaylor couldn't remember her name.

'Where have you been?' demanded Avery.

Confusion swarmed her head. 'Nowhere, I went to bed. I've just woke.'

They stared at her with incomprehensible looks on their faces.

'Where's my baby? Is she well? Can I hold her?'

Yeltzie glanced at the floor.

'What's going on? Where's my baby?'

'Kaylor, I think you should come and sit down,' said Yeltzie.

'What?' Fear gripped her like a vice. 'Please, tell me, where is Starliah?' she appealed to Avery.

'Kaylor, I don't know how to tell you this, but you've been gone for three days,' said Avery.

'Oh. Gone where, hospital?'

'No Kaylor, just gone.'

Kaylor rubbed her forehead which was fuzzy. There was a memory but it seemed distant, like a dream she couldn't recall. She allowed Yeltzie to guide her into the lounge room where she sat down. Avery used the two-way radio and asked Sarah to come at once. The other woman handed her a glass of water which Kaylor drank down in one go.

'She's dehydrated,' proclaimed the woman.

Avery manoeuvred the pouffe closer and sat on it facing her. Gently taking her hands he said, 'What can you remember?'

Kaylor cast her mind back. 'Starliah was kicking more than normal. I went to bed. I must have fallen asleep.'

'What else?' he beseeched her.

She strained her mind. Someone had reassured her that Starliah was safe and they'd be reunited shortly. 'I woke up. I was thirsty. I'm still thirsty. Do you know where our baby is?'

A vehicle pulled up outside and Sarah came running in.

'Sarah, thank god,' said Avery jumping up.

Sarah noticed Kaylor. 'When did she get back?'

'Just now,' replied Avery.

'She should be in hospital. Let's get her to hospital.'

'I'm not hurt.'

Sarah looked her up and down curiously.

'I need you to check her out Sarah. I mean, you've done medical training, right?'

'I have.'

'She's not physically hurt. We need to know where the baby is. She doesn't remember. Can you use hypnosis?'

Sarah blinked. 'I don't know. Maybe, but it could be too soon.'

Avery grabbed her by the shoulders. 'We need to find Starliah. The longer we wait, the harder it will be.'

'Yes, alright, I'll try, but I'll need the room.'

'Everyone out,' barked Avery.

Yeltzie headed outside, while the other two headed for the kitchen.

A memory stirred in Kaylor's mind. Faces looking down at her. Small grey faces with big black eyes. They didn't speak, but through telepathy, they were reassuring her. She smiled. 'It's alright, they're coming back.'

'Who is?' asked Sarah.

Yeltzie gave a short sharp squeal and walking backwards she re-entered the room. 'Avery.'

'They're here,' said Kaylor.

A bright light appeared outside.

'Avery!' shrieked Yeltzie.

Kaylor stood up and began walking towards the light. 'Let's see if they returned Starliah.'

'Um Sarah, can you bring her back now,' asked Avery.

'She's not hypnotised; we hadn't started.'

Kaylor walked outside onto the deck. There were two lights. Three little greys emerged from one and walked across and into the other. It lifted off and disappeared. 'But what about Starliah?' Tears rolled down her cheeks. 'You were supposed to give her back. You weren't supposed to keep her.'

*****

Avery stared dumbfounded, unsure what to make of what had just occurred. The bright light had dimmed to become a small silver spaceship no bigger than a fleet jeep. It stood on four legs, a narrow ladder protruding from the base. Round in shape, it rose to a sharp point like a teardrop.

'Okay, that was just plain queer,' said Dee who was striding towards it. Without asking she climbed three steps of the ladder only to be denied access by a forcefield. She yelped as it knocked her backwards. She landed sprawled on her arse.

Avery approached cautiously. En route, he picked up a thin piece of stick from the ground. He used it to test the forcefield but failed to find it. Gingerly he touched the ship. It was cool and highly polished like thin sheets of metal electroplated with chrome.

Still probing with the stick, he climbed up two rungs and tested the opening. There was no forcefield — at least not for him. He climbed some more and stuck his head inside. The space within was three times as large as it should be.

'Wow, check this out.'

'I fully intend to.'

Avery frowned. The voice sounded like Sparta's. Hurrying down he looked around. Sparta stood nearby, a laser pistol in each hand. Where he'd acquired them, Avery could only guess.

'Danny.'

Sparta fired a shot setting a bush in the nearby garden on fire. 'Call me that again, I dare you to.'

Thankfully the plant was a megglie bush and contained so much natural fire retardant that the flames just petered out.

Avery held his hands out in front of him in a non-threatening manner the way he'd been trained. 'Okay, let's just calm down. There's no need for violence. Just tell us what you want and we'll see if we can accommodate you.'

'I told you what I wanted. A time machine and it's just been delivered.' He grinned wickedly. 'I have to say, I had no idea if the Zetas would honour the deal, but I had to hang around to see.'

'Avery, what's he talking about?' asked Kaylor.

'Oh, you poor thing. Didn't he tell you? He sold your baby for this machine.'

'That's a lie,' spat Avery.

'Really, then where's the baby?'

'How should I know.'

Sparta tut-tutted. 'No point in lying. Not that I suppose it matters to me.' He moved closer while maintaining a gun trained on Avery and the other on Dee. He didn't seem to be worried about Sarah, Kaylor or Yeltzie.

'So, this is how it's going to be. I'm taking Avery and the time machine and we are going back to put things right. *Comprende?*'

No one moved.

Sparta moved towards the ladder. 'On board.'

Avery climbed up and on.

Sparta walked to the foot of the ladder, shoved both pistols into the back of his pants and climbed as fast as he could. Like Dee had been, he was struck by the forcefield. Yelping he landed on his arse. He squirmed so badly that he collided with one of the spaceship's legs. It shocked him again.

'That machine doesn't like you,' said Dee. 'I wouldn't take it personally. It doesn't like me either.'

Sparta went for his pistols, but Dee through a small rock at him which struck the side of his face. He squealed in pain and Dee used the opportunity to run at him. Rather than wrestle him to the ground, Dee punched him four times.

Sparta went down. His nose bleeding; his eyes watering. 'Fucking bitch. That's excessive force.'

'Would be if I was a cop, but spooks like me,' she leaned in closer, 'we get away with murder, literally.'

Terrified, he tried again to go for his pistols, but Dee forced him onto his stomach and pinned him to the ground with a knee.

'No, you, stupid fucks. I'm trying to do the right thing. I'm trying to set things right.'

Kaylor ventured forward as if she were in a trance. 'It's not meant for you. It's ours. Our chariot of fire.'

Dee screwed up her face. 'You hit your head or something?'

Kaylor ignored her and climbed the ladder. As it had with Avery, the ship let her onboard.

Shaking her head with disbelief, Dee hauled Sparta towards the jeep and literally tossed him in the back. She might be short, but she was bloody strong.

Sarah approached holding a stick the way Avery had. Like the other two, she was thrown backwards.

Yeltzie never bothered trying, she just walked closer so she could look up at Avery. 'Where are you going?'

'Where ever it takes us.'

'I see. Well, how long will you be gone?'

'I don't know.'

'Please come back and bring Starliah with you.'

'We will if we can.'

Yeltzie had a thought. 'Wait, I'll just be a moment. Sarah, help me please.'

Sarah followed Yeltzie inside. When they returned, Sarah had a duffle bag full of clothes; Yeltzie had thrown together a picnic which included two bottles of water.

'Kaylor can't represent Ria or Ziana in her pyjamas can she, and who knows if there'll be food or water where you're going.'

Fair point. Avery climbed down to retrieve the offerings.

Sarah grabbed his arm. 'Come back fleetman, that's an order.'

Looking her in the eye he nodded and climbed back onboard.

Chapter 40

There was no cockpit or windscreen. Just a small seat beside a ball thirty centimetres in diameter suspended on a shaft. Avery gently laid his hands on it and closed his eyes. He could feel the ship as if it were touching a living, breathing entity.

Letting his mind go free, he explored the ship moving through the circuits at lightning speed. The ship was alive. A biological entity encased in a metal shell.

Did it need to feed?

No, the ship was like an ascended being, it lived off of *Xean*, the universal lifeforce of the universe. All it needed was love and guidance.

Avery relaxed his mind and moved into a meditation. With each inhale he absorbed *Xean*; with each exhale he let love flow from his fingers. The ship responded allowing him to merge deeper and deeper with its consciousness.

The ladder retracted, the door shut and the legs folded away so the ship was hovering. Ready to fly, the ship hummed and shone brighter and brighter. The walls disappeared and Avery could see everything. The others were shielding their eyes from the brightness, but they could not see him or Kaylor.

A moment later they shot upwards into space faster than Avery ever had before, yet there were no g-forces. It was like flying a simulator.

Avery focused on his daughter. He didn't know what she looked like, but he'd spoken to her in the womb. He knew what her love felt like and he held onto that memory. They disappeared in a flash. A moment later they'd arrived.

Below was a small green island that contained an enormous pyramid. It was surrounded by blue water as far as could be seen in every direction.

Avery brought the ship in slow and steady. It responded to his mind, all he had to do was guide it. Ever so gently he landed it at the base of a great staircase that led up to the top of the pyramid. The door opened and the ladder descended.

'We're here,' said Kaylor.

'Yep, where ever here is.'

The place seemed real, but Avery wasn't convinced it was. Reality at present was like delirium.

'I'll just get changed, and I think we'd best take water with us, there're quite a few stairs.'

Avery descended the ladder into a life-supporting environment. He watched as a small flock of birds flew by. Thankfully the ship hadn't taken them to a planet whose environment would kill them. Shading his eyes, he craned his head to look up. She was right about the stairs. 'Perhaps I should look for a lower door or go up and check it out first.'

'No, we go together.'

She emerged in three-quarter hemp pants and a tunic with a cord tied loosely at the waist.

'Shoes?' asked Avery.

'Won't need them.'

Avery kicked off his boots and socks and tossed them back on board. Having placed the water bottles in a small backpack Sarah had thought to pack and put it on his back, he offered Kaylor his hand and said, 'Shall we?'

She held his hand. 'Indeed.'

They took their time, pausing to rest and drink frequently. There were two-hundred steps to the top, Avery counted them. They discovered a flat landing and a roofed entrance with a solid wooden door that was open.

Kaylor sat down on the top step. 'I should have brought a slinky.'

Avery didn't know that word. 'A what?'

'It's a toy I had as a child. It's a spring that bounces down the stairs. Amazing piece of engineering, but unfortunately there weren't many decent stairways on Ria when I was growing up.'

Avery looked down and could easily imagine Zianan children playing with such a toy and squealing with joy as they chased it down the stairs. He smiled at Kaylor who to his surprise removed a wide-toothed comb and a portable mirror from the pockets of her tunic. She took a moment to comb her hair and otherwise tidy her appearance.

'How do I look?' she asked standing up.

Avery shrugged.

'Thanks for the vote of confidence.' She stomped towards the door but paused to glance back over her shoulder. 'It's not every day one gets to meet an ascended master. Still, this is my second meeting with Moir.'

'What?'

She continued on without him.

'Wait up. You were going to tell me about the first meeting.'

'You never reminded me.'

'Well, should we knock or something?'

Kaylor continued through the open door without the slightest hesitation.

Feeling protective, Avery went after her and found himself in the Master's chambers. A simple yet elegant room, lit by slanting windows. There was a square fireplace in the centre of the room, a variety of comfortable looking chairs and a large wooden table.

A Zianan woman stood by the table dressed in a simple cream robe, her belt platinum, her long green hair unfettered.

Avery came to a standstill and just stared.

'My son,' the woman gasped. She hurried towards him and pulled him into a firm embrace.

He gently patted her back.

She stepped back and looked directly into his eyes. They were lilac like his own. Full of warmth and kindness, but also radiating power.

Squeezing his upper arm, she said, 'You've grown into a strapping young man.'

'I work out,' he replied, then cussed. His first words to his mother and he'd said, I work out. She must think him an empty-headed fool.

'There she is,' said Kaylor removing a baby from a cradle and holding her against her left breast.

Avery hurried over. The baby had light gold skin and his own lilac eyes, but her dark hair was that of her mothers. The baby grinned at Avery when he approached.

'She recognises her parents,' said Moir.

Kaylor glanced at the woman. 'Master Moir, does she have a name.'

'In her last life, she was known as Starliah the Beloved Star. I named her Starliah the second, but we've taken to calling her simply Stella.'

'We?' enquired Avery.

'Forgive me, where are my manners. Welcome to the initiate school Quorana. I have many students.'

'Of course,' replied Kaylor as if she'd been struck by a thought. 'Ascended masters are allowed to teach.'

'Where exactly are we?' asked Avery.

Moir hesitated to answer, but then said, 'A world beyond your star charts.' She busied herself arranging clay mugs before fumbling with a teapot. 'Tea?'

'I'd love one,' replied Kaylor.

Moir turned to lift an enormous cast iron kettle from a hook above her fire.

Avery automatically rushed forward, 'Can I help you with that?'

She smiled warmly. 'Chivalrous, you were raised well.'

Avery filled the teapot and placed the kettle back on its hook. Anger stirring beneath the surface.

'Say what you want to say. I promise I won't strike you down with lighting.'

Pain gripped his heart. 'If you didn't want me, why did you have me?'

Moir closed her eyes. 'I did want you. I loved you deeply. I wanted to bring you with me, but I couldn't.'

'If the legends are true, you are a master capable or bio-location. Who could stop you?'

'This house, it's alive and it deemed you … unready.'

Avery lowered his eyes. Knowing that the ship that had brought him here was also alive and it had prevented people from boarding. He knew she wasn't lying to him.

'I was forced to choose. You or my students. It was not an easy decision, but surely you understand that I have the gift of future sight. I could see potential timelines and I knew how things were meant to be. You were meant to remain on Ziana.'

Shame overcame him. 'I'm sorry, I should not have spoken to you in such a manner.' He stepped towards her and hugged her again, this time with more sincerity.

When they separated, he said, 'You should know, I was raised in love, and by and large, I've had a good life.'

Amusement flashed in her eyes. 'I know, I was never truly far away.'

Avery cussed again. Of course, she was an ascended master and omniscient.

Moir poured the tea, 'You have more questions.'

'Millions,' replied Avery picking up the mug of tea she'd given him and following her to comfortable looking chairs where they all took a seat. 'Will you tell me of my father?'

Moir winced as if ashamed of something. 'He was a strapping young man on leave in Port Town from a fleet ship called *The Vander*. I seduced him as a means to an end. He didn't know who I was and he was killed in the line of duty before I could tell him he'd fathered a son.'

Avery stared into his teacup. His mother's actions weren't that unusual for a woman who wanted a baby, but not a relationship. Less common on Ziana; more common on Earth, or so he'd heard. 'What was his name?'

'It's not important. I named you after his true love, the ship he served on.'

Avery sighed. At least he now knew where his desire to serve in fleet came from. 'How much of what has happened was your influence?'

Moir gazed at him lovingly. 'Very little. We met in the light before you were all born. You all planned your lives and I did my part, giving you life. Since then, I have had to watch things play out.'

'Because you can't interfere in free will?' said Kaylor.

'That's right. You've done so well since your NDE. I'm so proud of you.'

The anger stirred again. He'd always had difficulty understanding how an ascended master with so much power, was powerless to interfere. 'What of Starliah, our baby daughter?'

'She made a promise to Ziana and its people and she intends to keep it. She knows if she doesn't, her soul will hold her to it until she has fulfilled it regardless of how many lifetimes it takes.'

Avery understood. Promises were recorded by a person's soul were deemed unfinished business until fulfilled. Death did not resolve you of a promise, although the reincarnating person could not always remember what they'd agreed to. That was why certain people continuing repeating things again and again, even when it caused them pain.

'Starliah is to be our saviour then?'

'She will play her part as will you all.'

Right. Avery drained his mug. 'Thanks for the tea, it's been great catching up, but we must be going. We have a war to fight.'

'No rush, the war will still be waiting when you return. Stay the night, I have things to tell you and to show you. In the meantime, finish your tea.'

Avery glanced at his mug which was now full again. She hadn't needed to make it the way she had, she'd just done so in order to appear humble and normal. Fear fluttered through him. 'Are we prisoners?'

Moir laid a hand on her throat. 'Goodness no.'

Avery narrowed his eyes and pointed to Starliah, who was still being held by Kaylor. 'Is our daughter a prisoner?'

'No, but this house has accepted her enrolment.'

'So, you intend to take her from us?'

'Starliah wants to stay.' Moir paused as if to consider her next words carefully. 'You will only be separated for three days.'

'She's not going to learn much in three days, it's hardly worth her staying.'

Moir folded her hands in her lap. 'Take her if that's what you desire, but you should know the full story.'

On cue, a tall thin adolescent of about fifteen appeared from an internal staircase. Her gait a graceful glide. Her pale green skin and raven blue-black hair assured them she wasn't human. It wasn't her large oval ears, which seemed to have a life of their own or her big blue eyes that held Avery's focus. She was Kelidarian, a species, he'd read about many times previously. They were an ancient race of spiritual beings more advanced in their knowledge than even Zianans were.

'She's beautiful,' whispered Kaylor.

The Kelidarian didn't acknowledge the compliment, but held up the harp she was carrying. 'Master, you called me. Shall I play for Stella and our guests?'

'Later, for the moment I want you to show them what the consequences will be if they take Starliah to Ziana.'

The girl bobbed her head. It wasn't an act of servitude but a deep show of respect. She put down her harp and made her way to an open area within the room.

'Do not fear Jillharile, she will not harm you.'

Kaylor put the baby back in her cradle and walked over to the teenage girl. She had Avery and Kaylor stand facing her in a way that formed a triangle.

Jillharile placed her pressed hands in front of her and slowly drew them apart. As she did a vision appeared. It took Avery a moment to realise the planet he was looking at was Ziana. Brown in colour the planet was clearly dying. Torn apart by mining and deforestation and finished off with a devastating war. It was sickening that a single dictator could create such destruction.

The vision stepped back in time to before the war. There was a sound that Avery recognised as the music of the spheres. Zianas spherical music. It was beautiful, but the music changed and kept changing until it was so horrible that Avery covered his ears.

The vision changed abruptly and they were watching their future selves from a distance.

'I fucking hate the pair of you!' screamed a teenage Starliah.

Avery recoiled, but some invisible force disallowed him to leave the triangle.

'We thought we were doing the right thing bringing you home,' replied the future Avery.

'I had a destiny and you stole it from me!'

'I love you,' sobbed Avery.

'You're still a child. You don't know what love is. There is love in the stars you can't even fathom. I would have sung for them and dispelled the disharmony. I would have prevented this, but I needed Moir's training.'

Avery struggle against the triangle.

'That will do Jillie,' said Moir.

Jillharile released them.

Tears streamed down Avery's face as he stepped away. 'Alright, she stays.'

'A wise decision.'

As Jillharile disappeared down the steps the way she'd arrived, Avery used a clean handkerchief to wipe his eyes and nose. 'I still don't understand how a few days old baby can prevent the invasion that's imminent.'

Moir avoided eye contact.

'Oh great, more withholding. Why am I never told the full story?'

Moir pursed her lips. 'I'll tell you, but you won't like the truth.'

'Let me guess, I can't handle the truth.'

'Know it's not that; you actually have a great capacity to hear truth whilst remaining calm. It's more you're not particularly agreeable when certain actions concern you.'

Avery made a grumbling sound.

'For example, no one could have told you, look sorry Inglis is out of control. He had your wife murdered, but hey, have a child with Kaylor, because your daughter is Starliah and she'll be able to help.'

Avery folded his arms but conceded her point. 'Fine, but why did the Zetas take Starliah and leave us that spaceship.'

Moir wrinkled her nose. 'I'm sorry, that was mostly my doing.'

'You interfered.'

'Not exactly. I made a deal before I ascended.'

'Which you are going to explain to us.'

'Alight, but you are going to have to bear with me because it is quite a story.' In customary Zianan fashion, Moir got up and retrieved a bottle of red wine and three goblets.

'In my four-hundred and twenty-third year, as time is recorded now, I was made aware of the discordance in the music of the spheres. The knowledge came from beings from other planets. They came to Ziana seeking help. They knew we were not a space-faring world, but they also knew that we'd kept our planet musically tuned for millennia.

'I sort out our greatest singer and in time found Starliah. The pair of us were brought here to study under a master teacher who has since moved on. We trained and we became masters in our own right earning our platinum belts.'

Moir took a sip of her wine. 'As powerful as we were, our skills were not enough. We were able to prevent Captain Sorensen from invading Ziana, but we were not able to repair the discordance at its source. The reason was, that our minds could not override the consciousness of an entire race of beings. Are you following me?'

They both replied that they were.

'The race of being was the Zetas. A technologically advanced race whose scientists were second to none. They believed there was nothing they couldn't do with technology. In time they merged with it so that their bodies became machines. Over time the machines became more advanced and before long they were cyborgs completely disconnected from the natural world.'

'It's starting to sound a little too familiar,' said Kaylor.

'Indeed. Zianans knew of the dangers because our ancestors had seen dynasties fall victim to the allure of technology and what it caused. The train system is a legacy of a once technological savvy race. Thankfully our ancestors found their way back to spiritual connection and the rest is history.

'The Zetas, however, were now trapped inside their machines. Only flesh and blood can produce emotions. Worse still, only flesh and blood can reproduce. The Zetas were a dying race. As they always had, they attempted to use technology to solve the problem. They produced clones.

'Flesh and blood bodies that could theoretically reproduce except they discovered they couldn't. Without emotions, there is no sexual urge. No children were born from the first clones and a lot of the deceased souls used to living in machines refused to take them up. The flesh and blood bodies were just too fragile.

'The solution was to find genetic donors from other races, gene splice and create better bodies. So, they set out to find genetic material and to colonise. Emotionless as they were, the Zetas could not see the harm they caused by abducting people as part of a genetic harvest. Worse, it didn't stop there, they also began impregnating human women with genetically modified embryos and then stealing the foetuses from the womb prior to birth. They became known as the Raiders from Above.'

Kaylor went to speak, but Moir held up a finger.

'Children were now being born, with emotions. Children who cried tears were seen as miracles for the Zetas had not seen tears for millennia. Against the odds, the Zetas are saving their race from extinction. It's beautiful, but there is still a problem.

'There are, hundreds of colonised worlds where no one sings. Hundreds of planets with discordant music of the spheres. A problem they cannot fix for Zetas had long ago given up speech, let alone singing.

'Starliah went there and sang, but her body was not of those worlds and so the songs she sang were the wrong frequency. Desperate, she tried to teach them to sing, but it was no use. The new children's vocal cords were too poorly developed. She donated some of her DNA so they could make a clone, but there was no soul among the Zetas who could take up Starliah's clone for it was too spiritually advanced.

'Desperate, I met with a group of unborn souls getting ready to reincarnate. Beings who had died at the hand of Captain Sorensen and would thus return when Sorensen's own soul was reincarnated. Both of you agreed that you would give Starliah a new body. The others, well they agreed they'd assist where they could.

'The idea being that a body created with only a small amount of Zianan genetics would be much more compatible to create a clone, yet have Starliah's ability to sing. So, I made a deal with the Zetas. In exchange for one of their spaceships, they could be present at Starliah's rebirth and collect the blood from her placenta. Being full of stem cells it's the best specimen for gene splicing and creating a clone.

'Unfortunately, the Zetas misunderstood my instructions. Language was never their forte. Rather than bring you both here for the birth of your daughter, they simply abducted Kaylor and removed the baby from her womb. They healed Kaylor, even dried up her milk and she was returned from whence she was taken while Starliah was brought here. No one was intentionally mistreated; they did not realise Kaylor would need sustenance. They frequently neglect to feed their own cloned children.

'Anyway, no serious harm done. I have foreseen that the new clones will be born with Starliah's voice, and with training, she will be able to sing the songs needed to repair the music of the spheres. It's an exciting time for the Zetas right now. Those who have emotions are eternally grateful. I would like to introduce you both to them this evening if you are agreeable.'

Avery was overwhelmed at what his mother had just told him. Yet he still had questions. 'I'm troubled by an event that happened. On the day I proposed to Leda, was she meant to die?'

'It was an intersection of timelines. There is no doubt that if she had not worn a harness, she would have died. Then your life would have been very different.'

'But I caused us to stray from the agreed plan we'd decided prior to birth.'

Moir sighed. 'You need to understand something. The power of God is yours to command and God is commanded through decisions that have the support of a resolve.

'You decided you were going to marry Leda. God gave you the means to make that happen and you did not falter.'

'But the greater plan demanded she die.'

'There were many minds working to restore the plan. Prior to birth, Leda had agreed she would not stand in the way. That was why she was born unable to have children. She agreed to die if need be.'

Avery looked at the floor a glum expression on his face.

'My son, you are not to blame. The timeline you chose had greater adversity, but that only means the overall result will be grander.'

'Because I created more opportunity for people to suffer.'

'For them to experience. Whether they suffered was their own doing.'

Avery wanted to believe what he was being told but he doubted. How could his baby daughter lead them to victory? She should have been born years ago.

Moir glanced out the window. The sun now sat low in the sky and the shadows were growing. 'Look it is getting late. When the sun sets my students will be wanting their dinner. Two floors below is a bathhouse. Head down there and mull things over in the steamy water for a while. A bell will sound when it is time to head to the dining room.

Chapter 41

The pyramid was made of stones with beautiful swirling colours of browns and reds. Its walls and corners were decorated with great works of art that had no doubt been made by students past or present. The place was immaculately clean and en route to the bath house, they spired acolytes sweeping, dusting and mopping.

Avery bobbed his head to them and they returned the gesture. Polite and humble the place reminded him of the house he'd grown up in. Rians would call it an orphanage, but the word was too cold for Avery as it implied the children were unloved and unwanted.

It wasn't true because every child had been loved and wanted. Avery had been made offers of adoption by many families. He'd politely declined them. In his heart, he'd always knew he'd be reunited with his mother; he just hadn't realised how old he would be when it happened.

In the home, everyone was given chores because that was the way of *sheesha*. Avery had never minded doing seemingly menial work for it allowed him to work on humility and to ward off arrogance and entitlement. It didn't mean he couldn't focus on what he wanted, it was more he needed to understand, every manifestation comes with a cost and a responsibility.

At the time he'd thought he'd understood. He hadn't, but he did now.

'I think it's this way,' said Kaylor. 'That's steam I can see.'

He'd thought that Kaylor might remain with Starliah but their daughter was sleeping and Kaylor seemed content to leave her be.

The bathhouse was a room filled with steam. It contained a series of large round holes in the floor filled with gently bubbling water. Avery looked around. Some of the baths contained student both male and female. There didn't seem to be any segregation.

Lack of segregation was common on Ziana. Fourth seal beings did not have uncontrollable sexual urges. There was beauty in a person's bodily form, but Zianans were taught as children that true beauty came from a person's spirit and soul. To see it, Zianans did a discipline in which they sat comfortably on a cushion and stared into another person's eyes. Avery had practiced this growing up, but he soon discovered that Rians were extremely uncomfortable with this practice.

Kaylor did not hesitate to strip off and step into one of the chest deep baths that had steps leading into them and seats running around the edge.

Avery followed. 'You are not upset about what's happened?'

Kaylor recoiled. 'Goodness no. When I woke, I knew in my heart that no evil had befallen me or Starliah. I knew she was safe and she'd be returned. I just couldn't remember the details.' Her eyes softened. 'It's such an honour to have been chosen with a task of such responsibility. What will be achieved will be the stuff of legends and I was a part of it.'

'True. In time, an historian will want to interview you and others to write a book about these events.'

Still, Avery considered what had happened to them. When he'd first met Kaylor she had thought of herself as naught but a simple scientist who'd never expect to achieve any fame. Now she was rubbing shoulders with masters who were helping to heal entire civilisations and she'd given birth to one of them.

Avery closed his eyes and must have fallen asleep for a moment later a soft bell was chiming. They got out of the bath, dried off with towels readily available in the bathhouse. He was about to dress when Jillharile glided towards them carrying two robes.

She did not speak, just handed them over, bobbed her head and glided away.

'She's a woman of few words,' said Kaylor.

'Her race is deeply spiritual, but like the Zetas, they prefer telepathy to talking. I think she's had to be taught how to speak and she's self-conscious of how she sounds.'

'I think you're right. When she spoke to Moir it was with a bit of a hiss.'

Having dressed, they followed the procession of students to the dining hall. A great room lit by the flames of candles and bowls, which burned ethanol. The house did not appear to have electricity or any other forms of technology.

Avery knew why. Simplicity provided fewer distractions from study and practice. The dining hall was furnished simply by a great round table in the centre of the square room.

The students, a mix of people from many worlds, stood in front of their chairs. They did not sit until Moir strode in and gave them leave to do so. Then they bowed their heads and spoke a prayer in Zianan expressing their thanks for life and the food they were about to receive. Again, it reminded Avery of the home he'd grown up in.

Moir removed a cauldron from the top of a methane gas burner and sat it on a wooden chopping board that had been placed on the table. Using a silver ladle, she filled a clay bowl with thick vegetable soup. The bowl was passed along and Moir kept ladling until everyone had a bowl in front of them.

As he'd watched his mother serve the soup, he'd noted that no matter how much she took from the caldron, the level never changed. It prompted Avery to remember something he was taught as a boy. Everyone who's prepared to focus can manifest, but the difference between a philosopher and a master is quite specific. A philosopher understands the theory as a principle; a master can make it so.

'You're perplexed,' said Moir.

'I feel I am a disappointment to you. You're a great master and I'm so ordinary. Not even worthy to study in this school you preside over.'

Moir smiled at him. 'You judge yourself too harshly. You've lived with Rians who die before they reach one hundred, so you think of yourself as middle aged, but it's not so. You're not yet an eighth of the way through your life.'

'I see.'

'You don't, but you will. Trust me, you have my genetics or else you wouldn't have been able to fly Mystique. That's what I call your spaceship.'

'So, it is mine to keep.'

'Yes, you will need it.'

Avery wasn't sure why, but time would no doubt unveil the reason. 'Why did those men Black, White and Sparta think they could sell Starliah for it?'

Moir smiled. 'They are greedy. Through unscrupulous means, they intercepted a communiqué that was intended for a friend of mine, Steven Cadel. The criminals took it upon themselves to try and steal Mystique. By torturing a Zianan telepath, they also asked the Zetas for that influencing program that's still causing problems. You mustn't blame the Zetas for giving it to them, they don't know any better.'

'Why does it not work on Kaylor and me?'

'The reason you two agreed to have Starliah is that you both have a rare gene that gives you a greater amount of will power.'

That made sense. 'And Cadel knew about Starliah and the spaceship?'

'Of course, as did Mark Gorman. He also wanted the spaceship for himself which is why information was withheld from you.' Moir grinned. 'I wouldn't worry, Mystique's a little choosy about who she lets on board.'

'Yes, so we discovered. What about Dee?'

'Deanna is a tortured soul, beaten and abused as a child she's suffered greatly in this life. I feel for her. She wants to do the right thing but she's been fed so many lies she no longer knows right from wrong. She needs your love, Avery.'

'But she's gay.'

Moir looked at him patiently.

'Oh, right, that sort of love.' The same type of love he had for Sarah.

'She admires you and you'll need her before the end.'

*****

After dinner, they returned to Moir's chambers where Jillharile played her harp for them. Starliah sat on Avery's knee content to just listen. Kaylor leaned against his shoulder, a look of bliss on her face.

'Can we adopt her?' asked Kaylor when Jillharile finished playing.

'No, she's meant to be here,' said Avery.

Jillharile slipped away down the stairs and Moir took Starliah and laid her back in her cradle.

'The Zetas will be along in a while.'

Avery closed his eyes. He must have nodded off again for when he woke, he could sense the presence of the Zetas. He opened his eyes, but they were not in the room.

Shh, do not frighten them, Moir telepathed.

A bright light appeared in the room. Then they appeared. Four little grey beings. It wasn't so much like watching them across the room. It was more akin to watching the vision that Jilharile had shown them earlier.

Avery was not prepared for what he saw. Once his mind stopped seeing their strange bodies as a threat, he was able to gaze upon them in a more affable way. They were not ugly, not evil, not even threatening. They were a different form of sentient being who was entitled to mutual respect as humans were.

318

A fifth and sixth being appeared. They were different from the Zetas. Their bodies seemed more robust and less frail. Their eyes were not black but blue. They were crying. The Zetas were harvesting their tears. Not for genetic use, but as mementoes stored in vials. Artefacts to be cherished. Proof that they were succeeding in bring back emotions to their offspring.

Avery was so overwhelmed with a sense of love that he could do nothing but be in that moment.

*****

Moir served them a light breakfast of fruit and nuts for breakfast and then they sat on the platform outside her chamber and watched the sunrise.

'You're perplexed again Avery.'

'It's the Zetas. Their actions have caused such disharmony across the galaxy. It may not have been intentional, but it led to wars and the annihilation of entire worlds.'

'That's true,' replied Moir.

'As an officer of fleet, I'm trained to deliver justice in the form of punitive punishment, yet it does not seem appropriate for the Zetas.'

'Then what do you think should happen?'

'Well, I was taught that nothing is done onto another that wasn't first created by them, even if it was in a previous life. In other words, the destruction may have been fuelled by the discordance, but it would not have led to war if there weren't beings who'd agreed to participate in that event. Therefore, responsibility for the crimes committed must be shared. The Zetas need to be forgiven, and in time, their focus will shift away from technology towards awareness.'

The stones beneath Avery's bare feet vibrated for a moment.

'Quorana's opinion of you has shifted. She wishes me to tell you that you will be welcome to study here in a time of your choosing.'

Kaylor smiled.

A feeling of relief washed over Avery and he suddenly felt worthy to be Moir's son. 'Inglis and Peterson are a different matter. I believe they do need to be gaoled.'

'I agree,' said Moir. 'Last time the elders let Sorensen go because Ziana had no prisons and the concept of detaining someone was a foreign concept. He never learned his lesson; I think he will this time after he's spent many years in a prison cell on Isla.'

Avery stood up and walked over to Starliah who was seated in a bouncy chair. 'Three days you said.'

'That's correct,' said Moir.

'Do I need to come back for her?'

'No, she'll come to you.'

Avery gently kissed his daughter and hugged his mother before heading down the stairs with Kaylor towards Mystique.

Chapter 42

The night was darker than any other night Avery had ever experienced previously. It was because none of Zeus's other moons shone in the sky. A rare event that only occurred every seven hundred years.

Both Avery and Sarah had been ordered to remain at his house. Captain Loody had been sent back up to command *The Zee* and Commodore Erikson had been reinstated as base commander. By whose orders, Avery didn't know, but it wasn't his place to question.

Avery and Sarah both stood in full fleet combat gear ready for orders. A shuttle sat in the driveway. Dee was also here. For what purpose Avery didn't know, but if she insisted in coming into battle with them, he wasn't going to argue.

Yeltzie sat with her boyfriend Kanchan and they were both anxious. Kaylor was the only one who was calm and she sat quietly in contemplation.

Three days had passed as far as Avery reckoned. He hoped in some ways that Moir decided not to return Starliah because she was too young to be caught up in this. If she did arrive, Avery was going to take Kaylor and the baby and run. He wasn't sure where, but he hoped that the Kelidarians would grant them asylum at least until Starliah came of age.

There was a bright light outside which was followed by three sharp knocks on the door. Avery hurried to answer it and was confronted by a teenage girl. Her build modest, she wore a sleeveless cream tunic over black three-quarter length leggings. Her black hair was pulled back into a braid despite one side of her head being shaved. Green war paint striped that side of her face.

Avery stood frozen as a pair of blazing lilac eyes stared into his own.

'Father, so good to see you.' She stepped forward to embrace him before kissing both his cheeks in the customary fashion.

Avery might have stepped away, but his legs refused to move forward or back.

'Starliah?'

She grinned. 'Expecting someone younger, was you?'

Avery just stared. Again, he'd been withheld from, but naturally it made perfect sense. The Zeta ships couldn't just take you to a where, but a when. He cursed himself for a fool.

Starliah could have returned a moment after Kaylor and he had left Quorana, but she'd waited three days for the invaders to get closer. Now was the optimum moment for defence.

He saw movement around Starliah's legs and realised she wasn't alone. Four next generation Zetas stood in hooded cloaks; their big blue eyes wide with wonderment. They looked ridiculous, likes blue smurfs ripped from a comic book and dumped into a reality they knew nothing of.

Starliah strode in and took in the others, her eyes came to rest on Kaylor. Starliah produced a slinky from a small waist bag. Thanks for this, I had immense fun with it when I was younger. I hope you don't mind, but Moir borrowed it from your possession in storage on Ria.

Kaylor hugged her while smiling and mother spoke to daughter but too quietly for Avery to hear.

'Mother, go to your lab. You'll have a job only you can do. You'll be told what when the time comes.'

Kaylor bobbed her head and walked out the door.

Starliah turned to Yeltzie. 'Go, you know what to do and take these four ambassadors with you. They've trained to sing and they want to help. An apology of sorts for the crimes of the forbears.'

Yeltzie sprung to her feet.

Kanchan hesitated. 'Are you sure she's Starliah.'

'You want to question her?'

'Ah, no, not really.'

They hurriedly left with the smurfs shuffling after them.

'Father, I see you still have the spaceship you sold me for.'

He folded his arms. 'I never sold you.'

Her eyes twinkled and he realised she was taking the piss. 'Take Mystique and go and arrest Inglis. If you will it so, the spaceship will become undetectable. Inglis and Peterson are not on the flagship; they're hiding on *The Agile* at the back of the fleet.'

Avery wanted to salute but thought better of it.

'Take her with you.'

By her, she meant Dee.

'It won't let me on,' cried Dee.

'Try asking nicely. Sarah, you'll come with me.'

Trusting that his daughter knew what she was doing, Avery didn't wait to find out where Sarah was to take Starliah. Mystique was parked in pride of place right out the front. He scuttled up the ladder. Dee approached cautiously and made it a few rungs up before she was denied access. She again fell backward onto her arse.

'I'm fucking trying to help,' she cried.

Avery was sure that didn't qualify as asking nicely. He placed his hands on the control ball and said, 'Mystique, please. I know she tried to steal you, but this time I think she'll do the right thing.'

There was no response.

'Mystique, please, I can't do this on my own.'

Avery felt the ship respond. He couldn't be sure if it was a yes or a no, but there was one way to find out. 'Try again.'

This time Dee was permitted to board. She immediately noticed Mystique was three times larger on the inside than she was on the outside.

'This is queer.'

The ship shuddered.

'Okay, so the thing you need to understand is that Mystique is a living being and quite sensitive.'

Dee cocked her head. 'Yes, by queer I just meant gender fluid.'

Avery snorted. 'You just made that up.'

She smiled, 'Spooks need to be able to think on their feet, it's a job requirement.'

He looked at her until she said, 'What?'

'You're pretty when you smile.'

She stuck his arm hard enough to leave a bruise. Good, she was starting to like him.

She sat in one of the little Zeta seats. 'There're no seatbelts.'

Avery's own seat had grown considerably since he last piloted. 'Don't need them.'

She wasn't reassured. 'How does it fly?'

'No idea, some quantum thing, I think. To pilot, I have to give directions via telapathy.'

'Eek, wouldn't a couple of joysticks be easier?'

'Then anyone could fly it.'

'Point taken.'

Avery focused and a moment later they were in space with transparent walls.

Dee clutched the side of her chair. 'Crap, they do know we'll implode without walls right.'

Avery was more worried about being seen then the lack of walls. Inglis's fleet was only three-hundred thousand kilometres out. It was deaccelerating as it approached Ziana. Mystique suddenly darted left then right.

'What's happening?'

'They is frightened,' he replied, using the gender-neutral pronoun the same as Dee had. He focused on love, reassurance and undetectability before guiding the ship above the fleet where he could peer down upon them. Starliah had said Inglis was on *The Agile* and the ships names were printed in giant letters on the roofs.

They found the right fleet ship and Avery guided them in close. The hangar bay was closed, so Avery visualised them in the hangar bay. A moment later they were.

Dee looked at him sternly. 'That was too easy.'

'Agreed.

*****

Sarah hurried outside with Starliah who ran straight past the other parked Zeta ship.

Sarah pointed, 'We're not taking …'

'No, it's not mine and I'm not a pilot.' Starliah headed up the ramp.

'But you just sent the pilot away.'

'You're a fleet officer. You can fly, can't you?'

Sarah gulped. Technically she could, but she didn't fancy flying Avery's daughter, who was dressed like an Amazon and more or less a goddess.

'We're in a bit of a hurry.'

Sarah hurried on board and sat in the pilot's seat. Having belted herself in, she automatically reached for the AI switch.

'Leave that off.'

Damn it. Sarah had practiced flying without the AI in the base simulator and botched it every time. Her hands shook as she flicked switches. The engine started; she closed the ramp and completed a pressure test before lifting off.

'Where to?'

'Port Town.'

Damn it, they could have driven there. Sarah had learned to drive a jeep, well sort off. 'The base?'

'No, the council chambers.'

What? There was nowhere to land except the car park, which they could land in if Avery was flying.

Sarah did a flyby. There were no jeeps in the way, so she attempted to land. Crashed into a tree, thankfully gently, and set another on fire with the rear thruster.

Starliah pretended not to notice. As soon as the ramp lowered, she ran inside. Sarah hurried after her and found Renee in her office sitting beside Cadel. She skidded to a stop before snapping a salute.

'Sir, I…'

'Thought I was dead?' he replied.

'Yes.'

'No, just badly wounded. As I was being taken to the healing centre, I realised I needed to fake my death or else Peterson would just keep sending assassins after me. However, it's time for me to take back command of fleet.'

Sarah wanted to kiss him, but it wouldn't be becoming especially since he was her superior officer.

'Hang on a sec, I'm coming with you,' said Renee who was hugging Starliah. The Chief Minister directed her attention towards the tracking bracelet on her left wrist and using telekinetic force shattered it into a dozen pieces.

'Sure, okay,' said Sarah who had no idea Renee had such power.

They hurried towards the shuttle. Starliah directed her focus towards the burning foliage and began singing. The flames disappeared as if they'd been bombarded with a sound wave fire extinguisher.

'Show off,' said Renee.

'Like, you weren't just now,' retorted Starliah.

Sarah just stared, a sense of inadequacy sweeping over her.

'Wait a minute, where's Avery?' asked Cadel.

'Avery went on ahead with Dee,' replied Starliah.

Cadel frowned. 'Now I've got no pilot and without a mediator, those two will kill each other.'

'No, Sarah will fly and after this, Father and Deanna will be best friends.'

Cadel glanced white-faced at Sarah.

'Shall I run and grab a pilot, Sir.'

'Yes.'

'No, there's no time. Sarah can do this; I have every confidence in her.'

Cadel's lilac eyes bored into Sarah's, but he gave one stiff nod.

Sarah re-sat in the pilot's seat, half expecting Cadel to sit in the co-pilot's seat. He didn't and having belted up she lifted the shuttle off the ground. 'Where to?'

'*The Zee*,' replied Cadel.

Damn it. *The Zee* was in space and without an AI she'd have to calculate the gravitational exit angles manually. Her hands shook on the joystick causing the shuttle to jitter. She couldn't do this. Best if she admitted it before she killed everyone.

Starliah, who was sitting behind her, suddenly laid her hands on her shoulder. A warmth spread through Sarah and her mind buzzed for a second. She stopped shaking.

'What did you just do?'

Starliah was doing up clips and straps. 'Transferred a selection of my father's memories, inlaid in my DNA, via a telepathic transfer.'

'Oh wow, can I have your memories as well?'

'Not a chance. Open the door.'

'Sorry?'

'Open the door.'

Sarah realised Starliah had donned a parachute. Trained to obey orders without question, she flicked the switch to lower the ramp.

Screaming a war cry, Starliah ran and jumped out the back. Below were the high peaks of the Cathell alps. Starliah clearly intended to stand atop of them and sing whilst telepathically connecting to the Zianan populace who'd sing with her.

'Rebirth hasn't made her any less crazy,' pronounced Renee.

'No, if anything she's gotten worse,' replied Cadel. 'You good now Commander.'

'Yes, Sir.'

Sarah lightened her grip on the joystick, gave both shoulders a shrug and forced the shuttle into a nose dive. The deck rushed towards them and Sarah used the gravity boost to gain speed before curving them back upwards. Now she opened the throttle the way Avery did. Not bothering to even glance at her gauges, she felt the ship as if it were an extension of her own body. There was no need for calculations; Sarah simply connected to the greater mind of the universe and just knew what angle to fly at. They shot into space and straight into a dogfight.

*****

Eternally grateful for her father's memories, passed on genetically and awoken using ancient meditative techniques, Starliah glided in and executed a perfect landing. Her bare feet sunk into the snow up to her calves and she quickly unclipped the parachute. A moment later, before she froze to death, she began the discipline of tahumo. A meditative practice that caused her auric energy to spin around her at increasing speed. In doing so, it generated immense heat warming her from within.

With steam rising off her and snow melting at her feet, Starliah began to sing. Reaching out her mind she telepathed with the people of Ziana. Every man, woman, and child who stood ready to sing with her.

They began and with Starliah's guidance synched into one voice forming a gestalt. The wordless singing contained the intent of pure love directed towards the incoming armada.

*****

With laser pistol drawn, Avery descended the ladder and Dee followed.

'Where are the hangar guards?' whispered Dee also clutching a pistol.

Even in space there was always meant to be two guards in the hangar. Just to ensure no one departed without authorisation.

'I don't know, but we're too exposed here.' Keeping low he hastened to the wall. There was no one, not a soul.

They made their way along to the door. It was closed and locked. Avery had intended to stun the hangar guards and use one of their hands to open the biometric lock. To his surprise, Dee laid her hand on the reader and it flashed green.

'What the fuck?' he whispered.

Her finger flew to her lips. 'We spooks have access to everything.'

Figures. No wonder they frigging knew everything.

The corridor was also empty. Avery assumed Inglis would be on the bridge and went to head that way, but Dee motioned in the other direction. Avery, guessing she had the drop on the evil would-be dictator, followed her. They made their way passed cabins and stopped in front of the captain's cabin.

Doors began to open and fleetmen emerged pointing pistols at them. They'd unwittingly walked straight into an ambush.

Chapter 43

Laser shot passed as Sarah dodged. Three shuttles chased her and all she could do was use evasive manoeuvres.

'Can I return fire, Sir?'

'Not to kill, we need to give Starliah a chance to work her magic. Just get us to *The Zee.*'

The Zee began to return fire, but it was just cover fire. Sarah used it to swing around in a large arc. As she headed for *The Zee,* she fired a few shots of her own, deliberately wide.

A voice came over the radio. 'You couldn't hit the side of a barn.'

'Look who's talking,' replied Sarah, again dodging and flying like she never had before.

Laser struck The Zee but deflected harmlessly off the shield. During the wait, *The Zee's* generators had been upgraded meaning her shield should hold for longer.

Sarah looped around and flew straight at the open hangar bay doors. At the last second, a hole appeared in the shield permitting her entry before snapping shut behind her. The three pursuing ships only narrowly avoided crashing into the shield which would have destroyed them.

'No hard feelings, but the better pilot won today,' said Sarah.

'That'll do Commander,' said Cadel, but his eyes twinkled with amusement.

Sarah landed and waited for the hangar door to close and the hangar to pressurise before lowering the ramp. Cadel and Renee hurried off heading for the bridge and Sarah followed.

As expected, Captain Loody was on the bridge. He snapped a salute. 'Sir, it's good to have you back.'

'It's good to be back,' replied the Admiral. He turned to the communication officer. 'Open a line of communication broadcasted simultaneously on all frequencies.'

'Yes, Sir.'

Cadel cleared his throat. 'This is Admiral Cadel, I'm countermanding all existing orders and ordering all fleet ships incoming to Ziana to stand down. I repeat, stand down.'

There was no response.

*****

Avery and Dee had had no choice but to lay down their arms and surrender. Their hands cuffed behind their backs they were taken to a cell in the brig and thrown in. The forcefield door was raised and now they were bound and detained.

'Damn it, we were too predictable.'

'Of course, but now they've underestimated us.'

'They have?'

She moved closer and lowered her voice to less than a whisper. 'There's a copper pin in my hair. Grab it with your teeth.'

Avery spied it and taking it in his teeth he knelt down and positioned his mouth near her hands. Dee's hands were small, but her fingers were dexterous. She shaped the pin into a hook and used it to unlock her cuffs. Having done so, she also unlocked Avery's before moving to the door.

The cells had a biometric reader on the inside built as a safety feature, in case pirates seized the ship and locked them in. Naturally, a senior officer would remove access to genuine prisoners when they were detained. Dee placed her hand on it and it lit green. She hadn't been joking when she said she had access to everything. The how wasn't that difficult to fathom. As the techie Hugh had once told him, all programming has backdoors.

Obviously, the spook's techs had used them to give themselves access.

The shield fell away, and without hesitation, Dee ran at the two guards stationed outside. She kicked the first one in the head dropping him. The second one went for his pistol. He fired, but missed as Dee threw herself into a roll.

He was ling up for a second shot when Avery grabbed him from behind and threw him on the floor. A well-placed kick sending his pistol from his hand. Before the guard could regain his feet, Dee relieved him of his sparker which she made use of. His body went limp.

The guards were relieved of their weapons. There was no point putting them in the cell because Avery wasn't authorised to withdraw their biometric access. When they came to, they'd just let themselves out.

'Do you reckon Inglis is still in his cabin?' asked Avery.

'I do. He'd have his own control room in there; why would he leave it?'

It made sense to Avery. Inglis was clever, but he was also a coward. He wouldn't command from the bridge until Ziana was his.

They made their way back to Inglis's cabin and found two guards in front of the door. Taken by surprise, they were stunned before they knew what had hit them. Dee placed her hand on the biometric reader, but it flashed red. That was bound to happen sooner or later. Undeterred, Dee tried the hands of the guards, but neither had authority to open the door.

'Damn it. Now what?'

Before Avery could answer the question, a ghastly deafening noise forced him to place his hands over his ears.

'It's metal,' yelled Dee.

Avery had no frame of reference for what she meant, but it sounded like metal being ground, pounded and torn apart while someone screamed in agony and another yelled swear words.

'He's using it to counteract the singing.'

It was all Avery could do to remain upright because all he wanted to do was crawl into the foetal position and beg it to stop.

*****

'Make it stop!' yelled Cadel covering his ears.

'I'm trying Sir,' replied Ralph who was scrolling screens trying to find the off switch.

It seemed like longer, but it was only thirty seconds before *The Zee* fell silent.

'What in damnation was that?' screeched Cadel.

'Heavy metal music Sir,' replied Ralph.

'Music? A choir of demons couldn't make such a din.'

'It was developed on Earth Sir,' said Sarah. 'It's been used as a weapon to fuel base emotions in soldiers. During the twenty-first century wars, tank operators would play it with lyrics repeating words like burn, kill, and die motherfucker, while shelling a city.'

'Good grief, that's barbaric,' said Renee.

'Yes, but effective,' replied Cadel. 'I'd wager gold that this metal racket is counteracting Starliah's loving messages of peace.'

'I agree, Sir,' said Sarah.

'Is there any way we can switch it off on the other ships?'

'Not from here, Sir,' said Ralph.

A hologram of Vice-Admiral Peterson appeared. 'Stand strong fleet. I assure you Admiral Cadel is deceased. The message you received was, of course, a fake. A desperate ploy by Chief Minister Hardy and her despotic government to lead us into a trap through trickery. Now they are trying to glamour you with singing. It is nothing short of witchcraft, but don't fear, whilst the music plays, you will remain unaffected.

'I now speak directly to the captain and crew of *The Zee*. Stand down and let justice prevail or I will be forced to order a full-scale attack. Believe me, when I tell you, I will destroy you if need be. You have five minutes to comply.'

Renee's eyes flared. 'Let me speak with him.'

'It's no use, Ma'am, since the Admiral's address, they've begun jamming our communication signals,' said Ralph.

If Sarah had been playing a game of chess with Avery, he'd had proclaimed she was in check. It wasn't the end, but it did mean their next move had to be considered carefully or else it would be game over.

'Are you sure there's no way to shut off the metal music being played on the other ships?' asked Sarah.

'I'm sorry,' replied Ralph. 'The only way would be to use a brute force AI that can hack through military grade security. Regrettably, we don't have one, and even if we did, we can't risk Inglis using the persuasive program.'

Sarah's stomach lurched. It was mental, but the only way. She turned to Cadel. 'Sir, I have a crazy idea.'

He stared intently at her and just listened. 'That's not crazy, that's insane.'

'They've begun firing on us, Sir,' said Captain Loody. 'Shields are holding, but they won't indefinitely.'

They were never meant to hold indefinitely, just long enough for the fourth way to work its magic and end this.

'Sir,' pleaded Sarah.

Cadel stared directly into her eyes. 'Alright, but try not to die will you. The paperwork will be horrific if you do.'

Sarah fled trying not to smile at the Admiral's joke. She had to return to Ziana, but she couldn't use the teleporter because all the ship's power was needed for the shield. She also couldn't use a shuttle. Lady luck had helped her dodge the lasers on her way up, but it wouldn't work a second time. Her only option was to take a shielded escape pod.

Sarah climbed into one, closed the hatch and belted in. The pod was designed for two people and it provided a one-way trip to the surface.

She flicked switches and a moment later she was shot out of *The Zee* like a bullet from an old-fashioned gun. Caught by the planet's gravity, she was hurled through the atmosphere like a chunk of space rock. The pod erupted in flames and the cabin temperature began to rapidly heat up. All Sarah could do was pray the heat shields held.

On Earth, during the early days of space travel, the astronauts used to land them in the ocean. These days the pods had a bit more manoeuvrability. As she shot through the cloud layer two sets of retractable wings extended turning the pod into a glider. As she rocketed towards the ground, Sarah set a course for the fleet base.

If she'd been in a simulator, it would have screeched at her that she was coming in too fast and she was going to overshoot. Normally she'd have attempted to bank around in a large ark, but there wasn't time. When Port Town appeared below her, Sarah flicked switches, retracting the wings, which sent her into a free fall. She deployed the parachute and extended the landing legs, which were big springs.

Sarah's pod hit the parade ground and bounced her thirty metres into the air. Her stomach lurched and she feared she'd vomit. She bounced a second time, but rather than going straight up, she veered at an angle hitting the side of a building. Ricocheting off the wall, she was propelled through the glass entrance of the tech building.

The inertia would have killed her if it wasn't for the emergency landing jell. A green slime that rapidly expanded into semi-hard foam when it came in contact with air. It filled the cabin and saved her life.

Encased in slimy foam in a confined space, claustrophobia threated to send her into a panic. Fleetman had been known to survive pod landings, only to kill themselves with fear trying to get out.

Sarah closed her eyes and meditated. She'd never been good at it, but with Avery's memories, she found it remarkably easy. In moments she was in bliss.

There was a screeching of metal as two heavily muscled fleetman reefed the hatch open. Strong arms reached in and Sarah was dragged out.

'Commander Bartell.'

Sarah had no time for formalities. 'Find Hugh!'

They stared incomprehensibly at her.

'The techie, Hugh! Find him!'

Amid a chorus of "Yes Ma'am", Sarah was left to wipe the slimy foam off her face. Thankfully the tech building also housed the science labs and the bathrooms were fitted with showers. Sarah stood under one clothes and all.

There was a knock at the door.

'Who's there?'

'Kara.'

Sarah wracked her brain, but she couldn't remember who Kara was. She opened the door to discover a young Zianan woman holding an armful of clothes and several towels. 'How the fuck?'

'I saw your pod coming in, so I remote viewed what you'd need.' She swallowed. 'I'm sorry, but we needed access in a hurry and your apartment is going to need a new door.'

A door was the least of Sarah's concerns. She began to rip off her wet slimy clothes.

Hugh skidded to a stop, saw Sarah in a state of half dress and avoided eye contact. 'Commander.'

'I need Tank, Sparta's AI.'

'I have it, Ma'am, but we can't use it. It's too dangerous with …'

'Kaylor can use it.'

'I'm sorry, who?'

'Dr Kaylor Emerson. Like Avery, she's immune to the persuasive program.'

'Right. Shall I summon her?'

'No, we need a fleet jeep.' Sarah realised as kind as Kara's intentions were, she didn't have time to properly wash and change. Now topless, she wiped off the worst of the water and slime, pulled on a clean tank top and ran.

Outside one of the large men who'd pulled her from the pod screeched to a stop in a jeep.

Without opening a door, Sarah leaped into the back and barked, 'Research Centre Science Labs! Yesterday!'

Hugh had tried to jump in the same way Sarah did. Not being as athletic, he botched it. He'd have fallen if Sarah hadn't grabbed his shirt and reefed him in. The jeep was already moving kicking up dirt as it hurried towards its destination. Having grasped the urgency of the situation the driver did not stick to roads but cut across the base taking a direct route for the gates. Having speed between building and flattened gardens they emerged on the training ground and speed towards the exit. Sarah waved her arms, but the watchmen didn't understand.

The boom gate snapped like a twig as the bulbar on the jeep careened into it. The driver spun the steering wheel this way and that to avoid potholes in the gravel road that led to the Research Centre. All the while they bounced in the back desperately trying to remain in the vehicle. At the entrance, Rian guards stepped out of the gatehouse and demanded they stop.

They never even slowed. The jeep crashed through the large mesh gates ripping one off its hinges. Without the bulbar, the jeep would have been killed. Now it wore one of the gates as a hood ornament.

A klaxon alarm sounded as the Research Centre security was breached. Fearing they'd be locked out of the science building; the driver drove straight into the glass doors. Caught in the metal frames the jeep finally came to a standstill.

'Well driven.' Sarah leaped out of the jeep. 'Shoot to stun.' She ran for Kaylor's lab.

*****

When the alarms sounded Kaylor feared the worst. Were the invaders taking over the Research Centre? Would she be raped and killed? She looked for a weapon but there was nothing that would suffice against armed troops.

'Kaylor!'

The voice sounded like Sarah's. Kaylor flung open the lab door to discover Sarah running up the stairs. Bits a glass clung to her hair and clothes and her bare arms were covered in small cuts. One was bleeding profusely. The bottom half of her was wet and dripping green slimy foam.

'Oh my God.'

'I'm fine, but I need your help.'

Kaylor decided Avery was correct about the use of the word fine.

A panting techie was lumbering behind Sarah.

'For god sake man, give it here,' yelled Sarah snatching a communicator from his hands.

Kaylor backed into her lab. 'Please, my equipment is sensitive.'

Sarah remained outside but thrust the communicator at her. 'I need you to use this to hack into the fleet ships and shut down the PA systems.'

Kaylor blinked.

'Time is against us. Please, I know how crazy I look and sound, but you are the only one who can do this without being taken over by that evil program.'

Kaylor recalled her daughter's words to her. "Something only she could do". She fitted it to her ear and switched it on. 'AI, can you hear me?'

'Access denied.'

There was a commotion in the atrium below them.

'Ma'am, Commodore Erikson ordered us to bring Sparta here.'

'Let him go, that's an order.'

Sparta took the stairs two at a time, burst into the room and held out his hand for the communicator. Kaylor handed it to him and he fitted it behind his ear.

'Tank.'

'Daniel.'

'Tank, I authorise you to give Dr Kaylor Emerson your full co-operation.'

'Certainly Daniel.'

He handed the communicator back to Kaylor.

Kaylor fitted it and repeated what Sarah had told her. A moment later her head buzzed. She fought and relayed Tank's questions through Sarah.

A radio squawked. 'Commander Bartell, come in please.'

The fleetman who'd driven the jeep handed Sarah a handheld radio.

'This is Bartell, go ahead.'

'The is Kara, Ma'am. I received a telepath from Avery, I couldn't make it out, so I remote viewed.'

'What did you see?'

'Door eleven-eighty-six. I think Avery needs it opened.'

Sarah directed her attention at Kaylor. 'He's on *The Agile*. Open it, if you can.'

*****

'Shields are down to thirty percent! They won't hold for much longer!' someone yelled.

Cadel knew they were out of time. He couldn't risk the crew of *The Zee* a moment longer. It was over, they'd failed. 'Flash white light.'

'Sir?' queried Captain Loody.

'That's an order. We're surrendering.'

In space, a flashing white light was akin to raising a white flag of surrender. Moments after it was activated, the bombardment of laser stopped. A hologram of Inglis appeared smug-faced. 'Is this an unconditional surrender?'

Cadel answered him. 'It is.'

'Very well. Prepare to be boarded.'

*****

Avery prided himself on his ability to remain calm even under extreme duress. As a fleet officer, he'd been subjected to all manner of advanced training, including being placed in a pod filled with rats and being launched into space. That had been horrific, but this metal was far worse.

Still holding his hands over his ears, he sat on the floor with his back to the wall and meditated until his mind cleared. What did he need?

The noise off and the door opened.

In meditation, the means to achieve ends would come if you allowed it. It was, however, not always as one would expect. He saw Kara's face. The young fleet woman with a gift for remote viewing. Using all of his will, he attempted to make contact with her. Words flashed but Avery had never had the gift of telepathy. Still, he refused to give in.

Dee seemed unaffected by the music. She just stood there like a viper ready to lash out at anything that threatened them.

The music stopped suddenly. The silence was eerie. Avery stood up just as the door panel flashed green. Dee burst through the door. Inglis was standing with his back to it looking at Ziana through a large glass window. He turned to look at them and revealed that he held the device in his hands.

'Ah, daughter, have you come to beg my forgiveness and swear fealty to the new Emperor? I just accepted Ziana's unconditional surrender.'

'The only thing you'll be Emperor of is a prison cell,' she snarled.

He returned a disappointed look and began swiping the screen of the handheld. Avery waited for troops, under the influence of the persuasive program, to storm the room, but nothing happened.

'Did Black and White neglect to tell you that the program had an expiry date? That's remiss of them.'

Concern flashed in Inglis's eyes. Without the program, becoming Emperor wasn't going to happen even if he won this battle, he'd lose the war. People only obeyed without question for two reasons, extreme fear of retribution or devout love, and Inglis could command neither.

Avery pointed his laser pistol at Inglis. 'On your knees, hands behind your head.'

Inglis refused to comply.

Without warning, Dee fired at him repeatedly, but the laser bounced off a body shield.

'Did you think I'd leave myself open to attack? You stupid lesbian wench.'

Yelling like a mad woman Dee ran at him only to bounce off his shield. She rolled to her feet and stood crouched; her teeth bared like a mad person.

Avery wracked his brain for a solution and it came to him. There was only one way to fight against an electrically shielded opponent and it was as low tech as it came. Leaving Dee to keep him busy, he hastened into the cabin's en suite. On the handbasin was a cup, which he filled it with water.

Inglis had drawn a laser pistol and was now shooting at Dee, but surprisingly lithe on her feet she kept dodging. Avery ran at Inglis and flung the cup of water in his face.

In a spectacular display of sparks, the shield short-circuited. Sensing her opportunity, Dee ran at Inglis again and crash-tackled him to the ground. Her fist smashed into his face repeatedly.

'Enough you'll kill him.'

'Raging with fury, she kept striking him.'

Avery grabbed her from behind and hauled her backward. They fell to the ground in a tangle of arms and legs. It took all of Avery's considerable strength to restrain her. Suddenly, she went limp and to Avery's bewilderment began to sob uncontrollably.

Patting her awkwardly, Avery did his best to console her. She stopped crying, but refused to speak. He got up, cuffed an unconscious Inglis and cautiously made his way to the bridge. En route, he discovered the crew were crying and hugging each other.

On the bridge stood Vice-Admiral Peterson. Unaffected by the love of the fourth way, he punched and kicked the bridge troops who refused to comply with his orders. Avery looked to see why he was unaffected and discovered Peterson had earphones in his ears.

Avery was sure Peterson would also have a body shield and so refrained from shooting at him. Avery looked for water or any other kind of liquid. In hindsight, he should have refilled the cup and brought it with him. He hadn't so he looked around. There had to be something, a water bottle, an undrunk coffee, anything. There was nothing. Peterson, aware of the Achille's heel of his shield, had ordered all liquids be banned from the bridge.

Laser narrowly missed him as Peterson open fire. Avery ran. He needed to find liquid and ran towards the galley. Peterson pursued firing at every opportunity. For the first time ever, Avery was glad of fleet ship's internal design that was a maze of passageways.

He made it to the galley only to discover no water came from any of the taps. Damn, Peterson must have accessed the ship's computer and ordered the water be shut off. Avery searched for a substitute but failed to find anything. It was ludicrous.

Peterson entered the galley and fired at him. Avery picked up a copper saucepan and threw it at him. It hit the shield and arced but failed to short-circuit it. He ran, not really knowing where he was going, he found himself in the hangar.

Mystique was still there. Should he board and leave? No that was the coward's way. He needed to stop Peterson. Think.

A laser flashed towards him again. Avery ran blindly but was confronted by a dead-end containing a hatch. He hadn't meant to come this way and now he'd cornered himself. The first airlock door was open, but even if Avery shut himself in all he'd do was trap himself.

Knowing he'd won, Peterson took his time approaching. Without fanfare, he raised his pistol. With his death imminent, Avery saw his life flash before his eyes.

There was a vacuous noise. Avery recognised it as the hatch opening. Instinctively he grabbed hold of a rail and clung on for life.

Peterson flew past him and into the vacuum of space. The hatch snapped shut. Starring through the porthole window, he waited for Peterson to implode. He didn't. The shield had to be protecting him, but it would last only until the batteries ran out.

Peterson fired his pistol at Avery's face, but the laser from a pistol was too weak to penetrate the ship's hull or its reinforced windows. All the shots did was create sparks.

Avery looked up to see Dee standing by the control panel. She too was wearing earphones. She must have known to use them and now she'd saved his life just as she'd predicted she would. Avery approached her and gently removed them before pulling her into a hug.

*****

Starliah finally stopped singing. She was tired now and becoming cold. She needed to get off this mountain and down into the valley below where she could get warm, rest and sleep. Once she had, she'd be able to catch a train back to Port Town. She picked up the parachute harness and removed the first chute. The pack came with two chutes and so she put it back on and did up the straps.

She took off running and yelling yahoo, as she jumped off the mountain.

Chapter 44

Kaylor conceded Yeltzie had been right, love conquered all. Under Admiral Cadel's leadership, the invading fleet ships had stood down. Rather than demanding punishment, the Zianans had welcomed the crews to come planet-side and celebrate a renewed peace with a feast. Bonfires burned and music and cheer filled the air.

Kaylor had been dancing, but now she rested for a moment while she enjoyed a glass of wine.

A woman approached.

'Chief Minister,' said Kaylor.

'Please call me Renee,' she replied taking a seat.

'I heard you were offered a crown for what you did during the battle.'

'Yes, I was, but I refused it. Ziana doesn't need a queen. I'll serve as Chief Minister for a while longer, then Avery can retire from fleet and have my job.'

'Seriously. Do you think he will accept the position?'

'I know he will and he'll administer with a firm belief in justice.'

'Yes, I can imagine that.'

'Anyway, I trust you'll have a bit to do in the coming months.'

'Yes, I've so many finding to write up, I scarcely know where to start.' She sipped at her wine. 'Yeltzie tried to explain fourth seal love to me but I couldn't comprehend what she was saying. I certainly couldn't imagine that it was so powerful that hardened troops would lay down their arms and start crying and hugging.'

'Love is all sentient beings natural state and even those separated from it yearn to find it. When it is felt for the first time, especially after lifetimes of separation, it is all consuming.'

'I can relate to that, but why wasn't Avery affected by it the same way?'

'Avery was raised in love and when he is encompassed in it, he doesn't react to it the same way. Plus, his entire focus is about justice. It's what he lives for and until he owns that, unless he's chasing criminals, his life will seem pointless.'

'The same way my life would seem pointless if I wasn't studying sound frequency.'

'Yes. It is your soul's purpose in this lifetime.'

Kaylor hesitated, but then decided to ask. 'I know it's a lot to ask, but I was wondering if my research budget could afford to teleport me to Earth. When I've got my papers in order, I'd like to present them at the World University.'

'Splendid idea, but you won't need to teleport. Simply ask Avery to take you in his chariot of fire.'

Kaylor's heart fluttered. 'I don't want him to feel obliged.'

'He's very fond of you Kaylor and I know you feel the same way about him. His late wife's murderer is about to receive the full weight of union law. Once that occurs, he'll be free to pursue you, if you'll let him.' She patted Kayor's hand. 'I'd expect you'll be invited on a date shortly and given he has a chariot of fire, think of the location possibilities. Not to mention the research opportunities.'

Kaylor smiled as butterflies fluttered in her stomach.

*****

In full dress uniform, Avery exited the courtroom on Isla. It had been an exhausting two-weeks. Admiral Cadel was now back in charge of fleet and without Inglis to prevent it, Renee's speeches had been broadcast on Ria's RBC.

The Rian people were outraged at the lies and deception. Naturally, the Inglis government had fallen and in the days that followed, the arrests had been too numerous to count. Not that Avery had been involved in any of that. Instead, he'd been summons to Isla to testify against Inglis, Peterson and Sparta.

It did not matter that the device no longer worked because Sparta had broken down and confessed to everything. He was yet to be sentenced, but Avery was sure the judge would take his remorse into account and lessen his sentence.

Inglis had so many charges against him it had taken an hour for the court clerk to read them. Even so, he'd refused to plead guilty to any of them. Hence the boring and pointless fortnight-long trial, but still, everyone was entitled to due process. He'd be sentenced to prison in a maximum-security cell on Isla for the rest of his life. As Moir had said, he'd have a long time to consider his actions. Hopefully, he'd be reborn a better man.

Peterson had been rescued from the vacuum of space before his shield batteries ran out and he imploded. He'd face a court-martial, be dishonourably discharged and like Inglis, be gaoled for life.

Daniel Sparta was again represented by Brooke. He was again granted conditional bail, to be sentenced at a later date since the courts on Isla were overwhelmed. This time he chose to remain on Isla for what reason Avery didn't know.

Overall, it was a good result and having finally secured justice for Leda, Avery wanted nothing more than to spend time with his daughter, as well as, her mother Kaylor. He planned to win her heart and marry her.

Hearing hurried footsteps behind him Avery turned to see Dee hurrying after him.

'Could I buy you a coffee?'

Avery disliked Isla's coffee, that was weak and tasteless, but Dee's beseeching eyes made him agree. They headed for the nearest café and having secured coffee at the counter, sat down.

Dee looked at him with her dark eyes. 'I wanted to apologise. I lied to you, withheld from you and tried to steal your spaceship.'

Avery nodded slowly. 'But you did the right thing in the end and you saved my life.'

'Yes,' she looked away.

Avery reached out and gently touched her hands, to his surprise she didn't withdraw them. 'Look, if there's something you want to tell me, I swear it will be just between us.'

She looked at him with a never-before-seen sense of trust in her eyes. 'I think I owe you an explanation about who I really am.'

Avery agreed, but, 'Telling me your true identity, would that not be a violation of SIA protocol?'

'Yes, but you just promised to keep what I tell you a secret.'

Avery understood. Dee desperately needed to unburden herself before pent up grieve gave her cancer.

'You have my unwavering fidelity.'

She took a sip of her coffee, made a face of disgust and pushed it away. 'My father is Inglis. He mistakenly thought my mother was a whore and when her contraception failed her, I was the result. Due to certain circumstances as an SIA agent, she couldn't keep me, so she'd left me at an orphanage on Ria.

'My father, never discovered me until I was eight. He insisted on taking me to his home. At first, I thought it was wonderful. I even got my own room and a soft bed.'

Tears escaped her eyes and she wiped them away with her palms. 'Five years later, he came into my room one night.' She looked away. 'Afterwards, were the usual threats. If I told anyone, well you know how it goes.'

She used a napkin in place of tissues. 'He kept me locked in that room for a year, beating and raping me and feeding me only when he remembered. Even years later, I still can't sleep in a bed without horrific nightmares.'

Avery's stomach churned.

'My mother broke me out. Father had told me there was nowhere I could hide that he couldn't find me, but he was wrong. I was given a new identity and taken in by the SIA as a child recruit.

'I vowed to kill him, but they wouldn't let me and trust me they have ways to stop agents going rogue.' She smiled weakly. 'Fucker has finally got his just desserts.'

Avery nodded in agreement. Inglis wasn't just facing a lifetime in prison on Isla, his nose and face required surgery to repair the damage Dee did to it. If the fourth way hadn't kicked in when it did, she might have shaken off Avery's restraints and killed her father. Then she'd be gaoled rather than him and there was no justice in that.

'I know we can't be friends, but I just wanted to thank you. Your relentless perusal of justice — it gave me hope and strength and I wanted to thank you for that.'

Avery frowned. 'What makes you think we can't be friends?'

'Well, I don't do friends. I'm not a befriending sort.'

Oh, you poor thing. Moir was right, Dee needed his love and Sarah's. 'Sure, I understand that, but look if you ever feel you need an acquaintance you should know you're always welcome to drop by, help yourself to food and sleep on the couch.'

'Thanks, that's very kind.'

He fondled her hands. 'I suspect you hate head quacks, but you should know that Sarah is very good at her regular job and she practices with the utmost discretion. Maybe talking to her, might help with the nightmares. She's helped a lot of people with trauma including myself.'

Dee looked thoughtful. 'I do trust Sarah, but she's fleet and can only treat fleet troops.'

Avery waved away her concern. 'Admiral Cadel is a great man. I'm sure he'd permit an exception.'

'Sure, well I'll talk to her when I see her.'

Carrying her own coffee Sarah came bumbling over and took a seat. In a way it was good timing. 'Good news on two fronts.

The Oversight Committee has awarded the three of us the Victoria Cross medal for bravery.'

Since they'd flown Mystique onto an enemy ship and fought two insane men who were wearing shields and were nearly killed, Avery thought it was well deserved. 'I heard you left the Zee in a pod whilst the ship was under attack from laser fire.'

'Yeah, it was absolutely insane, but I could think of no other way. I'm going to attend Daniel's sentencing and testify to what he did. I'm not saying he doesn't deserve to go to gaol, but he had the decency to help save Ziana at the darkest hour and then he confessed to everything.'

'I'm confused about something. Before Kaylor and I boarded Mystique, you', Avery was looking at Dee, 'beat the shit out of Sparta and drove off with him. Where'd you take him?'

'Back to his cell at the base. Commodore Erikson ordered his release and that he be taken to Kaylor's laboratory. Personally, I think Kaylor should be awarded a medal as well.'

'I agree,' said Sarah. 'Since she isn't with fleet it would fall to Chief Minister Hardy to award it to her.'

'Indeed, it would. What's your other news?'

'Mike has apologised and is grovelling for me to give him another chance. I will of course, but he can sweat for a bit longer yet. I don't blame him; I mean if I thought he was a treasonous traitor I'd have reacted the same way.'

'Fair enough. I don't wish to speak out of turn, but perhaps you should consider having that baby you desperately want.'

Sarah didn't reply, but looked dreamy.

'Anyway, Deanna, needs an appointment with Dr. Bartel, the psychiatrist.'

'I can't … actually fuck it. Let them court martial me if they dare.'

Avery smiled. That was the Sarah he knew and loved. Willing to risk the consequences of breaking fleet protocol to help someone in need. Avery squeezed Dee's hands. 'Bring your swimmers when you come and stay, the natural swimming pool is really relaxing.' He mouthed talk to Sarah, before taking his leave.

*****

Under lights, Avery and Sarah stood to attention in full dress uniform on the parade ground. They were joined by Dee who wore her customary black suit and Kaylor who wore a dark green pants suit.

Admiral Cadel held a wireless microphone and faced the audience, which included the crew of *The Zee*. 'My words cannot describe what bravery it took for Lieutenant-Commander Vander and Agent Deanna to fly a chariot of fire onto a fleet ship and battle two insane men during the greatest battle of my career.

'I cannot even begin to know what bravery it took for Commander Bartell to take of pod down to Ziana during that battle whilst *The Zee* was taking fire. Without her actions I fear we would have lost that battle and I shudder to think what former President Inglis would have done then. So, without further ado, I award the three of you the highest medal for bravery, the Victoria Cross.'

Commodore Erikson stepped forward and pinned the medal on Avery and Sarah's chest. When the clapping stopped, Director Gorman stepped forward and pinned the medal on Deanna's chest.

Chief Minister Renee Hardy took the microphone. 'Dr. Emerson was brought to Ziana under false pretences by Daniel Sparta. Having her as an honouree citizen and the mother of Starliah is a golden boon for Ziana. Her work must continue, but for the moment we must pause to consider what she did during the battle. With Daniel's authorisation, she used an illegal brute force AI to put an end to the horrible metal racket and also open a door on *The Agile* which allowed Lieutenant-Commander Vander and Agent Deanna to get at former President Inglis. Of course, the craven prick was hiding in his quarters like an extreme coward. Anyway, I award Dr. Emerson the Medal of Bravery.'

The minister for law and justice stepped forward and pinned the medal on Kaylor's chest.

'If you'll indulge me for just a few more moments, I have some additional news. I have spoken at length with the council of judges on Isla and they have agreed to sentence Daniel Sparta to a suspended sentence and place him on parole for two years. He is free to return to Ria, continue to live on Isla or come to Ziana provided he wear a tracking bracelet for the duration of his parole.

'Despite his former criminal lifestyle, I recognise his brilliance in problem solving. In light of this, I have offered him an honouree position on the Zianan council as an analyst. He has agreed to accept the position, but we are still negotiating his renumeration.

'Anyway, congratulations to everyone who fought in the battle regardless of which side you were on. I'm very grateful that no one was killed. It is my pleasure to announce that I have authorised a feast for everyone. So, enjoy the party.'

Chapter 45

Starliah stayed longer than she'd planned seeing as she'd had to take a choir to Isla and also to Ria. Avery flew them in Mystique. Thank goodness for the large interior.

Upon arrival, Starliah had led all who cared to join her in song sending the intent of love across the worlds. Now she had to return to Quorana to resume her studies. Avery had given her a lift in Mystique and Kaylor had come along for the ride. They'd returned to the spaceship at the base of the pyramid, but were yet to head home.

'I thought you might have taken up studies yourself,' said Kaylor.

'No, perhaps later. It would be awkward studying at the same place as my teenage daughter. You know college girls; they're so easily embarrassed by their fathers.'

Kaylor grinned at the joke.

'Anyway, I wondered, since we're out and about if you'd consent to a picnic date. I packed a hamper before we left.'

'Oh, you did?' She raised an eyebrow when she saw Zianan pink fizzy wine in the hamper.

Avery's face flushed red. 'Alright, Yeltzie did, but…'

She put a finger on his lips and silenced him before replacing her finger with her lips. There kiss was long and passionate.

'So that's yes to a date then?'

She placed a finger on her cheek. 'Hmm, I guess so.'

There was nothing more alluring than a woman who teased and then played hard to get. 'Did you have a picnic spot in mind?'

'Well, since you mentioned it, I would really love to see the Pink Nebula up close.'

'Splendid choice.'

'But I should probably mention something. I'd like to conduct a little science while we're there. I've never heard the music of a nebula before?'

Avery sighed, scientists, they were all the same.

'Oh, and one other thing. I don't mean to sound presumptuous, but if you should feel a burning desire to propose at any time, I'd be much obliged if you didn't push me off a rope bridge before you did so.'

'I didn't push her, she slipped.'

'So, you say, Mr. Vander, but I must ask, were there any witnesses, or am I to take your word for it?' She winked cheekily.

Avery rolled his eyes. He ought to run, he knew what he was in for. Leda had dragged him off hunting rare plants; Kaylor would run him ragged chasing unusual stars, moon, planets and anything else that made sound. It was too late now. He'd fallen in love again and he'd just have to live with the consequences.

THE END

About the author

Dion Perry is an Australian who was born in Townsville, Queensland. He spent the first eight years of his life living in a caravan and travelling around the eastern side of Australia before moving to Tasmania. He attended university in Hobart, where he did a BA with majors in sociology and Aboriginal studies. He writes mainly speculative fiction in the genres of science fiction and fantasy, but he also writes autobiographies. In May of 2021, he was diagnosed with viral myocarditis, and on 2 September 2023, he underwent a heart transplant. While the transplant was successful, the antirejection drugs destroyed his kidneys, and he now undergoes haemodialysis three times a week. He lives in Crookwell in the Southern Tablelands of New South Wales Australia with his wife, dog, and cat.

www.ingramcontent.com/pod-product-compliance
Lightning Source LLC
Chambersburg PA
CBHW071705120626
46550CB00001B/115